THE

Hip-hop

There are more than one hundred and fifty
Rough Guide travel, phrasebook, and music titles,
covering destinations from Amsterdam to Zimbabwe,
languages from Czech to Vietnamese, and musics
from World to Opera and Jazz

www.roughguides.com

Rough Guide Credits

Text editor: Orla Duane; **Series editor**: Mark Ellingham
Production: Michelle Draycott, Julia Bovis, Link Hall, Helen Ostick

Publishing Information

This first edition published January 2001 by
Rough Guides Ltd, 62–70 Shorts Gardens, London, WC2H 9AH

Distributed by the Penguin Group

Penguin Books Ltd, 27 Wrights Lane, London W8 5TZ
Penguin Putnam Inc., 375 Hudson Street, New York 10014, USA
Penguin Books Australia Ltd, 487 Maroondah Highway,
PO Box 257, Ringwood, Victoria 3134, Australia
Penguin Books Canada Ltd, 10 Alcorn Avenue,
Toronto, Ontario, Canada M4V 1E4
Penguin Books (NZ) Ltd, 182–190 Wairau Road,
Auckland 10, New Zealand

Typeset in Bembo and Helvetica to an original design by Henry Iles.
Printed in Spain by Graphy Cems.

© Peter Shapiro, 352pp
A catalogue record for this book is available from the British Library.

ISBN 1-85828-637-9

THE ROUGH GUIDE TO

Hip-hop

by Peter Shapiro

ROUGH
GUIDES

Contents

Introduction

Hip-hop may be all about the flow, but it has never been about narrative or smooth, continuous progressions. Like the music itself, hip-hop's history has been characterized by cutting and chopping segues, ludicrous leaps of imagination and wildstyle flights of fancy and derring-do. To constrain hip-hop culture within the framework of chronology seems sacriligious. But if you need a creation myth – you can have your Kool DJ Hercs, Grandmaster Flashes and Afrika Bambaataas – the real godfather of hip-hop might very well have been some guy called Robert Moses. Moses was an unelected New York City official who exerted tyrannical control over the Big Apple's city planning in the '50s and '60s. One of Moses' pet projects was the Cross-Bronx Expressway. Built in the early '60s, it became Route One for white flight from the city to the tony suburbs of Westchester County and Connecticut. In order to build this fifteen-mile stretch of road, several thousand people were displaced and large sections of The Bronx were levelled. This destroyed communities, necessitated the construction of ugly, modern housing developments and left large portions of The Bronx nothing but rubble and tenements.

With New York City bankrupt and beholden to the bond-holders who imposed austerity programmes on the city, The Bronx – with no incentive for civic pride – became a brutal place to live. The first generation of post-CBE children in The Bronx was the first group to try to piece together bits from this urban scrap heap. Like carrion crows and hunter-gatherers, they picked through the debris and created their own sense of community and found vehicles for self-expression from cultural ready-mades, throwaways and aerosol cans.

"New York, New York, it's a helluva town/The Bronx is up and The Battery's down", the song goes, and hip-hop was (and still is) largely a matter of geography. "If you can make it there, you can make it anywhere", another New York anthem goes, and it's amazing that in the '70s in capitalism's capital city the frame of reference was still so small. The ultimate dream was to make it all-city, to have your name known from the island of Staten to Manhattan, from Van Cortlandt Park to Rockaway Beach. The rep of early folk heroes like Taki 183 and Kool DJ Herc grew so big that they couldn't be contained by 183rd Street or Sedgwick Avenue, and they became Johnny Appleseeds planting the hip-hop virus throughout the five boroughs until, eventually, it went not only all-city, but all-world.

The Rough Guide to Hip-hop follows hip-hop culture in all of its aspects, both musical (DJing and MCing) and visual (graffiti and b-boying or breakdancing), from its origins as the urban folk culture of the mid-'70s Bronx to its present status as the most important and biggest-selling genre in modern music. Following hip-hop's basic tenet of competition, *The Rough Guide to Hip-hop* is a comprehensive reference guide, but it is an opinionated one and, hopefully, will spark as many debates and cause as many beefs as it quashes. As the RZA says on Ghostface Killah's "Nutmeg", *The Rough Guide to Hip-hop* is "In stereo/Crazy as Shapiro".

Acknowledgements

Thanks to everyone at the Rough Guides – particularly my editors Orla Duane and Jonathan Buckley – Mike Lewis, Pooh Daddy, YT, Michael Schenker, and thanks, most of all, to my wife Rachael, who is more inspirational than all the CDs and 12"s mentioned in this book put together.

Tha Alkaholiks/
Likwit Crew

Given their name and SoCal origins, it should come as no surprise that Tha Alkaholiks are protégés of legendary partier and St. Ides pitch-man King Tee. Tash (Rico Smith), J-Ro (James Robinson) and E-Swift (Eric Brooks) made their vinyl debut on King Tee's **Tha Triflin' Album** (1993) on the stellar "I Got It Bad Y'all".

Tha Alkaholiks' debut album, **21 & Over** (1993), was a collection of good old-fashioned party rhymes, stoner anthems and shout-outs to their favourite brands of malt liquor. "Hooked on gin and tonic like ya mama's hooked on phonics", the Liks cold-rocked the party with drunken juvenilia, but in the G-Funk era it was one of the more

MIKE LEWIS

refreshing sounds in hip-hop. "Make Room" was an enormous, floor-filling single with wailing JB horns and booming beats that had far more to do with the East Coast than LA, while "Likwit" was simply fat no matter where it came from. As if to fully prove their funk credentials, even the album's most stupid moment, "Only When I'm Drunk", featured J-Ro actually burping on beat.

The group somehow managed not to become a one-joke act and on **Coast II Coast** (1995) they matured without losing their sense of fun. While the Diamond D-produced "Let It Out" covered old territory (admittedly well), tracks like "Flashback" and "WLIX" saw the group reminisce about hip-hop's glory days like they were elder statesmen.

There were no signs of the Liks checking into the Betty Ford clinic on **Likwidation** (1997) as the inevitable collaboration with Ol' Dirty Bastard, "Hip Hop Drunkies", proved. However, the joy was no longer there: both "Killin' It" with Xzibit and "All Night" (a collection of old-school party rhymes over a Stevie Wonder Moog riff) had killer production, but Tash and J-Ro sounded ornery and tired.

Tha Alkaholiks' Likwit Crew (Defari, Lootpack and Barbershop MCs), however, kept the momentum going with a collection of superb underground releases. Defari's "Bionic" and especially "People's Choice" (both 1997) found the school teacher blueprinting an alternative LA style that would be picked up by groups like Dilated Peoples. His slept-on **Focused Daily** (1999) album was a collection of classic flows and undiluted beats like "Likwit Connection" and "Keep it on the Rise". Lootpack's **Soundpieces** (1999) followed suit with devastating tracks like "The Anthem", "Whenimondamic" and "The Long Awaited".

Tash's solo album, **Rap Life** (1999), managed to do what the Liks hadn't been able to as a group recently – sound like they were having fun. Catashtrophe didn't exactly break any boundaries, but the album was inebriating all the same.

⊙ **21 & Over**   Loud, 1993

It may have been nothing but "party and bullshit", but at least they didn't overstay their welcome or throw up on your sofa.

Artifacts

Coming out of "New Jeruzalem" (or Newark, New Jersey) in the mid-'90s, the Artifacts helped lay out the parameters and mind-set of much of the underground hip-hop that was to follow in their wake. Comprised of former graff writers Tame One and El Da Sensai, the Artifacts gave their DJ (DJ Kaos) some and wrote homages to the burners in the train yards at a time when rappers' egos and standard music-biz promotional practices were threatening to destroy the cultural aspects of hip-hop.

The Artifacts first appeared on "Do Ya Wanna Hear It" (1993), a collaboration with the Nubian Crackers. The group got widespread exposure on the East Coast with "Wrong Side of Da Tracks" (1994). With the oft-sampled line, "I'm out to bomb like Vietnam", on top of a Grover Washington Jr. loop, "Wrong Side of Da Tracks" was a tribute to aerosol culture that managed to find some space on the airwaves for itself when Biggie and Tupac were running things.

Between a Rock and a Hard Place (1994) followed a similar blue-print with crunching drums and catchy horn loops, particularly on the singles "C'mon Wit Da Get Down", which featured a pre-stardom Busta Rhymes as well as some of the first sightings of now classic breaks from David Axelrod and Galt McDermot, and "Dynamite Soul", with Timbaland's favourite rapper, Mad Skillz.

The mellow but eerily insistent "Art of Facts" followed in 1996, preceding their second album, **That's Them** (1997). The sequel to "Wrong Side ...", "Return to Da Wrongside", sported a killer Bennie Maupin sample and "Collaboration of Mics" featured Lords Finesse and Jamar, but the album was a bit too one-dimensional. After a single as the Brick City Kids ("Brick City Kids/What What") for Rawkus in 1997, Tame One and El Da Sensai, like Journey, went their separate ways.

Tame One has since appeared on tracks from Fatal Hussein and Redman and worked with his Boom Skwad posse. He has also dropped two solo joints, "In Ya Area" (1998) and "Trife Type Tymez" (1999), on his Boom Skwad label. El Da Sensai, meanwhile, has become something of a hired gun on the underground, working with everyone from Organized Konfusion and Mike Zoot (on Sensai's "Frontline" (1998) single) to Norway's Tommy Tee and the UK's Creators.

⊙ **Between a Rock and a Hard Place**   Big Beat/Atlantic, 1994

From its appreciation of graffiti to its beat archaeology, this is a classic of the underground aesthetic.

Audio Two

The duo of Milk Dee and Gizmo is in this book for one reason: one of the greatest singles, hip-hop or otherwise, of all time. A supercharged blast of noyze, "Top Billin'" (1987) was everything hip-hop was supposed to be about – drum machines that rumbled and screeched like the A-train, blunt cuts from Giz, a sample from Stetsasonic's "Go Brooklyn 1" in the background, and a rap from Milk that was all pumped-up b-boy attitude. Perhaps even better than the original mix was Clark Kent's remix, which introduced both the Jimmy Castor

"Going way back" intro and the piano riff from Rick James's "Mary Jane". If Milk has a resemblance to a certain female MC, it's not surprising: MC Lyte was Milk and Giz's half-sister. In fact, the whole family initially recorded for dad Nat Robinson's First Priority label.

"Top Billin'" anchored their debut album, **What More Can I Say?** (1988), which took its name from the hook from "Top Billin'". Although much of the album attempted to recapture "Top Billin'"'s energy burst to little effect, **What More Can I Say?** had some fine, disorienting production from Stetsasonic's Daddy-O, the inspired lunacy of "I Like Cherries" and the funny follow-up single, "Hickeys Around My Neck". **I Don't Care** (1990) was more of the same, but had a semi-classic in "Get Your Mother Off the Crack" and the reprehensible gay-bashing of "Whatcha Lookin' At".

By this time, hip-hop had largely passed the duo by, while their half-sis borrowed Milk's rhyming style and rode it to hip-hop stardom. The group split in 1992 and Milk released a solo album, **Never Dated** (1994), for American Recordings. The album's title wasn't entirely accurate, but it had a few moments where Milk almost reignited the flame of "Top Billin'", especially the stoopid fresh duet with the Beastie Boys' Ad-Rock.

⊙ **What More Can I Say?**   First Priority, 1988

A pretty typical album from the period (two great cuts and a lot of lame filler), but its high point is one of the genre's apexes.

B-boying

Despite worldwide successes from the Sugar Hill Gang, Grandmaster Flash & the Furious Five, Afrika Bambaataa and Run DMC, you've got to wonder if hip-hop would ever have made it out of New York if it wasn't for the infectious athleticism of the b-boys. The phrase may have been brought to mainstream attention by Run DMC's "Sucker MCs" ("Cold chill at a party in a b-boy stance"), but b-boying had nothing to do with cold chillin'. "B-boy" is short for "break boy", Kool Herc's term for the dancers who went crazy when he dropped the breaks (segments of records where all the instruments drop out to let the drummers do their thing) of records like The Incredible Bongo Band's "Apache" and Mandrill's "Fencewalk". In fact, without the b-boys (and b-girls) reacting the way they did to Herc's records, there wouldn't be any hip-hop at all.

Like all aspects of hip-hop culture, b-boying is ultimately a form of competition – a facet that was crucial to its original popularity since b-boying began, when New York's ghettoes were run by street gangs. Afrika Bambaataa's Zulu Nation organization helped channel violence into dancing competitions: where b-boys would uprock (criss-crossing their arms and Pro Keds 69ers-clad feet while keeping everything else still) and then drop and scuff the floor with their creased Lee jeans while performing backspins and turtles.

While breakdancing (a term disowned by all b-boys) began with crews like the Nigger Twins, the Zulu Kings, the Salsoul Crew, the City Boys, Freeze Force, Starchild La Rock, The Disco Kids and the KC Crew, the most influential was undoubtedly the Rock Steady Crew. Formed in 1977 by Jo-Jo Torres, Jimmy Lee,

Mongo Rock, Spy and Jimmy Dee, the Rock Steady Crew gathered together the best of the second wave of Latino b-boys who had come to dominate the field since it migrated out of the Bronx in the early '70s. The RSC's main innovation was to make b-boying more athletic, more gymnastic. Many of these moves were pioneered by the two b-boys who are generally considered the greatest: Richie "Crazy Legs" Colón and Ken "Swift" Gabbert. Moves like the windmill, the whip, the 1990, the chair and the spider are credited to Crazy Legs and Ken Swift, who helped the RSC become the dominant crew in legendary battles against the Dynamic Rockers, the Floor Masters and the New York City Breakers.

Meanwhile, in Los Angeles, a kid called Don Campbell invented locking (freezing in between moves). The dance became so popular that he formed his own troupe in 1973, the Campbellock Dancers, which included such minor celebs as Fred "Rerun" Berry, Toni Basil and "Shabba-Doo" Quiñones. The style was expanded by The Electric Boogaloos ("Boogaloo Sam" Solomon, Timothy "Popin' Pete" Solomon, Skeeter Rabbit, Twisto Flex Don, Creepin' Cid and Tickin' Will), who invented moves like poppin', boogaloo, tickin', twisto-flex and the old man while dancing to Zapp records. Less of a Mitch Gaylord floor routine than the East Coast style, poppin' and lockin' emphasized upper body movements in almost geometric patterns. Thanks to Pop'N Taco, Mr. Wiggles, Sugar Pop and Loose Bruce, the style continues today and continues to influence the legions of Europeans and Japanese who have helped keep breakdancing alive, while American hip-hoppers ran from its *Flashdance* associations.

Bad Boy Records

Sean "Puffy" Combs might provide proof of Freud's famous equation between shit and gold, but if someone's going to trade in hip-hop's cultural capital for million-dollar success, better Cream Puff than Vanilla Ice. Writing new lyrics to all your favourite hits, Puffy is hip-hop's Weird Al Yankovic – just replace Al's humour with a messianic belief in his own greatness (he once released an industry-only showcase disc called **Puffy Combs: Changing the Sound of Popular Music**). Making a mockery of hip-hop's much-vaunted skills culture, Puff Daddy has built a fortune from a stable of talent-deficient MCs, turning rock critic Lester Bangs' attitude-is-everything dictum into a Nietzschean will to power.

Before he became the only hip-hop mogul who could rival such legends as his future paymaster Clive Davis or Walter Yetnikoff, Combs was a kid from money earnin' Mount Vernon, New York, who started promoting parties while attending Howard University in Washington DC. On the recommendation of childhood friend Heavy D, Combs landed a gig as an intern at Andre Harrell's Uptown Records. At the same time he was pro-moting a series of successful parties at Manhattan's Red Zone club called "Daddy's House". At the end of 1991, he organized a charity basketball game that went horribly wrong as nine people were trampled to death in a scramble to get inside.

A year later he emerged as the brains behind both the "Queen of Hip-Hop Soul" Mary J. Blige and chief boot knockers Jodeci. In order to get his acts played in both the Jeeps and the bedrooms, Puffy almost invented the art of street promotion, hiring teams of kids to sticker anything stationary in New York

→

and litter the club scene with flyers. As a result, he was promoted to vice president of A&R at Uptown. While still in that position, he conceived his Bad Boy Entertainment label and was fired for insubordination by Harrell.

Bad Boy became an imprint of Arista and immediately ruled the streets of New York with Craig Mack's "Flava in Ya Ear" (1994). Mack, who had previously recorded MC EZ & Troup's "Get Retarded" (1989), brought things back to the old school with his b-boy with a cold flow and corny jokes on his underrated album, **Project: Funk the World** (1994). Mack's album was released on the same day as Notorious B.I.G.'s **Ready to Die** (see entry) and, although it went gold, quickly took a back seat in Bad Boy's plans. Mack left the label and released the dire **Operation: Get Down** (1997) and became the butt of jokes from every comedian on BET. He returned in 2000, however, riding a loop of Frank Sinatra's "High Hopes" courtesy of 45 King on the massive "Wooden Horse".

Unfortunately for hip-hop fans, Bad Boy had debuted with its two best artists and it was all downhill from there. After some R&B projects – Biggie's former wife Faith Evans, 112 and Total – and Biggie's weaker Life After Death (1997), Puff Daddy & the Family released the mind-bogglingly awful **No Way Out** (1997), which somehow managed to go seven times platinum on the back of the Police-sampling "I'll Be Missing You" tribute to Biggie. Believe it or not, it took a whole team of behind-the-sceners like producer Derric "D-Dot" Angelettie and ghost writer Sauce Money to make it as execrable as it was – perish the thought of what it would've been like without their input. Even worse was the collected oeuvre of sidekick

→

Mase (**Harlem World** (1997), **Double Up** (1999) and **Mase Presents Harlem World – The Movement** (1999)), who rapped like a deer caught in the headlights. Even though your kid sister could freak a beat better than Mase, he too sold several million records. Thankfully, he retired in 1999 to devote his life to God.

After being responsible in one way or another for a staggering 40 percent of *Billboard* #1s in 1997, Puff relocated Daddy's House to the exclusive beach community of the Hamptons so he could live by the sea like his magic dragon namesake and bum rush the upper echelons of American "society". It soon started to go wrong, however. After their gold debut **Money, Power and Respect** (1998), The LOX very publicly split from Bad Boy with their "Let the LOX go" campaign and defected to Ruff Ryders Records. One month later, just like Black-Scholes, P Daddy's hit-making equations failed him on his sprawling **Forever** (1999) album, which has sold six million less than his debut.

Black Rob's much-delayed **Life Story** (2000) and its hit single, "Whoa!", seemed to steady the ship, but with Puff in legal trouble (not for the first time) over an incident in a New York club, Bad Boy's CEO was living up to his label's name and Puffy threatened to go up in smoke.

⊙ **Various Artists – Bad Boy's Greatest Hits**	Bad Boy, 1999

It's got nowhere near all of the label's hits, but if you can't get enough of Puff and Mase mumbling and stumbling their way through the karaoke machine of your local pub, this is the least painful way to do it.

Afrika Bambaataa

T he moral guardians who think that hip-hop is nothing but a negative force need to take a look at the life of Kevin Donovan. In fact, if it wasn't for hip-hop, New York might very well be the anarchic hell envisioned by John Carpenter in his film *Escape From New York*. Once the leader of the Big Apple's most notorious street gang, the Black Spades, Donovan, inspired by the sight of Africans fighting the British imperialist overlords in the wretched film *Zulu*, renamed himself Afrika Bambaataa and turned his gang into the Zulu Nation, an organization dedicated to urban survival through peaceful means. With their party promotions and b-boy battles, the Zulu Nation gave disenfranchised kids in The Bronx, and soon all of New York and beyond, a sense of belonging and success that they had previously only found in the street gangs that ruled New York during the early '70s.

While Bambaataa would be a hip-hop figurehead for this fact alone, his legendary reputation was cemented by his role in some of the most epochal records in hip-hop history. When he graduated from high school, Bambaataa was given a set of turntables by his mother and, with a prodigious record collection, he was soon given the honorific title, "Master of Records". You can hear the Master of Records at work on **Death Mix** (1983), a less-than-lawful copy of a tape of Bambaataa playing a party at the James Monroe High School in The Bronx that was released on Winley Records apparently without his consent. Featuring MCs advertising the next party over incredibly rough and primitive cutting and scratching by Bambaataa and Jazzy Jay, and the most dire fidelity since Edison's cylinders, **Death Mix** is hip-hop's equivalent of cave painting.

Bambaataa's first appearance on wax was the similarly ancient-

sounding live recording, "Zulu Nation Throwdown" (1980), also released by former doo-wop impresario Paul Winley. Far more important, however, was his first single for Tommy Boy, "Jazzy Sensation" (1981), made with the Jazzy 5. Ironically, "Jazzy Sensation" was the closest Bam would get to "pure" hip-hop during his studio career. After the infectious group energy and Sugar Hill-style street funk of "Jazzy Sensation", Bambaataa would remake hip-hop in the image of his favourite group, Kraftwerk. Exploiting the surreal popularity of Düsseldorf's showroom dummies in New York discos and block parties, Bambaataa, keyboardist John Robie and producer Arthur Baker welded the melody of Kraftwerk's "Trans-Europe Express" to the synth-bass of Kraftwerk's "Numbers" and the percussion from Captain Sky's "Super Sperm" to create the song that taught the world that machines were just as funky as James Brown. Bambaataa & Soulsonic Force's "Planet Rock" (1982) was the Rosetta stone of electro and one of the most important records of the last quarter century.

They followed "Planet Rock" with the almost as good "Looking for the Perfect Beat" (1982) and "Renegades of Funk" (1983). These three early hip-hop masterpieces were included on his very late first album, **Planet Rock: The Album** (1986). However, in the lag between his singles and album, Bam hooked up with James Brown for the **Unity Pt. 1-6** EP (1984) – which contained the title track and so-so versions of every b-boy's favourite Godfather track, "Give it Up or Turn it A Loose" – and Bill Laswell as Shango for **Shango Funk Theology** (1984), which included a cover of Sly Stone's "Thank You Falettinme Be Mice Elf Agin". An even stranger cover could be found on Bambaataa's second Tommy Boy album, **Beware (The Funk Is Everywhere)** (1986): an electro-shocked version of The MC5's "Kick Out the Jams".

Since then, Bambaataa has been working with ex-members of P-Funk, remixing "Planet Rock" about a hundred times and forging links with the rave generation that "Planet Rock" helped spawn.

● **Planet Rock: The Album**　　　　　　　　　Tommy Boy, 1986

Bambaataa's legacy has not been properly preserved on CD, but dodgy vinyl bootlegs circulate everywhere. This package is the only place that you can find three of his most important singles in one place.

Rob Base & DJ E-Z Rock

obert Ginyard (aka Rob Base) and Rodney Bryce (aka DJ E-Z Rock) might have started their careers as ten-year-olds in Harlem, but they will forever be remembered for one single that they released in 1988. Called the greatest single of all time by *Spin* magazine in 1989, "It Takes Two" was an enormous club hit that ranks as one of the most breathtakingly immediate records ever made by someone who was not James Brown. Of course, the part of the record that grabbed you by the seat of your pants was a loop of a trademark JB yelp and grunt that electrified "It Takes Two" with Brownian motion. The loop (as well as the beat and the vocal hook) was taken from Lyn Collins' 1972 single, "Think (About It)", which was Brown's most influential outside production. Along with Eric B & Rakim's "I Know You Got Soul", "It Takes Two" heard Brown's disembodied shrieks and chopped-up beats as the main elements in a chaotic urban soundscape and helped make Brother Rapp an unavoidable presence in hip-hop.

While Base and E-Z Rock made Brown's energy positively bionic on "It Takes Two", their debut album, **It Takes Two** (1988), was filled with Base's straightforward raps layered on top of even more straight-forward samples. "Joy and Pain" was a respectable follow-up single in commercial terms (if not artistically), but Maze and Frankie Beverly later sued the duo for failing to clear the sample and for failing to properly credit the large chunk of the lyrics that the duo borrowed from the Maze song of the same name.

Base's follow-up, **The Incredible Base** (1989), ditched E-Z Rock, but followed the same format of simple cadences and familiar samples. Antic-ipating the Puff Daddy formula by a decade, Base laid tired rhymes over obvious samples of The Gap Band, Marvin Gaye and Edwin Starr. Reunited with E-Z Rock, Base tried to recapture the electricity and success of **It Takes Two** on **Break It Down** (1994) with predictably lame results.

⊙ **It Takes Two**   Profile, 1988

Most of the album is acceptable, although very dated, pop-rap; the title track, however, is one of the truly great hip-hop singles and the only reason Rob Base and DJ E-Z Rock are in this book.

Beastie Boys

In the liner notes to the **New York Thrash** (1982) cassette, the crucial document of New York hardcore punk, compiler Tim Sommer wrote, "Beastie Boys, brief stars somewhere in the fall, nutty, fun and a bit bizarre, unfortunately dissolving before they could reach their full promise". Doh! OK, so it's unfair to single out Sommer's boner: not even John Landau would have realized that these young, drunk and stupid high-school kids were the future of popular music.

Formed in May 1981, when bassist Adam Yauch joined the Young Aborigines – a punk group comprising vocalist Mike Diamond, drummer Kate Schellenbach and guitarist John Berry – the first incarnation of the Beastie Boys was inspired by Black Flag and Bad Brains to up the tempo of punk rock into masturbatory blurts of teen angst. Their **Polly Wog Stew** EP (1982) included such gems of breathless energy as the 23-second "Riot Fight", the 57-second "Beastie" and the positively epic, one-minute-and-20-second account of an ambush on a punk-rock doorman "Egg Raid on Mojo". Soon after the EP was released, Berry left and was replaced by former member of the Young and the Useless, Adam Horovitz.

The following year, the group released "Cooky Puss" (1983), a recording of a series of phony phone calls to various franchises of the Carvel ice-cream store chain. The record blew up on New York college radio to such an extent that a portion of it was actually used in a British Airways commercial, prompting the group to sue. The group soon started to get into hip-hop and hooked up with "DJ" and NYU student Rick Rubin, and Schellenbach gradually faded out of the picture.

Now young, drunk and stoopid, the Beasties were known as MCA (Yauch), Mike D (Diamond) and King Ad-Rock (Horovitz) and ran around in matching red sweatsuits and Puma Clydes. With Rubin producing and releasing the results on his new Def Jam label, they released the **Rock Hard** EP (1984) which featured John Bonham drums and Angus Young guitar riffs. More rock-rap, pro-wrestling shenanigans were to be found on "She's on It" (1985) from the *Krush Groove* soundtrack. Somehow, they got themselves the opening slot

on Madonna's Like a Virgin tour and offended a nation of pre-teens with their Dictators-set-to-a-drum-machine routines. When singles like "It's a New Style" and "Hold it Now, Hit It" (both 1986) came out, however, they began to apply their Jewish wise-guy schtick ("If I play guitar it'd be Jimmy Page/The girlies that I like are under age") to more conventional hip-hop beats.

They may have seemed like a joke, but **License to Ill** (1986) became the multi-platinum soundtrack to every frat party from Hilo to Harvard. Tracks like "Fight For Your

Right (To Party)" and "No Sleep 'til Brooklyn" were intended as paro-
dies of Neanderthal rock, but they were so perfect that, like other pop
burlesquers Steely Dan and Chic, the Beasties ended up becoming
what they were poking fun at. Nevertheless, it was a helluva lot of fun.

With their drunken stage antics and questionable sexual politics,
the three stooges became media pariahs. Retreating from the spotlight
and splitting from Def Jam, they relocated to LA to record **Paul's Boutique** (1989) with the Dust Brothers. A Salvation Army store of the
mind, **Paul's Boutique** was one of the high watermarks of the sampling era. The throwaway references to White Castle and Led Zep on
the first album were now a dense collage of name checks, allusions
and "B-Boy Bouillabaisse", enhanced by the Dust Brothers' thrift-store
clutter style of production.

The Beasties were inspired by the Dust Brothers to become dedicated crate diggers, but their growing affection for groups like The Meters
actually led them to pick up their instruments again. **Check Your Head**
(1992) fused laidback late '60s funk with arena-rock-sized, fuzzy grooves
and hardcore textures, creating the blueprint for skate and snowboard
music in the process. **Ill Communication** (1994) was more of the same.
"Sabotage" is the definitive song of this part of their career and its
accompanying video, directed by Spike Jonze, is one of the defining documents of the '90s. During this time, with their reformed attitude, attempts
to free Tibet, occasionally great magazine *Grand Royal* and clothing line,
the Beasties had become the darlings of the music and lifestyle press,
principally because just about every editor and writer wanted to be them.

After some fairly pointless EPs and vault-raiding exercises, **Hello
Nasty** (1998) found the former class clowns revisiting the old school
they had once terrorized. "Intergalactic" and "Body Movin'" were retro-
electro reminiscences crafted with the help of the superlative turntable
skills of new DJ Mix Master Mike, but their ears remained open

enough to include some bossa nova on "I Don't Know". Now firmly elder statesmen, the Beastie Boys had miraculously maintained the longest viable career in hip-hop, approaching their twentieth anniversary still at the top of their game.

⊙ **License to III** Def Jam, 1986

Disproves Dean Warner's pronouncement that "young, drunk and stupid is no way to go through life".

⊙ **Paul's Boutique** Capitol, 1989

The white **It Takes a Nation of Millions to Hold Us Back**.

Beatnuts

Among the finest producers in the biz, the Beatnuts were the logical progression from Pete Rock. Both melodic and head-snapping, the beats constructed by Psycho Les (Lester Fernandez) and JuJu (Jerry Timeo) defined the state of the art of New York hip-hop in the mid-'90s. Like most of the best producers, before getting into production, the Corona, Queens duo were aspiring DJs and as teenagers they ran in a clique with the X-ecutioners' Rob Swift. After stockpiling a massive record collection at the tail end of the golden age of sampling, Les and JuJu began their careers as producers with Chi-Ali's "Age Ain't Nothin' But A Number" (1991). Running with the Native Tongues, they soon produced tracks for Monie Love, the Jungle Brothers, Artifacts, Pete Nice and Kurious.

Joining forces with MC Fashion (aka Al Tariq, aka Bertony Smalls), the Beatnuts released the **Intoxicated Demons** EP in 1993. Sounding like the funkiest frat party you never attended,

Intoxicated Demons' best tracks – "Reign of the Tec", "Psycho Dwarf" and "No Equal" – combined cutting-edge, jazzy production from the labs with the rudest, crudest lyrics from the gutter. **Beatnuts** (1994) was more of the same: tracks about oral sex and fried chicken, jump-around party anthems, gratuitous gun play, scintillating beats and loops and a Das-EFX dis thrown in for good measure.

Despite their prodigious mixing-desk skills, the Beatnuts remained a strictly underground concern until their 1997 album, **Stone Crazy**.

MIKE LEWIS

Fashion left the group, but he was replaced with numerous cameo appearances from various MCs. The album's shining moment was the ridiculously catchy "Off the Books", which featured Big Punisher on the mic. Still, as hot as Pun's verse was, it was the flute riff that propelled the track into the charts. The rest of **Stone Crazy** was similarly loopy and established Les and JuJu as the finest East Coast knob twiddlers this side of DJ Premier.

Unfortunately, **A Musical Massacre** (1999) sounded stale by comparison. The lead single, "Watch Out Now", was a blatant attempt to recreate the success of "Off the Books", while the rest of the album just sounded like everything else that was around. Of course, when they felt like challenging themselves, the beats were as bumping as ever.

⊙ **Beatnuts** Relativity, 1994

Lyrically, it's not exactly appropriate for schoolchildren, but this album is a lesson in beatsmanship with model organ loops, Afro-Cuban percussion parts chopped into head-nodding patterns and guitar fuzz driving choruses.

Big Daddy Kane

King Asiatic Nobody's Equal is just that: perhaps the most complete MC ever. No one has managed to match Big Daddy Kane's combination of fierce battle rhymes, smooth lover's rap and Five Percent knowledge. Jiggy long before Puffy ever got busy, as intimidating as Rakim, dropping Muslim science on huns before King Sun, as funny as Chris Rock, Kane not only destroyed the mic device, he also ghost-wrote rhymes for Roxanne Shanté and Biz Markie.

Antonio M Hardy was introduced to the Juice Crew by Biz in 1986 and made his debut the following year with "Raw" (1987). With Marley Marl's killer production based on Lyn Collins' "Mama Feelgood", "Raw" must have given the Bomb Squad a few ideas. Even so, Kane stole the show with nimble battle rhymes like "Rulin' and schoolin' MCs that I'm duellin'/Watch 'em all take a fall as I sit there coolin'/On my throne with a bronze microphone/Mmm, god bless a child that can hold his own".

If it wasn't released in 1988, perhaps hip-hop's greatest year, **Long Live the Kane** would be hailed as one of the greatest hip-hop albums ever. Although it was overshadowed by Public Enemy, Boogie Down Productions and NWA, **Long Live the Kane** was nearly perfect. "Ain't No Half Steppin'" saw Kane slow the tempo, but remain as ferocious as he was on "Raw", while "Wrath of Kane" found Kane stomping MCs like they were roaches on top of a beat that would have had most rap-

pers hyperventilating after the second bar. While the rhymes were almost uniformly b-boy boasts, the cover hinted at Kane's future direction. Decked out in his "fresh Cameo cut", cloaked in a toga and gold rope chain with three female minions feeding him grapes, Kane started to think of himself as a ladies' man.

It's a Big Daddy Thing (1989) found Kane distancing himself from Marley Marl's hard funk production towards a *GQ* sheen. The album's biggest hit, "I Get the Job Done" (1989), featured fantastic New Jack beats from Teddy Riley and Kane still in impressive form, but the love-man schtick was just lame, and only made worse by tracks like "Pimpin' Ain't Easy". He started to wear designer suits in his videos, sipping champagne and macking, and, although he contributed a fiery verse to Public Enemy's "Burn Hollywood Burn", by his next album,

Taste of Chocolate (1990), he was duetting with Barry White.

Although he envisioned himself carousing in a penthouse, rubbing his girl down with essential oils like Teddy Pendergrass, **Prince of Darkness** (1991) and **Looks Like a Job For Big Daddy Kane** (1993) were treated like street trash by the hip-hop audience. Instead of changing his image for **Daddy's Home** (1994), he spent his time posing nude for *Playgirl* and Madonna's *Sex* and totally played himself out. **Veteranz Day** (1998) wasn't as horrific as it could have been, but it wasn't anywhere near as pretty as Big Daddy thought he was.

⊙**Long Live the Kane**   Cold Chillin', 1988

With Kane still hungry and Marley Marl at the peak of his powers, this is one of the true greats.

Big Punisher

The history books will remember Big Punisher as the first solo Latino rapper to go platinum, but hip-hop heads will honour Pun as one of the funniest, most nimble MCs of the '90s. Born Christopher Rios in November 1971, he started rapping at the end of the '80s under the name Big Moon Dog. With future members of his Terror Squad crew, Triple Seis and Cuban Link, the renamed Pun caught the attention of Diggin' In The Crates Crew's Fat Joe, who introduced Pun on "Firewater", the B-side to his "Envy" single from his Jealous One's Envy (1996) album. After matching Raekwon word for word on that track, Pun quickly became a fixture on the underground mix tape circuit.

It was Pun's verse on the Beatnuts' "Off the Books" (1997), however, that really turned heads. Riding the track's flute hook, Pun spryly dropped rhymes like "It's all love, but love's got a thin line/And Pun's got a big nine/Respect crime, but not when it reflect mine" and "My cream's fat/I smoke the greenest grass/My bitch got the meanest ass". His first single, "You Ain't a Killer" (1998), appeared on the *Soul in a Hole* soundtrack, but it was his second that made him a star. A massive summertime hit with its piano stabs and chorus from R&B singer Joe, Pun's "Still Not a Player (Remix)" (1998) saw him take over the title of "overweight lover" from Heavy D: "I'm not a player, I just fuck a lot".

"Still Not a Player" anchored his debut album, **Capital Punishment** (1998). Although his rhyme skills were evident throughout (particularly on "Twinz" and its superlative couplet, "Dead in the middle of Little Italy/Little did we know that riddled a middle man who didn't know diddly"), the production was too slick and pandered to hip-hop's pop contingent. It achieved its aims, though: **Capital Punishment** has sold some two million copies.

Along with Fat Joe, Cuban Link, Triple Seis, Armageddon and Prospect, Pun released the equally commercially minded **Terror Squad: The Album** (1999). By this time, though, Pun's health was becoming a serious issue. On February 7, 2000, he suffered a heart attack while staying at a hotel in upstate New York and died later that day. The cause was said to be health problems resulting from his obesity: at the time of his death, he weighed a reported 698 pounds (50 stone). He had completed **Yeeah Baby!** (2000) weeks before his death and it was released two months later. There were a couple of hardcore headnodders like "New York Giants" and "We Don't Care", but the out-of-place guitars on "Leather Face", the too-obvious "It's So Hard" with Donnell Jones, and the Simple Minds interpolation on "Don't You (Forget About Me)" meant that the album wasn't the memorial he deserved.

⊙**Capital Punishment**   Loud, 1998

"Still Not a Player" allowed him to mix with Jennifer Lopez, but there are enough bangers like "Dream Shatterer" to make this worthwhile to even player haters.

Biz Markie

T he clown prince of hip-hop, the one and only Biz Markie (Marcel Hall) may have been a pudgy guy in an ill-fitting T-shirt, but unlike the Fat Boys' "The Diabolical", Biz Markie was no novelty act. Biz's comedic talent was only one aspect of his formidable armoury. Biz Markie was a formidable beat boxer, as he proved on his first wax appearance, Roxanne Shanté's "The Def Fresh Crew" (1986). The human SP 1200 backed Shanté's ferocious rap with a symphony of Bronx cheers and an imitation of a cat-food commercial, and on the flip ("Biz Beats") he created one of the truly great saliva solos in hip-hop history.

Biz Mark was also a fine MC with perhaps the most engaging personality of any mic spitter. Just like Shanté, most of his rhymes were written by Big Daddy Kane, but it was the Biz's delivery, rather than the words that mattered. "The human orchestra"'s first single, "Make the Music With Your Mouth Biz" (1986), featured not only Biz's beat boxing, but it also introduced his singular, drunken rhyming style over a crashing drum beat and an Isaac Hayes piano snippet. With its killer production (based on Steve Miller's "Fly Like an Eagle"), "Nobody Beats the Biz" (1987) parodied New York electronics chain The Wiz as Biz dropped the immortal, and much imitated, line, "Reagan is the prez, but I voted for Shirley Chisholm".

Going Off (1988), which included his singles, remains a classic. Riding the beat from James Brown's "Papa Don't Take No Mess", "The Vapors" was a savage and funny attack on jealous neighbours that could've been written by Leiber and Stoller. "Something for the Radio" was another instant classic, but the landmark cut was probably "Pickin' Boogers". While hip-hop was turning hardcore and political, Biz was rapping about flipping snot into other people's lunch over the groove from Graham Central Station's "The Jam".

The Biz Never Sleeps (1989) saw Biz take over production duties from Marley Marl. While Biz has a record collection that is probably equalled only by Afrika Bambaataa (according to legend, he had to buy a second house just to store his records), his mixing-desk skills couldn't match Marl's. Nevertheless, the album had the absurd "Just a Friend", which found Biz singing like a dying swan – on the radio it was the perfect antidote to the narcissism of Bobby Brown and his ilk.

I Need a Haircut (1991) was again produced by the Biz. While he dug deep in his crates on tracks like "Check it Out", the album became more famous for his failure to dig deep enough. He was sued by Gilbert O'Sullivan for his use of "Alone Again (Naturally)" and Judge Kevin Duff ruled that sampling was theft under copyright law. Biz was threatened with time in the slammer and hip-hop's golden age of sampladelia was over. **All Samples Cleared** (1993) may have featured production by Large Professor, but it largely comprised obvious samples and uninspired raps. Ever since, Biz has basically traded on his cartoon persona and shows up in cameo appearances for the likes of the Beastie Boys singing "Benny and the Jets" and Handsome Boy Modeling School singing "Night Fever".

Mike Lewis

⊙**Going Off** Cold Chillin', 1988

With Marley Marl's stellar production and Biz's inspired lunacy, this is damn near a perfect album.

Black Eyed Peas

oming out of the LA live scene like some Sunset Strip metal band (complete with long hair and scarves), the Black Eyed Peas earned their reputation with their high-energy, stage-diving performances years before they ever got a record contract. Perhaps because of their rock-like dues-paying and "progressive hip-hop" mentality, Will.I.Am, Appl D App and Taboo were, along with Jurassic 5, the toast of hip-hop tourists in 1998.

With live instruments, thrift store garb and anti-gangsta lyrics, their debut album **Behind the Front** (1998) was a cause célèbre among European dance mags. The breakthrough track was "Fallin' Up", a plea for peace in hip-hop's intercoastal rivalry. "Karma" interpolated the chorus of Blondie's "One Way or Another" to warn gangsta rappers that there "Ain't no runnin' from karma". While their level-headed lyrics attracted pacifists, hippies and people who didn't understand metaphor, it was their warm, mellow production that really got heads turning. "Clap Your Hands" sampled both The Meters and Inner Circle to recreate an old-school block party vibe, while "What it Is" swiped a lick from Tom Browne's "Funkin' for Jamaica". There were also plenty of acoustic guitars and basslines that were as warm and fuzzy as a Guatemalan sweater. It wasn't all jazziance and Brazilian percussion, however: they also sampled Laid Back's lost

'80s classic, "White Horse", and made like Frankie Valli on "Joints & Jams".

Following the same blueprint but without any inspiration or passion, the title of **Bridging the Gaps** (2000) seemed to indicate the only places that would play such insipid hip-hop.

⊙**Behind the Front**   Interscope, 1998

With Interscope running scared from anything gangsta-ish, the Black Eyed Peas capitalized with this pleasant, harmless album.

Black Moon

As is typical of the cities' histories, in the early to mid-'90s, LA rap made everyday violence cinematic and ultra-stylized, while New York hip-hop presented it raw and unmediated. Emphasizing pure skills, dusty samples and murderous metaphors, Black Moon represented the grim inverse of Dr. Dre's well-polished G-Funk.

The trio of Buckshot, 5Ft. Excellerator and DJ Evil Dee exploded on to the scene with their debut single, "Who Got the Props?" (1993). On top of a deceptively mellow Fender Rhodes loop from Da Beatminerz production team (Evil Dee and his brother Mr. Walt), Buckshot Shorty "sounded like an automatic" as he delivered this deliriously combative anthem to "Crooklyn, better known as Brooklyn". **Enta Da Stage** (1993) featured more gun-clapping lyrics and denuded smooth soul samples like "How Many MCs?", "Black Smif-N-Wessun", "Son Get Wrec" and "Slave". A Barry White-heavy remix of "I Got Cha Opin" found the group breaking through to mainstream radio, but aside from an unauthorized collection of B-sides and freestyles, **Diggin' in Dah Vaults** (1996), the group wouldn't be heard from again until the so-so **War Zone** (1999), credited to Buckshot, 5Ft. and Evil Dee rather than Black Moon.

In the meantime, however, Buckshot (with Dru Ha) started the Duck Down label and management team. Part of Buckshot's Boot Camp Clik, Smif-N-Wessun (the duo of MCs Tek and Steele) followed in Black Moon's orbit with the magnificently moody "Bucktown" (1994). **Dah Shinin'** (1995) was similarly slow and dusty, seething with menace and punctuated by blasts of rude bwoy reggae – an absolute underground classic. After being forced to change their name by the Smith and Wesson gun company, Tek and Steele re-emerged as Da

Cocoa Brovaz on the surprisingly good **Rude Awakening** (1998), which featured a stunning collaboration with reggae star Eek-A-Mouse on "Off the Wall".

The Boot Camp Clik continued to come kicking with Heltah Skeltah (Rock and Ruck) and the Originoo Gun Clappaz (Starang Wondah, Louieville Sluggah and Top Dawg Da Big Kahuna). With new Beat-miner Baby Paul behind the boards, Heltah Skeltah and OGC's "Leflaur Leflah Eshkoshka" (1996) introduced the "Fab Five" on top of a serene synth loop. Heltah Skeltah's **Nocturnal** (1996) was an overlooked album of weeded beats and laidback flows, while **Magnum Force** (1999) suffered from awkward and money-grubbing collaborations with the likes of Tha Dogg Pound. OGC's **Da Storm** (1996) was similarly slept on, which was hard to believe with the fire of "Wild Cowboys in Bucktown" and "Hurricane Starang". Their **M-Pire Shrikez Back** (1999), however, suffered from the absence of Da Beatminerz, stranding the OGC's hardcore styles in a morass of sterile live instrumentation.

⊙ **Enta Da Stage**   Wreck/Nervous, 1993

Gritty, dusty, nasty New York hip-hop at its best.

Kurtis Blow

G randmaster Flash may have a bigger profile in hindsight, but Kurtis Blow was hip-hop's biggest early star. The erstwhile Curtis Walker was a mobile DJ who was turned on to rapping by DJ Hollywood. Basing his smooth style almost entirely on Hollywood's, Kurtis Blow was spotted at an MC battle at the Hotel Diplomat by *Billboard* writers Rocky Ford and J.B. Moore, who were persuaded by

Blow's manager, Russell Simmons, to let him record their song "Christmas Rappin'". Released at the end of 1979, "Christmas Rappin'" followed the formula of "Rapper's Delight" by aping the "Good Times" bassline and Nile Rodgers' chicken scratch guitar, but it surpassed the Sugar Hill Gang's magnum opus with better rhymes and a hefty dose of seasonal cheer.

"Christmas Rappin'" moved crazy numbers and Blow became the first rapper on a major label when he signed to Mercury. The song

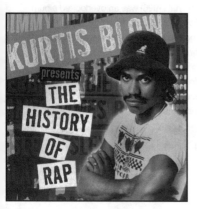

reached #30 on the UK pop charts and Simmons sweet-talked a place for Blow on Blondie's European tour. When he returned from Europe in 1980, Blow released one of the greatest singles in hip-hop history, "The Breaks". Complete with timbale breaks from Jimmy Delgado and spacy keyboard lines, "The Breaks" was a quantum leap from "Christmas Rappin'" in terms of musicality, but it was the sophisticated lyrics that really set the record apart. Bringing hip-hop out of the party and into the outside world, Blow rapped couplets like "If your woman steps out with another man/And she runs off with him to Japan" and "And you borrowed money from the mob/And yesterday you lost your job/Well these are the breaks". Of course, there was also plenty of "Just do it, just do it, just do it, do it, do it", but it only added to the atmosphere, and "The Breaks" became hip-hop's first certified gold single.

"The Breaks" anchored Blow's first album, **Kurtis Blow** (1980). Although **Kurtis Blow** had more developed social commentary in the form of "Hard Times", Blow, like all early hip-hop artists, was a singles artist and all of his albums have acres of filler and awkward, straight R&B tracks. While "Rockin'" (1981) was OK, it wouldn't be until 1983 that Blow would have another artistic or commercial success. "Party Time", a track that briefly ruled the East Coast, was a tribal percussion throwdown that featured Washington DC go-go artists EU.

However, a group that featured an MC who used to go by the name of "The Son of Kurtis Blow" soon emerged and made the old school redundant overnight. Unlike his contemporaries, however, Blow did manage to have a couple of hits during the Run DMC era. "Basketball" (1984) was omnipresent on blacktops across New York from the Boogie Down to the 'burbs, while the joyous but poignant "If I Ruled the World" (1985) from the *Krush Groove* soundtrack would eventually be the basis for Nas's "If I Ruled the World (Imagine That)". There was also the drum machine symphony, "AJ Scratch" (1984) – an ode to Blow's DJ – but by this time Blow was more of a producer than an artist, working with the Disco 3 (aka the Fat Boys), the Fearless Four and Dr. Jeckyl & Mr. Hyde.

Blow continued to turn out eminently forgettable albums until the very optimistically titled **Back By Popular Demand** (1988). He now lives in LA, where he hosts an old-school radio show. In 1997 he compiled the three-volume **Kurtis Blow Presents the History of Rap** series for Rhino.

⊙ **Best of Kurtis Blow**   Mercury, 1994

Definitive early hip-hop.

Bone Thugs-N-Harmony

It's a wonder no one thought of it sooner: combine gangsta realness with smooth vocal group harmonies, throw in some triple-time, tongue-twisting rhymes for good measure and sell more than ten million records. Cleveland's Bone Thugs-N-Harmony's multi-platinum style was allegedly devised when one of these former drug dealers, Krayzie Bone (Anthony Henderson), was in prison for shooting his fellow thug Wish Bone (Byron McCane). When he got out of the pen, Krayzie, along with Wish, Layzie Bone (Steven Howse), Flesh-N-Bone (Stanley Howse) and Bizzie Bone (Charles Scruggs), formed a group called Bone Enterprises and united the smooth music to which real gangsters listen when they need to escape with the titillating tales of guns and drugs that people not living the life love to listen to.

Relocating to LA in 1993, the group renamed themselves Bone Thugs-N-Harmony and caught the ear of Eazy E, who signed them to his Ruthless Records label and hooked them up with production whiz DJ U-Neek, who helped craft the group's successful sound. Their debut release, the eight-track **Creepin on ah Come Up** EP (1994), eventually sold three million copies. The fairly standard Dr. Dre-style funk production was fleshed out with their G-funk barbershop harmonies and largely indecipherable raps about the game, revenge murders and Ouija boards. The breakout single was "Thuggish Ruggish Bone", which introduced the world to their sing-song, rapid-fire rhyming style.

E. 1999 Eternal (1995) knocked Michael Jackson's **HIStory** off the top of the American pop charts with its contradictory mix of dead-homie sentimentality and unrepentant violence. Beginning with muezzin incantation of "Da Introduction" and moving through the graceful brutality of "Mo' Murda" and "Die Die Die", **E. 1999 Eternal** envisioned a world that wasn't all that different from a ghettocentric heavy metal, a vibe only enhanced by the skull iconography, supernatural shtick and biblical doomsday verses. Elsewhere, though, the album was less schlocky: "1st of tha Month" catalogued the creative ends to which you could put your welfare check, while the huge hit, "Tha Crossroads" (built on a sample of the Isley Brothers' "Make You Say it Again Girl"), was a saccharine, but ultimately effective, eulogy to their label boss who had died of AIDS a few months earlier.

With some seven million sales behind them, the group went about empire building. They started their own label, Mo Thugs Records, which debuted with the platinum **Mo Thugs Family Scriptures** (1996). 1998's sequel, **Mo Thugs Chapter II: Family Reunion**, included what was probably hip-hop's second country song (after Disco Four's "Country Rock Rap"), "Ghetto Cowboy", which spent seven weeks on top of *Billboard*'s rap chart.

The Art of War (1997) was a double album that showed the group had predictably run out of ideas, but Americans still bought a couple of million copies of the damn thing, proving that in hip-hop cheddar and cheese often go hand in hand. The group's solo albums were generally mind-bogglingly awful. The title of Bizzy Bone's **Heaven'z Movie** (1998) was an invite for wags, and the album was notable only for "Thugz Cry" – a pretty savage attack on Eazy E's widow, Tomica Woods-Wright, who had taken over Ruthless. Krayzie Bone's **Thug Mentality 1999** (1999) was a 32-track epic of indo smoking, disses (Twista and Three 6 Mafia) and more budda smoking that had Krayzie's light-speed patter matching the speed of a machine gun's rat-a-tat-tat-tat, only to hit with the force of a ten-cent water pistol.

BTNHResurrection (2000) was another endurance test, but the rapid-fire snares, stuttering kicks, "Little Red Corvette" interpolations and occasionally funny lyrics ("Ecstasy"'s "I was trying to call my dick, but it couldn't hear me") made it less of an ordeal than their previous record.

⊙ **E. 1999 Eternal** Ruthless, 1995

Their style is singularly annoying, but DJ Uneek's production and the amazingly garish "Tha Crossroads" eventually crawl under your skin.

Boogie Down Productions

Formed by DJ Scott La Rock and KRS-One at a South Bronx homeless shelter, Boogie Down Productions were hip-hop's militant minimalists. BDP's music was characterized by rhythms so sparse that there was rarely anything resembling a hook. This kind of spartan rigour mirrored the rigid but confused ideology of KRS-One (Knowledge Rules Supreme Over Nearly Everyone). Undeniably one of hip-hop's greatest MCs, the Blastmaster is, like most important figures in the music's history, a bundle of contradictions: he was an articulate spokesperson against black-on-black violence, yet made his battle rhymes flesh when he threw PM Dawn off of a stage; he railed against materialism and the commercialization of hip-hop, and then did a commercial for Sprite.

BDP's first album, **Criminal Minded** (1987), avoided any political commitment, concerning itself instead with reasserting The Bronx as hip-hop's home. BDP's first single, "South Bronx" (1986), was an attack on MC Shan's "The Bridge" and the Juice Crew, who were claiming that Queensbridge was where hip-hop

→

was at. BDP eventually won hip-hop's second most famous battle with the awesome "The Bridge Is Over" which interpolated
both Billy Joel and some Kingston dancehall chatter. The
album's clipped drum machine beats and bleak samples were
constructed with the help of the Ultramagnetic MCs' Ced Gee
and were a brutal response to what KRS-One and Scott La Rock
considered the "sweetening" of hip-hop.

The first track on the follow-up, **By All Means Necessary**
(1988), indicated BDP's future direction in the wake of the murder
of Scott La Rock by an unknown assassin in August 1987. From
here on in, BDP would pioneer politically conscious rap alongside
Public Enemy. The
album's title and cover
art, which explicitly ref-
erenced Malcolm X,
and BDP were largely
responsible for the
resurgence of his
teachings in the hip-
hop community. "Stop
The Violence" was
KRS-One's response
to the death of his
friend and musical

conspirator and introduced his use of the metaphor of drug peddling for the abuses by the white power structure.

The Weldon Irvine-sampling "My Philosophy" introduced KRS-
One as hip-hop's teacher. His music frequently descended into

pedagogy, but still had occasional moments of brilliance. He founded the Stop the Violence Movement, which released "Self-Destruction" (1989), an all-star jam featuring BDP, PE, Stetsasonic and Kool Moe Dee. **Ghetto Music: The Blueprint Of Hip Hop** was released the same year and featured their most austere music yet. It also featured some of KRS-One's best songs, "Who Protects Us From You?" and "You Must Learn". But his pedantic tone started to take over and **Edutainment** (1990) frequently devolved into lecturing. After a remarkably decent live album, **Live Hardcore Worldwide** (1991), **Sex and Violence** (1992) suffered from the fallout of his divorce from Ms. Melodie and declined into the grotesque sexism.

BDP disbanded after this album, although KRS-One had purged many band members beforehand. His first solo album, **Return Of The Boom Bap** (1994), was not only a return to form, but a stylistic leap as well. While not abandoning the stark arrangements of old, he successfully incorporated the rhythmic innovations of hip-hop's new school to make a record of brooding funk, with "Sound of the Police" being the standout. This pattern continued on **KRS-One** (1995), which featured "MC's Act Like They Don't Know", an excellent collaboration with the one and only DJ Premier, who at this point could even rescue Joey Lawrence's street cred. The minimalism was gone entirely by the time of **I Got Next** (1997), which featured the excellent "Step Into My World (Rapture)", a reworking of Blondie's "Rapture" and The Mohawks' "Champ".

Maximum Strength (1998) was an uncomfortable match of the Blastmaster's stentorian roar with contemporary, lightweight beats, but by this point KRS had become an A&R exec at Reprise and concentrated most of his efforts on his Temple of Hip-Hop project.

⊙ **Criminal Minded**   B-Boy, 1987

One of hip-hop's towering monuments. Its rhythmic minimalism and fierce tribalism stripped hip-hop to its purest essence.

Brand Nubian

One of the first hip-hop singles to engage with the Jamaican dancehall, Masters of Ceremony's "Sexy" (1987) was a sizeable underground hit and the best track on the group's underrated **Dynamite** (1988) album. The lead raggamuffin on "Sexy" and tracks like "Cracked Out" and Master Move" was Grand Puba (Maxwell Dixon), who would soon leave the group and found Brand Nubian with New Rochelle, New York homeboys Derek X (Derek Murphy), Lord Jamar (Lorenzo Dechalus) and DJ Alamo.

Their first album, **One For All** (1990), was a masterpiece of sound (one of the best examples of the freedom allowed by sampling technology – loose, free-flowing rhymes and funky fresh flows), but it was let down by scabrous Five Percent rhetoric and lyrical hypocrisy. "Slow Down" was ample proof of hip-hop's redemptive powers (it turned the ignorance-is-bliss hippy bullshit of Edie Brickell and the New Bohemians' "What I Am" into a dark, moody groove), but its cautionary tale of

BRAND NUBIAN • HIP-HOP

drug abuse soon turned into an irritating, all too predictable indictment
of skeezers. Picking up where Trouble Funk left off, "Drop the Bomb"
was a fine, black nationalist anthem, but Brand Nubian just as often
ignored Muslim teachings when it suited.

Grand Puba and Alamo left the following year to make Puba's **Reel
to Reel** (1992). While the album highlighted Puba's dexterous flow on a
bunch of so-so party jams, **Reel to Reel** is perhaps most notable for
one of the first (if not the first) Tommy Hilfiger shout-out in hip-hop:
"Girbauds hanging baggy, Hilfiger on the top" from "360° (What Goes
Around)". **2000** (1995) had even less substance, most of it taken up
with Puba's flirtations with R&B.

With DJ Sincere replacing Alamo and Derek X becoming Sadat X,
Brand Nubian continued with **In God We Trust** (1992). The album featured a more hardcore sound, both in sound and sentiment (particularly on the hot but loathsome "Punks Jump Up to Get Beat Down" and
the more overt Five Percent rhetoric on tracks like "Allah and Justice"
and "Meaning of the 5%"). **Everything Is Everything** (1994) found the
group struggling in a changing hip-hop climate. They eschewed East
Coast block rockers in favour of West Coast rollers and an atrocious
Simply Red interpolation on "Hold On".

After Sadat X's spaghetti western set in the Harlem badlands, **Wild
Cowboys** (1996), the original Brand Nubian reunited for **Foundation**
(1998), easily their best album. There were still disgraceful platitudes
and the older-than-King-Tim-III hip-hop chestnut – "girls didn't want
nothing to do with me until I got a recording deal"-type thing – but as far
as non-playa-hating mainstream hip-hop goes, this was about as good
as it got while Puff Daddy was still running things. "The Return" was
one of those killer laidback funk grooves that DJ Premier seemed to
churn out by the ton without even getting out of bed, while "Back Up
Off the Wall" sounded like it was constructed out of a Chopin *Nocturne*.

⊙ **Foundation**   Arista, 1998

Brand Nubian's rhymes won't blow anyone's mind, but even the dodgy
Five Percent rhetoric sounds positively liberatory compared to Mase's
drivel.

British Hip-hop

Despite the fact that the UK has produced one of hip-hop's most
revered MCs (Slick Rick), the British music press will never tire of
bemoaning the state of its homegrown hip-hop. Ignored by
record companies, journalists, shops and record buyers in favour
of their American brethren and dance music, UK hip-hop artists
have survived in a state of not so benign neglect for so long that
any attention, positive or negative, comes as a relief. Part of the
problem is that the Brits just can't see when they have a good
thing. Monie Love, who had worked with MC Mell "O" and DJ
Pogo, didn't receive any acclaim until she hooked up with
Queen Latifah on "Ladies First" (1989). Derek B's "Rock the
Beat" (1988), while viewed as something of a joke in its home
country, became a crucial part of the New Orleans bounce aesthetic when its drum beat was fused with The Showboys' "Drag
Rap", helping Louisiana labels No Limit and Cash Money go
multi-platinum. As an A&R man at the Music of Life label, Derek
B helped sign the Demon Boyz (Mike J and Darren). Many people have accused Das EFX of borrowing their raggamuffin-
inspired, motormouth deliveries.

Of course, prescience isn't always a blessing. The Cookie
Crew's "Rok Da House" (1987) is generally credited as being the
first hip-house track – not an achievement to be proud of. The

→

39

Wee Papa Girl Rappers' rap version of George Michael's "Faith" (1988) didn't lend the scene any credibility, either. The Cookie Crew, Wee Papa Girl Rappers and the She-Rockers, all all-female groups, unfortunately firmly established Brit-hop's identity as a novelty genre despite the best efforts of the Afrocentric Overlord X, the hardcore Hijack, the symphonic First Down and the East End gangsta style of the London Posse.

Comprised of Rodney P and Bionic, the London Posse were perhaps the first UK hip-hop crew to attempt to rhyme in a style that wasn't consciously imitating American flavours on their **Gangster Chronicles** album (1990). Rodney P later showed up alongside Roots Manuva, Phi-Life Cypher and the Scratch Perverts' Tony Vegas on DJ Skitz's fine rallying cry for UK hip-hop, "Fingerprints of the Gods" (1998). Despite excellent production, the single was dragged down by the MCs' proximity to the Queen's English: "Just like Man United relying on Schmeichel". Nevertheless, the track featured the artists who would help take Brit-hop ever so slightly out of the dark ages.

South London's Roots Manuva (Rodney Smith) had previously worked with North London stalwarts Blak Twang before releasing his **Brand New Second Hand** album (1999) on the best British hip-hop label, the avantist Big Dada. Like many Brit MCs his flow has got as much to do with Barrington Levy and Capleton as it does with Method Man and Rakim, but unlike too many Limey MCs he understands how to attack a beat with effective cadences. Phi-Life Cypher, on the other hand, are the most mellifluous, flowing British MCs around, best sampled on

$\rightarrow$

their **Earth Rulers** EP (2000). Where most MCs who speak the Queen's English go for a kind of gothic Busta Rhymes bluster because of their Caribbean origins or because they simply can't rap, Phi-Life could pass muster among the Rotten Apple's purists.

Separated by a common language, the UK hip-hop scene made its most impact on American heads in the realm of turntablism. The Scratch Perverts – Tony Vegas, Prime Cuts, First Rate, Mr Thing and Harry Love – were one of the world's most formidable DJ crews, winning numerous ITF and DMC competitions. Unlike many of his turntablist brethren, Jeep Beat Collective's The Ruf wasn't interested in defending the turntable's status as a musical instrument or in tearing apart syntax with lightning-speed juxtapositions and improbably named scratches. Instead, on his excellent **Repossessed Wildstyles** (1998) and **Technics Chainsaw Massacre** (1999) albums he slowed down the pace of the cuts, broke out some party tricks and packed his collages full of hooks and mnemonic devices.

In order to break the language barrier, many British producers worked with Yankee MCs. The Creators (Si and Juliano) provided beats for MCs like Mos Def, El Da Sensai and Mike Zoot on their very fine **The Weight** album (2000); The Next Men (Baloo and Search) delivered a smooth, Wes-Montgomery-on-qualudes EP, **Break the Mould** (1999), that fell somewhere between Shawn J Period and Pete Rock with Grap Luva, Soulson and Red Cloud; DJ Vadim teamed up with Iriscience from the great Dilated Peoples, Sarah Jones and the great British beatboxer Killa Kella on his excellent **USSR Life From the other**

Side album (1999), and with New York's brilliant avant-garde MC trio, Anti-Pop Consortium, for The Isolationist's **Isolationist** (1999).

⊙ **Roots Manuva – Brand New Second Hand**   Big Dada, 1999

Imagine early Wu-Tang with deconstructed dub loops instead of Shaw Brothers kung-fu samples.

⊙ **The Creators – The Weight**   Bad Magic, 2000

They may be cheating by using American ringers, but the 100 percent British production is smoking.

Canadian Hip-hop

Although "iced out" has a very different meaning in the Great White North, Canadian MCs don't exactly situate their raps in the tundra or brag about shooting caribous instead of five-Os. Nonetheless, hip-hop north of the 49th parallel inevitably lies in the shadow of the music made across the border, but this distance from the centre of the hip-hop community has allowed the Great White North to develop a number of artists who don't have to depend on the Canadian content law to get airplay and who have broadened hip-hop's sonic frontiers.

The first Canuck MC that anyone ever heard of was Toronto's Maestro Fresh Wes. Long before "T dot O" became common parlance in indie hip-hop circles, Wes and his Vision Crew were representing the 416. Wearing tie, tail and fade, Wes dropped "Let Your Backbone Slide" in 1989, which became a fairly size-

→

able radio hit on the strength of Wes's linguistics. His debut album, **Symphony In Effect** (1990), sold over 200,000 copies in Canada (double platinum in Canadian money). After a dud of a second album, however, Wes moved to Brooklyn and released **Naah, Dis Kid Can't Be From Canada** (1994), which situated Wes's dated rhyme style in contemporary production from Showbiz, making Wes seem more awkward than a Mountie in Bed-Stuy.

The Dream Warriors, a duo of West Indian immigrants King, Lou and Capital Q, had been around since 1988, but burst on the scene in 1991 at the height of the jazz hip-hop thing with "My Definition of a Boombastic Jazz Style". Sampling an old game-show theme tune, "My Definition", and the equally quirky "Wash Your Face in My Sink", remade hip-hop as a beatnik carnival, perfect for slumming indie kids and acid jazz fashionistas. The sound world displayed on **And Now the Legacy Begins** (1991) was undeniably impressive, but their rhyming skills left a bit to be desired, a fact only temporarily remedied by their excellent collaboration with Gang Starr, "I've Lost My Ignorance" (1992). Like similar artists from Digable Planets to Disposable Heroes of Hiphoprisy, Dream Warriors couldn't escape the coffee shop even when their core audience had moved on as well, and **Subliminal Simulation** (1994) was just dire. They disappeared for the rest of the decade, only to emerge on trip-hoppers The Herbaliser's **Very Mercenary** album (1999).

Kwest Tha Madd Lad took the opposite route: sex-obsessed juvenilia. Kwest's **This Is My First Album** (1996) had some amusing lines, but the tracks were two years old and sounded it

→

by the time the album was released. A better display of Kwest's skills can be heard on "Bathroom Cipher" from **Lyricist Lounge Volume One** (1998), where he rips freestyles with Hazadous, IG Off, Thirstin' Howl III and J-Treds.

With such high-profile failures, the Canadian scene has been sustaining itself on the underground. Despite local success for the likes of Thrust and Michie Mee, the only Canadian rapper signed to a major is Choclair, who debuted in 1995 with "Twenty-One Years". Word filtered down to New York, where Premier included it on his **New York Reality Check 101** (1997) compilation and scratched up Choclair's vocals from his second single, "Just a Second" (1996), on Gang Starr's "You Know My Steez". His debut album, Ice Cold (1999), however, was marred by his obsession with booty. Far better was a collaborative single with Frankenstein, Kardinal Offishall and Marvel, "Internal Affairs" (1999).

Those artists (except Frankenstein), along with Solitair, Saukrates, YLooK, Jully Black and Afrolistic, comprise Toronto's Circle Crew. The dancehall-inspired Kardinal Offishall's **Eye & I** (1997) included the undie anthem, "On Wid Da Show", but this seriously hyped (deservingly) MC's best track is "Ghetto" (1999), which features gems like "You know you're ghetto when your stuck inside a jail/And them Jordans on your feet's costin' more than your bail". Saukrates, on the other hand, sounded monotonous and anachronistic on **The Underground Tapes** (1999). While the Circle Crew run T.O, Frankenstein got heads nodding with his instrumental **UV EP** (1999), released on his own Knowledge of Self label, and Ghetto Concepts rocked the shores of Lake Ontario with "Precious Moments" (1999).

→

Across the country in Vancouver, The Rascalz (Red 1, Misfit, Kemo and Dedos) blew up with the trans-continental collabo, "Northern Touch" (1998). Along with Choclair, Thrust, Kardinal Offishall and Checkmate, The Rascalz spit battle rhymes over a slamming track that was like a jiggier version of EPMD's "So Watcha Sayin'". The Pacific Coast's best, however, are Swollen Members. They might have the worst name in the biz, but Madchild and Prevail are some of the most innovative artists in hip-hop. They debuted with the **Swollen Members EP** (1998), which featured the magnificently moody "Paradise Lost", a dense fog of dark strings and nails-across-blackboard scratching courtesy of Mixmaster Mike. At the drop of a Kangol, the epic **Balance** (1999) moved from fizzing, twisted dubscapes with stream-of-consciousness sci-fi metaphors to huge, piano-fuelled jump-up anthems and brought a new range of expression to the Aleister-Crowley-adept wing of hip-hop. While lines like "Mischievous elves cringe at my introduction" suggested that the MCs not only "drink with Dionysus" but also listened to Ronnie James Dio, the horror-show imagery was tempered by classic boasts like "Even Van Gogh looked at me and said, 'You're one piece of work'/So I said, 'Lend me an ear 'cause I'm the state of the art'", which elevated **Balance** above the merely cartoonish.

In Montreal, where aspiring hip-hoppers are shackled by the language barrier, the city's best and brightest have mastered the art of turntablism instead. Fifteen-year-old DJ A-Trak won the DMC world mixing championship in 1997 and laced Obscure Disorder's "Lyrically Exposed" (1998) with some of the wildest array of crabs and flares ever heard on a conventional

→

hip-hop record. Meanwhile, media fave Kid Koala rocked a little Genesis on his superlative **ScratchCratchRatchAtch** (1997) bootleg mix tape, which felt like one of those chase scenes that closes an episode of *The Benny Hill Show*. His **Carpal Tunnel Syndrome** album (2000) was proof that, where most turntablists are out to wow you with their prowess behind the decks, Kid Koala impresses you with sheer force of personality.

⊙ **Swollen Members – Balance**   Battle Axe/Jazz Fudge, 1999

Quite simply, one of the best undie hip-hop albums of recent years.

Capone-N-Noreaga

Renaming their Big Apple environment after Middle East trouble spots – Lefrak City (Iraq), Queensbridge (Kuwait), Brooklyn (Baghdad) – Kiam "Capone" Holley and Victor "Noreaga" Santiago, Jr. have taken Chuck D's pronouncement that "rap is black people's CNN" more literally than anyone else. With a street reportage style similar to their neighbours Nas and Mobb Deep, C-N-N are the Wolf Blitzer and Christiane Ammapour of the Queens housing projects.

The two met while they were both serving time at the Collins Correctional Facility in upstate New York. After Capone was released, he started working with Tragedy the Intelligent Hoodlum, and when Noreaga got out six months later they recorded "LA, LA" (1995) with Tragedy and Mobb Deep, a response to Tha Dogg Pound's "New York, New York". Anchored by the fearsome "T.O.N.Y." and the very Mobb Deep-like "Halfway Thugs", the duo's **The War Report** (1997) quickly became a classic of the stark, grim, chillingly hopeless sound of New York thug rap.

Soon after the album came out, however, Capone was arrested for a parole violation and was sent back to prison for another two years. Severing ties with Tragedy (and releasing the savage "Halfway Thugs, Pt. II" (1998) to mark the occasion), Noreaga went solo with **N.O.R.E.** (1998). Standing for "Niggas On the Run Eatin'", **N.O.R.E.** was a hungrier, more commercially savvy album than C-N-N's debut. The title track and "Superthug" featured bouncing synth stabs, lush production

(by the Trackmasters and the Neptunes), absurd rhymes ("Run laps around the English Channel/Neptunes, I got a cocker spaniel") and a catchphrase ("Whut?! Whut?!") that took over New York and helped make the album gold. "Body in a Trunk", a collabo with Nas, and its urban gothic production, didn't hurt either.

A composite of *Hustler* (and *Rap Pages*) publisher Larry Flynt and the Melvin Udall character from *As Good As it Gets*, **Melvin Flynt Da Hustler** (1999) was meant to unveil a new facet of Noreaga's persona, but it was the same old José Luis Gotcha without the hooks.

⊙**The War Report**   Penalty, 1997

Raw, gritty, grimy – the sound of two street kids with absolutely nothing to lose.

Cash Money

New Orleans is the cradle of modern popular music, but if you look at almost any history of the Crescent City's long and illustrious music scene it will tell you that New Orleans today is nothing but a museum for old styles like zydeco, swamp pop, Dixieland, Mardi Gras chants, cajun fiddle breakdowns and street funk. With the recent success of the Cash Money and No Limit labels, however, that notion has been shown up as the middle-class fantasy it is.

Cash Money is the leading purveyor of that peculiar sub-genre of hip-hop native to New Orleans called Bounce. Although it now encompasses drum machine versions of local Mardi Gras rhythms, Bounce was kick-started by a group from Queens, New York, The Showboys. The scattershot drums and the weird, digital-xylophone break of The Showboys' 1986 single, "Drag Rap"

→

C

(aka "Triggerman"), was a huge hit down south, and budding MCs from the Magnolia Projects in New Orleans' Third Ward would rhyme over the top of it. Instead of trying to match the rapid-fire beats, the rappers would use that molasses-slow Nworlins drawl made famous by such lazy soul singers as Lee Dorsey and Alvin Robinson. One of these MCs was Terius "Juvenile" Gray, whose "Bounce for the Juvenile" (1993) was a huge local hit when it appeared on DJ Jimi's **It's Jimi** album, which also featured another proto-Bounce hit, "Where Dey At".

In 1995 Juvenile recorded **Being Myself** for New York-based Warlock Records, but it went nowhere and Juvenile quit music to work on an oil rig. In 1996, however, he hooked up with Cash Money, who had been releasing New Orleans rap by groups like UNLV (whose "Sixth & Barone" and "Drag 'Em in the River" were the label's first hits), Pimp Daddy and B.G. (aka Christopher Dorsey) since 1991. In 1996, Cash Money reorganized around Juvenile and a trio of man-childs – sixteen-year-old B.G., fifteen-year-old Dwayne "Lil' Wayne" Carter and sixteen-year-old Tab

→

"Turk" Virgil – who had all been through more before the age of twenty than any person should go through in an entire life. With this first-hand knowledge of the dark side and a youthful, infectious esprit de corps, Cash Money quickly moved from local concern to one of the biggest labels on the hip-hop landscape.

The other ingredient in their transformation was producer Mannie Fresh. Like that other supernova producer, Swizz Beatz, Fresh created a seemingly endless storehouse of recoiling beats that were simultaneously old-school and futuristic. And, just like Swizz Beatz, he claimed it took him about fifteen minutes to come up with a beat. Cash Money's breakthrough track was Juvenile's "Ha" from his triple platinum **400 Degreez** (1998) album. "Ha" had great production – skittering snares and hi-hats, bizarre basslines ricocheting around the mix – but you couldn't understand a word he said: he rapped like he had a jar of peanut butter stuck in all those gold teeth. Called an "off-the-porch flow", Juvenile's style was like Snoop Doggy Dogg's in 1992: a completely original sound that took everyone by surprise. The mix of shine and grime continued on Juvenile's **G-Code: Live By It – Die By It** (2000) with tracks like "Take Them 5" and "Never Had Shit", which brought age-old Big Uneasy concerns into the present. However, "U Understand" was a discouraging novelty – a boring Mannie Fresh beat – that didn't bode well for the future.

Fresh was on top form, though, on B.G.'s **Chopper City in the Ghetto** (1999). Tracks like "Thuggin'" and "Trigga Play" may have chronicled smokin' fools with forensic detail over menacing beats reminiscent of Dr. Dre's heyday, but the best track here was "Bling Bling", a 'hood fantasy so garish that it viewed the world as one big Pen & Pixel album cover. The Hot Boy$' (the Cash Money supergroup featuring everyone on the label) **Guerrilla Warfare** (1999) followed a similar agenda and showed that the Mannie Fresh assembly line was still operating with maximum efficiency.

⊙**Juvenile – 400 Degreez**   Cash Money, 1998

The lyrics are nothing to write home about, but the flow and the beats are as hot as the album's title.

Cash Money & Marvelous

I n the mid-'80s enterprising DJs from Philadelphia looking to make a name for themselves in a hip-hop world ruled by New York invented turntable techniques that would make the City of Brotherly Love the centre of DJing excellence. Transformer scratching (clicking the fader on and off while moving a block of sound – a riff or a short verbal phrase – across the stylus) was invented by DJ Spinbad, but perfected by Cash Money, perhaps the best DJ ever to come out of Philly's fertile environs. As well as perfecting transforming, Cash Money's main advance was to make scratching more rhythmic with techniques like the shiver and the stutter.

Under the name Dr. Funkenstein, Cash Money recorded the seminal early scratch record "Scratchin' to the Funk" (1985), but he would really make a name for himself a couple of years later. With his arsenal

of skills, Cash Money won both the New Musical Seminar Battle for
World Supremacy in 1987 and the DMC Championship in 1988, a feat
duplicated only by DJ Cheese and DJ Noise. In 1987, he hooked up
with Philly MC Marvelous. Although Marvelous was nowhere near the
equal of "the brother with the green eyes", the duo were responsible
for some solid, if not great, moments. Signing to New York's Sleeping
Bag Records in 1988, they released the occasionally funny "All the
Ugly People Be Quiet". The humour was writ large on their only album,
Where's the Party At? (1988), which has dated better than similarly
styled albums from the era. The album's highlight was undoubtedly the
Cash Money showcase, "The Music Maker". An electric mash-up of

the Beastie Boys, Art of Noise, James Brown, Eric B & Rakim, *Batman* and very '80s horn stabs, "The Music Maker" made turntablism's weird science as infectious and as party-rocking as any Rob Base or LL Cool J track.

The demise of Sleeping Bag in 1990 drained the duo's momentum, but they re-emerged in 1993 with a classic single, "Mighty Hard Rocker", for Warlock. With Bomb Squad-style horn squeals and chunky breaks, "Mighty Hard Rocker" may have been passé when it was released, but for those who weren't fashion-conscious its huge beats and Marvelous's simple rhymes made the party jump. Concentrating too much on the DJ and with boasts that wouldn't scare an old lady, Cash Money & Marvelous were anathema to the current scene, but with the renewed interest in turntable skills towards the end of the decade Cash Money resurfaced with a large dose of his deck prowess, **Old School Need Ta Learn Plot II** (1997).

⊙ Where's the Party At?   Sleeping Bag, 1988

If you can find it, this is a fine example of what the non-conscious, non-gangsta hip-hop of its golden age was like.

Chill Rob G

Born Robert Frazier, Chill Rob G came to prominence as a member of the Flavor Unit alongside Queen Latifah, Latee, Lakim Shabazz, Apache and Lord Alibaski in the late '80s. With a flow that managed to be both declamatory and nimble, Chill Rob was probably the best of the Flavor Unit's MCs. Unfortunately, despite his mic skills, Rob's main claim to fame outside the circles of hardcore hip-hop fiends came as the result of a couple of European hacks who borrowed his vocals.

Working with producer the 45 King, Rob released a handful of classic singles for the Wild Pitch label: "The Court Is Now in Session", "Wild Pitch", "Let Me Show You" and "Let the Words Flow". All of these were collected on Rob's only full-length, **Ride the Rhythm** (1989). "The Court Is Now in Session" found Rob "puttin' heads to bed" over a fierce 45 King beat constructed from Graham Central Station's "The Jam" and a piercing, siren horn loop from Maceo & the Macks' "Soul Power '74". The 45 King pulled out more rabbits from his Kangol on "Ride the Rhythm", "Motivation" and the Kool & the Gang-juiced "Let Me Show You". "Let the Words Flow" featured Rob's stentorian voice rhyming at the speed of thought over a loop of The Police's "Voices Inside My Head".

German-based dance producers Benito Benites and John Garrett Virgo III (aka Snap!) took the a cappella version of "Let the Words Flow" and layered it over a Jocelyn Brown sample to create the massive hit "The Power". Both Wild Pitch and Chill Rob G objected to the track and Snap! remade "The Power" with a terrible rap by Turbo G, while Rob released his own version in 1990. Of course, it was Snap!'s version that was the worldwide hit and Chill Rob quickly faded into obscurity, releasing a single in 1996 that went nowhere.

⊙ **Ride the Rhythm**   Wild Pitch, 1989

With classic b-boy beat science from the 45 King and assertive raps from Chill Rob G, this is an undeservedly overlooked album (later versions also included "The Power").

Chubb Rock

B orn Richard Simpson in Jamaica, Chubb Rock brought the Kingston dancehall's love of deep, stentorian voices to hip-hop. After dropping out of college, he hooked up with his cousin Hitman Howie Tee and made the instantly forgettable **Chubb Rock Featuring Hitman Howie Tee** (1988). Somehow he managed to hang on to his recording contract and released the excellent "Caught Up" (1989). Based on a sample from Inner Life's disco classic "Caught Up (In a One Night Love Affair), "Caught Up" highlighted Chubb's rhythmic flexibility and made him one of the most popular rappers of the era.

"Caught Up" was the lead cut on his very fine **And the Winner Is ...** (1989). "Ya Bad Chubbs" found Chubb spitting on top of the beat from Lyn Collins' "Think", while on "And the Winner Is ... (The Grammys)" Chubb lectured the National Academy of Recording Arts and Sciences on hip-hop history.

In 1990 Chubb and Howie Tee continued their disco sampling with the classic "Treat 'Em Right". With string stabs and a chorus from First Choice's "Love Thang", "Treat 'Em Right" was an exhilarating whirlwind of Chubb's baritone moving at something approaching light speed, but never losing sight of the groove. **The One** (1991) followed and, while it couldn't maintain the high standards of **And the Winner Is ...**, it featured a couple of excellent cuts in the form of the anti-drug "Night Scene" and the #1 Rap hit "The Chubbster".

I Gotta Get Mine Yo! (1992) saw Chubb stagnating and getting left behind, although it did feature the moody and apocalyptic prayer for peace, "Lost in the Storm". Chubb Rock was definitely a product of the late '80s, however, and he wasn't to be heard from again until he released the surprisingly decent comeback album **The Mind** (1997).

With production now handled by Easy Mo Bee and KRS-One, **The Mind** ditched the light-hearted rhymes of old and followed where "Lost in the Storm" left off.

⊙ **And the Winner Is ...**   Select, 1989

Fast, furious, funny and great production – what more could you want from a hip-hop album.

Cold Crush Brothers

They weren't the first hip-hop crew to make a record, but unless you lived on Sedgewick Avenue in The Bronx in 1978, the Cold Crush Brothers' rhymes were the first ones you'll have heard. When Sylvia Robinson first heard Henry "Big Bank Hank" Jackson rapping along to a tape in a New Jersey pizzeria, he was listening to a tape of a Cold Crush Brothers show. When Big Bank Hank and the rest of the Sugar Hill Gang recorded "Rapper's Delight", they borrowed liberally from Cold Crush's Grandmaster Caz's book of rhymes. Despite laying the foundation for all subsequent hip-hop MCs, Caz, DJ Charlie Chase, Tony Tone, JDL, the Almighty Kay-Gee and Easy AD have never really made a record that lives up to their reputation. Nevertheless, the Cold Crush Brothers remain one of the most legendary crews in hip-hop history.

Despite their contribution to hip-hop's commercialization, Cold Crush would have to wait until 1982 to make their first record, "Weekend", for the Elite label. Most people's introduction to Cold Crush, however, was in Charlie Ahearn's 1983 film, *Wild Style*. With lines like "Charlie Chase as cute as can be/You'd sell your soul to the devil to play like me", their first appearance during the basketball court battle with their old foes the Fantastic Five might not have been awe-inspiring, but they had charisma to spare. That charisma came to the fore on their awesome performance at the Dixie. One of the definitive old-school

documents, their five-minute live showcase in the movie was simply electric and influenced all hip-hop live shows that followed. Unfortunately, very few have managed to match it.

Aside from their contributions to the *Wild Style* soundtrack, Cold Crush's best record was "Fresh, Wild, Fly and Bold" (1984). Featuring huge drum machines and electro blips, "Fresh, Wild, Fly and Bold" was packed with b-boy energy. The only problem was that, by the time it came out, Run DMC and LL Cool J were making the old school ancient history. Soon afterwards, Caz left the crew and released a few solo records for Tuff City like "The Judge" (1987) and "The Hitman" (1990), which showed that Caz was able to make the transition in rap styles better than any of his contemporaries. Meanwhile, Kay-Gee and Tony Tone continued the Cold Crush Brothers as a duo and recorded **Troopers** (1988) for B Boy Records.

With old-school nostalgia running rampant in the late '90s, some of Cold Crush's legendary performances have been released. **The Cold Crush Brothers Live in '82** (1994) on Tuff City and **Cold Crush Brothers Vs. the Fantastic Romantic 5** (1998) both captured Cold Crush at the height of their powers and are well worth searching out.

⊙ The Cold Crush Brothers Live in '82   Tuff City, 1994

Long before the advent of the DAT, the Cold Crush did it all the way live and better than anyone no matter how much technology they might have.

Common (Sense)

H ip-hop may have its Grandmasters, Lords, Kings and Big Daddies, but one of its biggest talents has taken a more run-of-the-mill name. Common Sense (Lonnie Rashied Lynn) burst out of the hip-hop backwater of Chicago at the beginning of the '90s with a nasal, b-boy with a cold flow, and one of the smoothest deliveries around. His debut album, **Can I Borrow a Dollar?** (1992), may be the work of an MC who had yet to find his identity, but it had enough pure skills and lateral thinking on display to let heads know that Common wasn't as workaday as his name implied. Although "Heidi Hoe" had production by the Beatnuts, the highlight was undoubtedly "Soul By the Pound", a serious head-nodder that had Common claiming he was "fatter than heavy metal and harder than punk rock".

By the time of his second album, **Resurrection** (1994), the laidback keybs of the debut had developed into a fully fledged jazz aesthetic and Common Sense had become as conscious as his mic name. "I

Used to Love H.E.R." was a dazzling extended metaphor that viewed hip-hop as an unfaithful lover and instigated a beef with Ice Cube. Tracks like "Resurrection", "Watermelon" ("I stand out like a nigga on a hockey team") and "Sum Shit I Wrote", meanwhile, proved that the callow rhymes of the first album had become a

warm and funny style that seemed to have faith in hip-hop's sacrament that wordplay can transform one's surroundings. He was so confident in his abilities that on "Pop's Rap" he invited his father to drop some knowledge.

Losing his "Sense", a rechristened Common's **One Day It'll All Make Sense** (1997), unfortunately, failed to build on the foundation of **Resurrection**. All the elements were there – particularly on "Retrospect For Life", a duet with Lauryn Hill that found him meditating on the meaning of life – but they didn't come together. Far better were his indie singles, "Like They Used to Say/1-9-9-9" (1999) and "Car Horn" (1999), on which

Common dropped a Gil-Scott-Heron-thinking-he's-Billy-Dee-Williams flow over Dug Infinite's easy-listening motif ("Like They Used to Say") and 45 King's loping, off-kilter shuffle that remembered the days when funky meant greasy and stinky, not David Axelrod and Jeff Lorber.

Like Water For Chocolate (2000) was hailed by many as a master-piece, but it was suffocated by its relentless bohemianism. The production (by Jay Dee, D'Angelo, ?uestlove, James Pyser and DJ Premier) was often staggering, but, like Common's rhymes, it was impressive rather than likeable.

⊙**Resurrection**   Relativity, 1994

A mesmerizing, infectious album, released before Common became all smug in his dashikis and knit caps.

Company Flow

Exploding out of Brooklyn with the wildest beats and illest rhymes, screaming that they are "independent as fuck", Company Flow are the most original hip-hop crew around. Unlike too many "independent" hip-hop artists who are merely minor league MCs waiting for a major label break, El-P (Jamie Meline), DJ Mr. Len (Leonard Smythe) and Big Jus create uncompromising, extremely challenging hip-hop that wouldn't know jiggy if Lil' Kim came up and shook her thing in its face.

Co Flow began when Mr. Len met El-P while he was DJing his eighteenth birthday party. The following year El-P and Len released "Juvenile Techniques" (1993) as Company Flow. With Big Jus on board, the **Funcrusher** EP (1995) followed on the group's own Official Recordings label. It would be "8 Steps to Perfection/Vital Nerve" (1996), however, that would establish Company

Flow as *the* voice of the underground. On "8 Steps to Perfection" a smooth '70s soul string part straight out of Dr. Dre's repertoire got

dissolved and acid-washed into an attenuated blur, while El-P bragged that he was "the third gunner on the grassy knoll" and that he had "manners like Bruce Banner when he's stressed". "Vital Nerve", meanwhile, was a savage battle rhyme that managed to be both brutally minimal and viciously funky.

After the brilliant "Info Kill" (1997) single, the group signed to indie titans Rawkus and released the devastating **Funcrusher Plus** (1997) album. Hearkening back to the raw old-school productions of Schooly D, Run DMC and Audio Two, **Funcrusher Plus** was filled with stale, musty atmospheres that were punctuated by shards of metal, tracks so disjointed that they felt like the nightmares in *The Manchurian Candidate* and scratching that lay somewhere between the battle scars of the X-Ecutioners and the switchblade slashes of DJ Code Money. As the stunning "Last Good Sleep" (that rarest of things in hip-hop, a track that not only confronts misogyny, but also admits to weakness and failure) showed, their emotional palette extended beyond their egos. While Big Jus pierced vital nerves with the brutal funk, the William Gibson/Philip K. Dick-inspired El-P was the "Triple felon MC minus the melanin/When I bomb I talk with the shit to make Baby Jessica jump back in the well again". Even with all of the science on display, Co Flow didn't neglect the groove. They had enough sense to quote professional wrestlers and specialized in the one-line mini-epiphanies that are hip-hop's *raison d'être*: "My shit is like *War and Peace*, yours is just the Cliff Notes", "Fuckin' with your theology like Darwinism in the Bible Belt". Just for good measure, **Funcrusher Plus** also included the mind-boggling Indelible MCs (Co Flow with J-Treds and The Juggaknots) track, "The Fire in Which You Burn".

The **End to End Burners** EP (1998) was another disorientating body blow to hip-hop syntax. As El-P rapped on "Krazy Kings Too", sounding like he was trapped in one of his own loops: "Kid, I feel asphyxiated/I wear the city air like wet leather/Alarmed that the populous dwells so closely together". The **Little Johnny From the Hospital** (1999) instrumental album attempted to shift paradigms once again. Trying to recreate the feeling of the mid-'80s when hip-hop was a gruff, assertive challenge of sheer attitude by aggressive drum machines, wayward video game noises and punitive basslines, El-P's soundworld was abrasive and menacing, where hip-hop's traditional funk snippets became de-funked, funcrushed. Like the Bomb Squad, George Clinton and Miles Davis, Company Flow rearranged and reinterpreted James Brown's original bitches' brew in a bubbling cauldron of seething funk.

⊙**Funcrusher Plus**   Official/Rawkus, 1997

Dropping the most inspirational sucker MC disses since Roxanne Shanté over the harshest beats since Schooly D, this was not only hip-hop classicism of the most brutal kind, but the most original hip-hop since Public Enemy.

Coolio

Long before he made his fantastic voyage to the top of the pop charts, Coolio (né Artis Ivey) was a reformed basehead who joined up with WC and DJ Crazy Toones to form WC and the MAAD Circle. The group's debut album, **Ain't a Damn Thing Changed** (1991), was a classic slice of West Coast hardcore funk that tempered its gangsta-isms with biting social commentary.

After working with the LA hip-hop collective 40 Thievz, Coolio went solo and recorded **It Takes a Thief** (1994) with DJ Brian "The Wino"

Dobbs. At the peak of G-Funk, "Fantastic Voyage", which liberally sampled Lakeside's funk-lite masterpiece of the same name, smoothed out the LA sound with more streamlined beats and a light-hearted fantasy of the good life. Its sense of humour, focus on the

MICHEL LINSSEN

lighter side of the gangsta lifestyle and inclusivity pushed "Fantastic Voyage" to #3 on the US pop chart. **It Takes a Thief** wasn't all about the good times, however, as tracks like "County Line" catalogued the degradations of poverty and welfare.

Although it darkened Coolio's vision considerably, **Gangsta's Paradise** (1995) was an even bigger success. The title track, which also featured on the soundtrack to the Michelle Pfeiffer movie *Dangerous Minds*, was one of the year's biggest pop hits, reaching #1 worldwide and staying on the charts for some 40 weeks. Based on a sample of Stevie Wonder's "Pastime Paradise" and making it sinister with slashing strings and a perilously deep bassline, "Gangsta's Paradise" proved that pop-rap didn't have to be as cartoonish as Jazzy Jeff and the Fresh Prince or as mindless as Tone Loc. While **Gangsta's Paradise** also included decent tracks like "Too Hot" and "Kinda High, Kinda Drunk", it featured lame covers of Smokey Robinson's "Cruisin'" and Billy Paul's "A Thing Goin' On" that threatened to undo any respectability earned with the title track.

Following the blueprint of "Cruisin'" rather than "Gangsta's Paradise", **My Soul** (1997) failed to build on Coolio's artistic and commercial success. Unsurprisingly, Coolio tried to be a Hollywood player with his role in the straight-to-video *Tyrone*, but all he proved was that he was no Will Smith. Now that radio and MTV have fully embraced Jay-Z's pottymouth and DMX's bark, it seems unlikely that Coolio will recapture his commercial pre-eminence.

⊙ **Gangsta's Paradise**   Tommy Boy, 1995

Coolio may be an object of scorn in real hip-hop circles, but, thanks largely to the title track, there's no reason to be embarrassed about owning this.

The Coup

Politics and music often make strange bedfellows, but along with
Public Enemy and Boogie Down Productions Oakland, California's The Coup have managed that all-too-rare feat of making great
political hip-hop that is also just great hip-hop. One of the reasons that
they succeed where so many others fail is that they walk it like they
talk it: MC Boots Riley has been a community activist since he was in
high school, while the group's other MC, E-Roc, is a union organizer.
On the symbolic front, DJ Pam the Funkstress is one of the most visible female DJs in hip-hop, working with Saafir and the Conscious
Daughters as well as The Coup.

Boots formed The Coup in 1990 after joining the Mau Mau Rhythm
Collective, an organization that used hip-hop to address community
and political issues. The group's debut EP, **The Coup: The EP**, was
released in 1991 without much fanfare on Polemic Records. Signing to
Wild Pitch, The Coup's message should have reached the masses, but
by this time the label was on its last legs. **Kill My Landlord** (1993)
mixed didacticism with rolling, East Bay funk, as revolutionary tracks
like "Dig It" and "Not Yet Free" moved both asses and minds by combining Paris with E-40.

1994's **Genocide and Juice** was a gangsta parody that, with
cameos from Spice 1 and E-40, was probably too close to its subject
matter to be really effective. Biting tracks like "Fat Cats, Bigga Fish",
though, made their intentions clear. Wild Pitch dissolved soon after
Genocide and Juice was released, however, and the group members
returned to community activism, with Boots founding the Young Com-
rades, a youth group that tackles the racism of the Oakland police.

In 1999 The Coup returned with perhaps their best album, **Steal**

This Album. Boots' flow had gotten progressively less stentorian and more typical of that Cali drawl, but instead of being a sell-out move it was really a clever strategy to get the group's message across. Tracks like "Me and Jesus the Pimp In a '79 Granada Last Night" might sound on a cursory listen like your average bitch-slapping, mack tale (even though details like "His name was Jesus/Slapped a ho to pieces with his plastic prosthesis" let you know that this was out of the ordinary),

but The Coup subverted the genre conventions and made it a moving, scary tale that was every bit the equal of Funkadelic's "Cosmic Slop". Unlike most politically motivated crews, The Coup didn't sacrifice pleasure for message: there's humour, someone pissin' on George Washington's grave and shockingly lush production from

such guerrilla operatives. Marx was probably spinning in his grave.

⊙ **Steal This Album**   Dogday, 1999

With blaxploitation beats, clever rhymes and well-thought-out politics, revolution hasn't sounded this good since the glory days of PE.

Cypress Hill

Rapping about la vida loca long before it became a mainstream concern, LA's multiracial group of vatos Cypress Hill changed the face of hip-hop in the early '90s. Enjoying and endorsing cannabis at a time when the inner city was still reeling from crack, Cypress Hill combined the Bomb Squad with a West Coast pimp roll to produce a dusty, blunted style that made it clear that "stoned was the way of the walk".

Lawrence Muggerud was a relocated New Yorker who had gotten his start with LA crew 7A3, who had a moderate hit with a hip-hop remake of Queen's "We Will RockYou" (1987). When they dissolved, DJ Muggs and 7A3 rapper B-Real (Louis Freese) hooked up with former DVX hype man Sen Dog (Senen Reyes) and formed Cypress Hill in 1989. Their eponymous debut album (1991) attempted to remake Cheech and Chong for barrio dwellers who came strapped with both a gat and a one-hitter. But where Cheech and Chong were just dopey, Cypress Hill were sardonic and menacing: they made funny nursery rhymes about killing cops, Muggs' production was murkier than month-old bongwater and B-Real's nasal whine was cartoonish, biting and "just don't give a fuck" all at the same time. Tracks like "How I Could Just Kill a Man" and "Hand on the Pump" were dripping with both THC and casual violence.

Black Sunday (1993) was a self-confessed, rushed follow-up to their double platinum debut. While their Mary Jane Gatling tales didn't break any new ground, it did feature the massive single "Insane in the Membrane", and pushed their sound into the paranoiac realm that inevitably comes with massive marijuana intake. **Cypress Hill III: Temples of Boom** (1995) continued their journey into the heart of darkness

with brooding atmospheres and creeping beats creating a kind of gangsta psychedelia. With the exception of "Throw Your Set in the Air", there were no moments of abandon where the crowd could throw their hands in the air; even the Ice Cube dis, "No Rest for the Wicked", could elevate the vibe of this discomfiting gangsta critique.

After a three-year lay-off which found Muggs producing **The Soul Assassins** (1997) compilation, **Cypress Hill IV** (1998) signalled the group retreating into the caricatures that they always threatened to become. **Los Grandes Éxitos en Español** (1999) was a somewhat artistically pointless, if rather culturally significant, greatest-hits album entirely in Spanish. **Skull & Bones** (2000) was one half vintage (or generic) Cypress Hill, half Limp Bizkit/Kid Rock rap-rock brio. The **Skull** disc was all eerie pianos, Latino lingo, zooted beats and their trademark, jump-around war chants. The **Bones** disc featured a wailing cameo from Fear Factory guitarist Dino Cazares, dishing out the thrash on "Get Out Of My Head", while "Dust" was pure heavy metal rowdiness.

⊙ **Cypress Hill**   Ruffhouse/Columbia, 1991

An absolute classic of avant-hardcore hip-hop.

De La Soul

L
ike their fellow suburban Long Islanders Public Enemy, Eric B & Rakim and EPMD, Amityville's De La Soul remade hip-hop in their own image. With their elliptical lyrics, in-jokes and lush samplescapes, De La Soul expanded hip-hop's emotional palette by introducing an almost pastoral quality to an urban grid of chopped-up drum breaks and sound-bite raps.

De La Soul's debut album, **Three Feet High And Rising** (1989), saw Posdnous (Kelvin Mercer), Trugoy the Dove (David Jolicoeur) and Pacemaster Mase (Vincent Mason) create the D.A.I.S.Y. Age ("Da Inner Sound Y'all"), its flower imagery reflecting their unmacho approach and their arty, suburban roots. Produced by Prince Paul from Stetsasonic, the album was a dense collage of samples that ranged from "A Little Bit of Soap" by The Jarmels through Steely Dan to French-language instructional tapes. Featuring cameos from members of the other Native Tongue posse bands (Jungle Brothers, A Tribe Called Quest and Queen Latifah) and a mellow, inclusive feel, **Three Feet High And Rising** fostered a communitarian spirit that was in sharp contrast to the "go for yours" mentality of standard hip-hop.

In a pattern that would become all too familiar among independently hip-hop crews, when the singles "Me, Myself and I" and "The Magic Number" crossed over to the mainstream, the hip-hop community took De La Soul's popularity with a white audience as proof that they were soft. De La Soul were out to regain their street cred with their 1991 follow-up, the dark, angry and frustrated **De La Soul Is Dead**. The album was populated with inside jokes aimed at black radio, Sylvester Stallone, fast-food restaurant employees and American chatshow host Arsenio Hall. Amidst the unpleasant vibe, there was some great music: the exposé of sexual abuse, "Millie Pulled a Pistol on Santa", "A Roller Skating Jam Named 'Saturdays'", which sampled Chic and Frankie Valli, "Bitties in the BK Lounge" (a dozens game set to music) and the uplifting "Keepin' the Faith". Ultimately, though, the album wasn't the masterpiece it could have (and should have) been because of its preoccupation with pop's worst subject – the burdens of fame.

Their obsession with the cross-over mentality continued on their third release, **Buhloone Mindstate** (1993). On both "Eye Patch" and "Patti Dooke", De La Soul declared, "It might blow up, but it won't go pop", reaffirming their commitment to the street. Despite brilliant sound

MIKE LEWIS

bites like "I'll make you lost like high school history" and "Fuck being hard, Posdnous is complicated", **Buhloone** was even more wilfully obscurantist than its predecessors. The skits were filled with a venomous black humour and the music was a languorous elegy to the blues that heightened the mainstream-damning references to hip-hop history (they quoted everyone from Melle Mel to Public Enemy).

The band returned with **Stakes Is High** (1996), distilling the frustrations of the previous two albums into a collection of bone-jarringly blunt, minimalist sketches. Both the title track and "The Bizness" revolved around two-note basslines and snapping snares to create bleak attacks on lame rappers and institutionalized racism. Once again, De La Soul had managed to change their flow and their style not to move with the times, but to stay ahead of them.

However, when they released the sprawling three-CD project, **Art Official Intelligence** (2000), the group seemed shackled by label expectations. While tracks like "Oooh!" (with Redman on the hook) and "Foolin'" were good radio records, **Mosaic Thump**, **Art Official Intelligence**'s first instalment, lacked direction and was caught in the digital mire.

⊙ **Three Feet High And Rising**   Tommy Boy, 1989

A landmark hip-hop record. Their surreal humour and light-heartedness works perfectly with the disjointed artistry of the music to create an album that inherits George Clinton's mantle of politico-socio-sexual funk.

Death Row

Shady connections to organized crime, questionable business practices, beatdowns, lavish expense accounts: Death Row was business as usual for the music industry. Nevertheless, as the most prominent proponent of that media shibboleth, "gangsta rap", the label acquired a notoriety that belied the normality of such practices in the industry. From the lyrics of the label's artists right down to founder Suge Knight's garish, red jacket and the label's logo (a hooded man sitting in an electric chair), everything Death Row did was designed to inflame a racist media and the white establishment. However, even if you're trying to sidestep the devil, if you play with fire you're gonna get burnt.

Death Row was formed in 1991 when Knight, an ex-football-player-turned-bodyguard, and a gang of similarly proportioned, pipe-wielding men, allegedly "persuaded" Ruthless Records owner Eazy-E to release Dr. Dre from his contract with the company. Knight negotiated an unprecedented contract with Interscope that allowed Death Row almost complete autonomy and ownership of the master tapes. The Death Row era actually began with a song that was released on Epic, Dr. Dre's title track from the *Deep Cover* soundtrack (1992), which featured Snoop Doggy Dogg. Snoop's Southern gothic drawl introduced a new style to hip-hop, while Dre's streamlined P-Funk was irresistible. The sound, dubbed G-Funk, was writ large on Dre's **The Chronic** (1992), which achieved pop music's ultimate triumph of making rage and alienation sound sexy and cool and appealing.

→

Snoop's **Doggystyle** (1993) followed in a similar, if less sophisticated, style and Death Row had sold eight million copies of its first two albums. The *Above the Rim* soundtrack (1994) and Tha Dogg Pound's (Kurupt and Dat Nigga Daz) unredeemably gratuitous **Dogg Food** (1995) both went multi-platinum as well. Those whining synths and Parliament samples were everywhere and Cali was ruling the hip-hop world. The East Coast came up with its own cartoon CEO, Sean "Puffy" Combs, who attempted to replace G-Funk with his karaoke hits. The rivalry between the two seemed to extend beyond the marketplace when Knight

dissed Combs at *The Source* awards in 1995. In 1995 Tupac Shakur signed a four-page, hand-written contract with Knight in exchange for him posting Shakur's bail money while he was in jail on a rape charge. Tupac released **All Eyez on Me** (1996) a few months after being released. The double album went seven times platinum, but the label was in trouble: Dre wanted out; Snoop was in court on a murder charge; Knight was involved in numerous court cases; and the East Coast–West Coast beef was transcending the realm of metaphor.

The inevitable results of this embrace of gangsta glamour were realized in September 1996, when Tupac was murdered in

→

Las Vegas. Knight, who had symbolized a kind of fuck-you, independent black capitalism, was incarcerated and forced to sell his masters. Nevertheless, Death Row continued to release records: Lady of Rage's much-delayed **Necessary Roughness** (1997), Tha Dogg Pound's **West Coast Aftershock** (1998) and **Suge Knight Represents: Chronic 2000** (1999). Extricating themselves from Death Row, Dat Nigga Daz and Kurupt both released solo albums, most notably Kurupt's **The Streetz Iz a Mutha** (2000), which featured the brutal dis cut, "Calling Out Names". A rumoured deal with former Ku Klux Klan member and Louisiana politician David Duke only made the Death Row saga even more bizarre, yet utterly typical for the music biz.

⊙**Death Row Greatest Hits**   Death Row, 1996

Not the greatest selection (too many lame remixes, and where the hell is "Dre Day"?) and filled with Suge's venom (the inclusion of Ice Cube's "No Vaseline" and J-Flex's "Who Been There, Who Done That?"), but still the best available label overview.

Def Jam

"Musical myth-seeking people of the universe, this is yours" – with those words the biggest label in hip-hop history began its fifteen-year reign. T La Rock & Jazzy Jay's "It's Yours" (1984) was the first record to feature the Def Jam logo, but it was actually released on Arthur Baker's Partytime label. It was an amazing record – the densest rhymes this side of Rammellzee Vs K-Rob's "Beat Bop", production from Rick Rubin that sounded like Stockhausen and was almost as unfunky – but a strange beginning for such a commercial juggernaut.

It was Bambaataa associate Jazzy Jay who first introduced Def Jam founders Rubin and Russell Simmons, who at the time was running Rush Artistic Management, which oversaw the careers of Kurtis Blow and Run DMC (Jazzy Jay's "Def Jam/Cold Chillin' in the Spot" (1985) featured Russell Simmons showing why he wasn't a rapper himself). Made in Rubin's dorm room at New York University, the first proper Def Jam record, LL Cool J's "I Need a Beat" (1984), sold 100,000 copies and firmly established the label as a force.

In 1985 Def Jam signed a distribution deal with CBS, becoming the first label to be backed by major-label money and immediately knocking all competition out of the water. Of course, having LL Cool J, the Beastie Boys and Public Enemy on the roster didn't hinder Def Jam from becoming the genre's most important and successful label. Even such artistic disasters as smoove loveman Oran "Juice" Jones couldn't stop the Def Jam steamroller.

Although Rubin and Simmons brought hip-hop into the mainstream, they also held it down on the underground with Original Concept's "Knowledge Me/Can U Feel It" (1986), introducing the world to future *Yo MTV Raps!* frontman Dr. Dre. While Rubin was getting more into heavy metal, Def Jam continued to innovate hip-hop with Slick Rick, stealing EPMD away from Fresh and forming 3rd Bass from two distinct entities. MC Serch, Prime Minister Pete Nice and Sam Sever released the classic **The Cactus Album** (1989), which proved the white men could funk on tracks like the Beasties dissing "Gas Face", "Steppin' to the AM" and "Product of the Environment". Unfortunately, their **Derelicts of Dialect** (1992) couldn't keep up the momentum, with easy disses of Vanilla Ice and, ironically, overly commercial production.

Although Rubin left the label after a feud with Simmons' right-hand man Lyor Cohen, who soon became the label's CEO, Def Jam didn't miss a beat with Redman, Onyx, Warren G, Montell Jordan (the '90s version of Oran "Juice" Jones) and Method Man. Feeling like he couldn't miss, Simmons diversified into fashion with his Phat Farm line, film and TV projects, and an ad agency. Even though the *Def Comedy Jam* and *The Nutty Professor* had Simmons looking elsewhere, hip-hop acts like Foxy Brown, Ja Rule, Jay-Z and DMX championed the thug/Cristal aesthetic and continued to pay his rent.

⊙ **Various Artists – The Def Jam Music Group**
10th Anniversary Box Set   Def Jam, 1995

Hip-hop heads will own most of this already, but this 59-track overview of the label's first ten years is pretty unimpeachable, aside from the random programming.

Def Squad

EPMD originally debuted their Hit Squad on tracks like "Hardcore" and "Brothers on My Jock" from their **Business As Usual** album (1990). K-Solo (Kevin Maddison) was the first to go for dolo with **Tell the World My Name** (1990), which featured a moderate hit in "Your Mom's in My Business". However, his workmanlike raps would be eclipsed by fellow Hit Squaders Redman and Das EFX and after a couple more albums he faded away.

Das EFX, the duo of Krazy Drayz (Andre Weston) and Skoob (Willie Hines), emerged out of Virginia State University after being discovered by EPMD at a talent contest. Although they attracted the most fame for their stiggedy stuttering, diggedy dancehall-inspired mic styles, their pop

culture references were far more appealing. On **Dead Serious** (1992) they talked about giving Sinead O'Connor her crew cut and tracks like "They Want EFX" and "Mic Checka" blew up. However, they were quickly revealed as a one-trick pony, and **Straight Up Sewaside** (1993) and **Hold it Down** (1995) went nowhere (partially abetted by their siding with Parrish during EPMD's feud) and **Generation EFX** (1998) was a most unwelcome comeback.

The only member of the Hit Squad to enjoy continued success and good rep was Brick City's Redman (Reggie Noble). Like Das EFX, Funk Doctor Spock came with an original style, but from the beginning it was clear it wasn't a gimmick – he was simply unhinged. **Whut? Thee Album** (1992) was produced by Erick Sermon and the hard funk paralleled Redman's guttural, crazier-than-Busta-Rhymes flow perfectly. While he was inspired by horror flicks, Redman never dwelled in splatter schtick; instead he dropped rhymes like "Snapped the neck of Michael Myers, then I freaked it/'Cause it was August when he was takin' this trick or treat shit," on "Rated R". He told you "How to Roll a Blunt" on **Whut?**, but **Dare Iz a Darkside** (1994) was stickier than Northern Lights and the album's vagueness and blurriness suggested that Redman smoked one too many trees. Tracks like "Tonight's Da Nite" and the Hawaiian guitar-tinged "Green Island" stand out from the haze. **Muddy Waters** (1996) and **Doc's Da Name 2000** (1999) were more of the same, marking Redman as one of the most consistent MCs around. **Black Out!** (1999), meanwhile, saw Redman duetting with Method Man to similar effect, with great lines like "Cereal Killer"'s "Take nuts and screws outta ferris wheels".

When E and PMD split, Sermon renamed his crew the Def Squad. Keith Murray debuted on "Hostile" from Sermon's **No Pressure** (1993) album. His debut, **The Most Beautifullest Thing in This World** (1994), displayed Murray's smooth skills on the mic to fine effect, going gold on the strength of the superb title track. **Enigma** (1996) and **It's a Beautiful Thing** (1999) both followed in the same style, but without any hits to leap out of the lyrical drift. Murray, Sermon and Redman joined forces for Def Squad's **El Niño** (1998). While the album was largely lifeless, there were, as always, great lines like "You're soft like CD 101.9" to keep your interest.

⊙ **Redman – Whut? Thee Album**   Def Jam, 1992

The debut of one of the decade's most original, most consistent MCs.

Digable Planets

 formed in 1991 while students in Washington DC, the Digable Planets picked up where A Tribe Called Quest's **Low End Theory** left off and took be-bop hip-hop into new areas of abstraction and quirkiness. Instead of leaving their jazziness in the production, Butterfly, Doodlebug and Ladybug inflected their raps with beatnik slanguage and hipsterisms, briefly becoming the house band of the black bohemian intelligentsia in the process.

The group's first album, **Reachin' (A New Refutation of Time and Space)** (1993), was a big cross-over hit among those who got into hip-hop during its sampladelic golden age, but were now scared off by Dr. Dre's amorality. Based around a sample from Art Blakey & the Jazz Messengers, "Rebirth of Slick (Cool Like Dat)" fingerpopped its way into the pop consciousness with boho flows and mellow, mellifluous swing. The album wasn't all grainy, thrift-store appeal, though. It also had bite: "La Femme Fetal" worked a soundbite from the Last Poets into the mix as the Planets spun a pro-choice yarn that didn't hold back on the political content.

Riding black-style politics for all they were worth, **Blowout Comb** (1994) brought a streetwise nationalism to the fore. Featuring cryptic lines like "makin' bacon" (i.e. killing cops), the lyrics may have been as oblique as those on **Reachin'**, but it was no longer wordplay for word-play's sake. Like just about every other group whose success came from a kinder, gentler form of hip-hop, the Digable Planets ditched their pop appeal in an attempt to become more street. Unsurprisingly, it didn't work and **Blowout Comb** precipitated the group's quick slide into obscurity.

⊙ **Reachin' (A New Refutation of**
Time and Space)   Pendulum/EMI, 1993

Unfortunately, the group couldn't do as the title suggested and this fine album of unconventional hip-hop remains very much situated in the climate in which it was released.

Diggin' in the Crates

Naming themselves after the science of record collecting, New York's Diggin' in the Crates crew have held it down for hip-hop purists since 1990. The crew's linchpin DJ/producer Diamond D (Joe Kirkland), who had worked with Jazzy Jay since the early days, first appeared on wax as part of Ultimate Force with MC Master Rob (who "had more hair on his chest than Chuck Norris") on the blues guitar-based "I'm Not Playing" (1989). DITC started taking shape the following year when Lord Finesse (Robert Hall) asked Diamond to work on beats for his **Funky Technician** album (1990). With fellow residents of The Bronx's Forrest housing projects DJ/producer Showbiz (Rodney Lemay) and MC AG (aka Andre the Giant, aka Andre Barnes), Diamond helped make **Funky Technician** one of the most butter albums of the early '90s.

After working on Lord Finesse's album, Showbiz and AG teamed up again for the legendary **Can I Get a Soul Clap** EP (1991). With the title cut and "Party Groove", the EP was a classic of raw Bronx rhymes teamed with dusty but motorvating production. The vibe was writ large on **Runaway Slave** (1992) which, in addition to cuts from the EP, featured the smoking "Fat Pockets" and the jazz cut-ups of "Silence Tha Lambs". Their **Goodfellas: The Medicine** album (1995), however, suffered from an identity crisis and, aside from the hot "Next Level", couldn't sustain the duo's momentum.

In 1992 Diamond took to the mic for **Stunts, Blunts & Hip Hop**. He couldn't match the skills of either Finesse or AG, but Diamond's simplified rhyme style helped make **Stunts ...** a classic. His streamlined vocal rhythm allowed him and co-producers 45 King, Large Professor, Showbiz and Q-Tip to make a club-friendly but complex collection of slamming beats. "Best Kept Secret" and "A View From the Underground" introduced Fat Joe (Joseph Cartagena), while "Comments From Big L and Showbiz" featured the wax debut of Big L (Lamont Coleman). Although his mic technique had improved, Diamond succumbed to the trend for more melodic, less loopy production on his delayed follow-up, **Passion, Hatred and Infidelity** (1997).

Fat Joe released the fairly mediocre **Represent** (1993) (which included the hit "Flow Joe") and **Jealous One's Envy** (1995), but his thug-life Darwinism was at its best on **Don Cartagena** (1998). Big L, meanwhile, made a name for himself with scene-stealing guest appearances on Lord Finesse's "Yes You May (Remix)" (1992) and Showbiz & AG's "Represent" (1994). His debut album, **Lifestylez Ov Da Poor & Dangerous** (1995), was a rugged affair that burst to light on "MVP" and the posse cuts, "8 Iz Enuff" and "Da Graveyard".

"8 Iz Enuff" was produced by Buckwild (Anthony Best), who had previously been Finesse's tour DJ. Buck had also produced OC's (Omar Credle) underground anthem "Time's Up" (1994). OC had debuted on Organized Konfusion's "Fudge Pudge" (1991) and Buck helped produce their **Stress: The Extinction Agenda** (1994). OC's own debut album, **Word Life** (1994), marked the emergence of one of indie hip-hop's greatest, most reflective, most commanding MCs and aligned DITC with the underground.

Loved on the streets but ignored by consumers, DITC focused on the independent scene and started their own DITC label in 1997 with the posse cut, "Day One", which featured OC, Fat Joe, Big L and Diamond spitting to a Diamond-encrusted beat. Although DITC remained a largely cult phenomenon, Fat Joe was awarded the ultimate accord: he had a sandwich (grilled turkey, fried eggs and American cheese) named after him at New York's Stage deli. Meanwhile, Big L torched the underground with "Ebonics" (1998), which saw him play the slang teacher like Wide Boy Awake. On February 15, 1999, however, Big L was gunned down in Harlem and the posthumous collection of his rhymes, **The Big Picture** (2000), reveals how much New York hip-hop will miss his presence.

As a group, DITC signed to Tommy Boy and released **Diggin' in the Crates** (2000), largely a compilation of tracks they had released on their label, but featuring new cuts like the smoking Premier-produced "Thick".

⊙ **Showbiz & AG – Runaway Slave**   Payday, 1992

No-nonsense, true-school Bronx hip-hop at its finest.

⊙ **OC – Word Life**   Wild Pitch, 1994

Both deep and hard-knock, his debut album showed that OC is one of the most complete MCs around.

Digital Underground

Exploding out of the Bay Area with the utterly amazing "Doowutchyalike" (1989), Digital Underground brought George Clinton's Parliafunkadelicment Thang back to the public consciousness. At the outset of their career, ringleader Shock G (and his alter ego Humpty Hump), Money B, DJ Fuze and Chopmaster J made some of the most delicious, party-rocking hip-hop ever, only to get paralysed by formula.

It may have introduced a new, funkier sound into hip-hop, but "Doowutchyalike" was everything old-school hip-hop was about: jokey, cornball rhymes that had one object and one object only – to cold-rock a party. With stoopid fresh lines like "Help yourself to a cracker with a spread of cheddar cheese/Have a neckbone, you don't have to say please" on top of some serious handclaps and P-Funk punctuation, "Doowutchyalike" was the year's most irresistible single.

Sex Packets (1990) was thoroughly Clintonian in its conception: the album was based around a putative narrative in which a mad scientist unleashes a drug that causes those who ingest it to have wet dreams. The music was equally rooted in the Mothership. With its grinding bassline, numerous Parliament samples and hilarious rhymes like "Crazy, wack, funky/People say, 'You look like MC Hammer on crack Humpty'", "The Humpty Dance" was even better than "Doowutchyalike" and is undoubtedly the greatest dance craze that never was. The bizarre sense of humour and Parliamentarianism continued on "Freaks of the Industry", which highlighted the mic skills of Money B.

This Is an EP Release (1990) was a bit short on new material, with two remixes of tracks from **Sex Packets**, including a great reworking of "The Way We Swing". Of the new tracks, "Same Song" was the most notable, not only for its bumping rhythm, but it also marked the vinyl debut of Tupac Shakur. **Sons of the P** (1991) had more P-Funk stylings, but it didn't have the same effervescence of the debut. However, the album's best track, "No Nose Job", was exactly what George Clinton should have been singing about in the '90s: a funny, clever, cartoonish critique of black people who want to switch.

Money B and DJ Fuze formed the DU offshoot Raw Fusion in 1991 and released **Live From the Styleetron**, an underrated album that blended speeded-up dancehall beats with hip-hop and featured the great "Throw Your Hands in the Air". Raw Fusion's follow-up, **Hoochified Funk** (1994), however, was as stale as the main band had become by this point.

Digital Underground's **Body Hat Syndrome** (1993) was another concept album about sex and prophylactics, but it was nowhere near as inspired as **Sex Packets**. It was perhaps notable only for debuting Saafir. **Future Rhythm** (1996) continued the losing streak with abominable cyber-sex cover art and equally abysmal music. **Who Got the Gravy?** (1998) found Shock G and Money B teaming up with such East Coasters as Biz Markie, Big Pun and KRS-One in an effort to regain some momentum. While it was a significant improvement on the previous couple of releases, it still wouldn't make enough noise to register on the radar of public consciousness.

⊙**Sex Packets**   Tommy Boy, 1990

It might not be as great as its inspiration, but Shock G and crew don't embarrass themselves on what may be hip-hop's best party album.

Dilated Peoples

Perhaps *the* sensation of the hip-hop underground, LA's Dilated Peoples eschew any geographical stylistic boundaries in favour of a kind of hip-hop purity. Indie hip-hop scenesters continually rant about staying true to the culture, but no one epitomizes this more than Dilated Peoples' commitment to unadulterated mic and turntable skills. A member of the World Famous Beat Junkies, DJ Babu (Chris Oroc) "is so nice he don't slice, he severs", while MCs Evidence (Michael Perretta) and Iriscience (Rakaa Taylor) pop your eardrums with cutting battle rhymes and detailed strings of images.

Evidence and Iriscience were both graffiti artists who dropped the aerosol in favour of mics in 1992. The duo became Dilated Peoples in 1994 and soon inked a deal with the Epic-distributed Immortal

Records due to their affiliation with House of Pain's DJ Lethal. Their first wax appearance was "End of the Time", which was featured on **The Next Chapter** compilation (1996). The Peoples finished recording their debut album, **Imagery, Battle Hymns and Political Poetry**, but Epic dropped Immortal and the album has never seen the light of day.

MIKE LEWIS

Undeterred, Evidence and Iriscience appeared on Defari's "Bionic" (1997), which was released on Bay Area DJ Beni B's ABB Records. Always Bigger and Better then released the singles responsible for Dilated's formidable rep. "Third Degree" (1997) featured both Defari and Babu's first cuts with the group. "Work the Angles" (1998), though, was the breakthrough and it remains the closest thing the underground's got to an anthem. Produced by Evidence, "Work the Angles" had the scything guitar stabs that characterize their sound, cadences that only emphasized the track's head-nodding factor and the most outrageous scratching ever to feature on a non-DJ track. On the flipside, "Main Event" had Evidence "spray[ing] rain on your parade" over a beat by Alchemist and "Triple Optics" was Iriscience's fresh spin on hip-hop's evergreen "third eye" metaphor.

Evidence and Iriscience laced Joey Chavez's (who had produced some of their unreleased album) "After the Heat" (1998) before releasing the equally superb **Re-Work the Angles** EP (1999). They then signed to Capitol and their debut album, **The Platform**, finally dropped halfway through 2000. Although it suffered slightly from cadences that were too similar, **The Platform** highlighted why hip-hop sucked so much in the new millennium. In an iced-out world, no one cared much about skills any more, a sorry state made all the more obvious by Dilated's excellent live shows, which were always punctuated with Evidence's stage dives during "Work the Angles".

⊙ **The Platform**   Capitol, 2000

This features "Work the Angles", "Main Event" and "Triple Optics" and, as Iriscience says, it moves like "John Coltrane pushing a blue train".

Divine Styler

One of hip-hop's most celebrated mystery figures, Divine Styler has forged a path that is pretty much unique in the music's history. Part of Divine Styler's originality comes from the fact that he's a Brooklynite who came to prominence as a member of Ice-T's West Coast Rhyme Syndicate posse. His geographical non-alignment means that he has been able to pursue his own unique, personal muse – even if he takes no more than a handful of people with him.

His 1989 debut album, **Word Power**, was a dense paean to Islam that explored the coded complexities of mysticism a couple of years before the Five Percenters rose to prominence. Although musically similar to the Native Tongues albums of the same era, Styler's word-play and bizarre stream-of-consciousness conceptual drift on tracks like "Divine Stylistics" staked out new territory and was the first equation in Styler's "ill black calculus".

The follow-up, **Spiral Walls Containing Autumns of Light** (1992), was as psychedelic as its title and saw Divine playing most of the live instruments himself. Against a forbidding wall of noise constructed from atonal synth squall and feedback guitar that at times recalled fusioneers like Herbie Hancock and Larry Young, Divine called himself "Your blackest fathom", delved even further into the mystical depths of Islam and made his flow even more dervish-like.

SØLVE SUNDSBØ

Then, unless you count working with House of Pain on their third album as keeping in circulation, he more or less vanished. His disappearance from the scene prompted a 'zine called *In Search of Divine Styler*, and Divine became an object of trainspotting fascination. In 1997 Divine made the pilgrimage to Mecca and the experience renewed his faith both in Allah and in music. El Hadji Divine Styler released the brilliant 12" "Before Mecca" (1997) soon after he returned, which set the stage for his comeback album, **Word Power 2 – Directrix** (1999). His return was marked by a muezzin calling the faithful to prayer and after an instrumental and spoken-word invocation, Divine started to "refine the myth". Where most MCs who praise Allah couch their beliefs in scabrous rhetoric and arcane numerology, Divine's raps were filled with the kind of twisted images and labyrinthine logic that made you want to take the time to unravel his metaphors rather than leave them for the adepts. In fact, unlike his Five Percent peers, Divine's most pious tracks were the most accessible. The rough, bruising synth-lines and knock-your-wind-out drum beats cohered into a kind of future gothic symphony. Whatever his commitment to language, Divine didn't forget that Allah created noise before he made the word.

⊙ **Word Power 2 – Directrix**   DTX/Mo' Wax, 1999/2000

"Logos" may be a Christian concept, but with his lyrical originality – and (crucially) equally original production – Divine tried to make the word of God flesh.

DJ Jazzy Jeff & The Fresh Prince

The Philadelphia duo of DJ Jazzy Jeff (not to be confused with the Funky Four's Jazzy Jeff) and Fresh Prince are responsible for one of hip-hop's best trends and one of its worst. As a deck technician, DJ

Jazzy Jeff (Jeffrey Townes) was almost without peer in the '80s: his development of the transformer scratch and invention of the chirp scratch helped propel the art of DJing from the ground zero of Flash's backspins to the current hamster-style state of the art. On the other hand, the Fresh Prince (Will Smith) was the first rapper to become a TV and movie star, thus beginning the trend of rappers as entertainers rather than musicians.

The two got together in 1985 in South Philly and landed a record contract after Jeff won the New Music Seminar DJ Battle for World Supremacy in 1986. Originally released on Word Up, **Rock the House** (1987) featured the poptastic, *I Dream of Jeanie*-sampling "Girls Ain't Nothing But Trouble" alongside more radical, proto-turntablist fare from Jeff like the awesome "A Touch of Jazz".

MIKE LEWIS

He's the DJ, I'm the Rapper (1988) had more turntable antics from Jeff, but it was dominated by cross-over material like "Parents Just Don't Understand" and the album went triple platinum and clinched the duo the first rap Grammy. **And in This Corner** (1989) was even more of a grasp at pop stardom and hit with the pretty dire "I Think I Can Beat Mike Tyson". **Homebase** (1991) followed suit with more soccer-Mom-friendly hip-hop, but they reached rock bottom with the scandalously bad "Boom! Shake the Room" from **Code Red** (1993).

By this time, however, Smith was starring in *The Fresh Prince of Bel-Air* and he soon began his movie career with *Six Degrees of Separation.* Several box office smashes later, Smith deigned to bless the mic again on the *Men in Black* soundtrack with the pointless remake of Patrice Rushen's "Forget Me Nots", "Men in Black" (1997). Smith got jiggy wit' it on **Big Willie Style** (1997), selling five million and becoming one of the biggest stars on the planet. **Willennium** (1999) had more ghost-written rhymes and obvious samples and it too went multi-platinum.

⊙ **Rock the House** Jive, 1987

Not even Puffy would touch it nowadays, but "Girls Ain't Nothing But Trouble" was fine, brezzy pop way back when and there was plenty of Jeff on the decks to make this their least cringe-worthy release.

DJ Quik

Although David Blake had connections to the Tree Top Piru Bloods and left the "c" out of his mic name because it represented the Crips, DJ Quik is less of a gangsta rapper than he is a continuation of the traditions of street corner signifying and filthy party comedy of Rudy Ray Moore and Redd Foxx. As a producer Quik was one of the first Left Coasters to develop the rolling version of the P-Funk. Despite his mixing-board chops, Quik will probably always be associated with what may be hip-hop's most devastating series of dis records: his battle with MC Eiht.

After lacing LA underground mix tapes for a couple of years, Quik emerged with **Quik Is the Name** (1991). "Tonite" was a Top 50 single about the pleasures of "getting bent" and playing celo that rode a huge synth/vocoder groove from Kleeer. Quik drawled fast and furious on the title track, which was based on snippets from Brass Construction and Cameo, while "Born and Raised in Compton" sampled Isaac Hayes over a slamming kick drum.

Way 2 Fonky (1992) followed **Quik Is the Name** as a gold album largely thanks to the fearsome single, "Jus Lyke Compton". **Way 2 Fonky** also escalated his wax war with MC Eiht on the title track and "Tha Last Word", which also responded to Tim Dog's Compton baiting. However, **Way 2 Fonky** made no advances on his debut's sound and the only growth was in the number of pussy references.

Reeling under the sheer weight of Eiht's "Def Wish" records, Quik released the absolutely savage "Dollars & Sense" (1994) after hooking up with Death Row's Suge Knight. Based on the groove of Brick's "Dazz", "Dollars & Sense" was merciless in its slander of Eiht: "'E-I-H-T' now should I continue?/Yeah, you left out the 'G' cause the G ain't in you". The battle continued on **Safe & Sound** (1995) with "Let You Havit", but the vast majority of the album was taken up with pseudo-comic tracks about his prowess in bed that wouldn't have made anyone in the locker room laugh, and flaccid, back-in-the-day reminiscing like "Summer Breeze".

Rhythm-al-ism (1999) was a major progression in production (Quik played most of the keyboard, bass and drum parts himself). The fuller, warmer sound apparently had its effect on the lyrics, too: on

"You'z a Ganxta" Quik made peace with Eiht in the fallout of the deaths of Tupac and Biggie. Of course, the old macking lyrics like "Hand in Hand" were there too, but the beats were so good that you didn't mind. Unfortunately, **Balance & Options** (2000) followed too quickly on the heels of **Rhythm-al-ism** with a brace of uninspired covers of Eazy-E and Digital Underground tracks. The only bright spot was a collaboration with Raphael Saadiq, "Well", which was the most tasteful and moving meeting of hip-hop and R&B in a long, long time.

⊙ **Quik Is the Name**   Profile, 1991

Perhaps the most well-produced West Coast album this side of Dr. Dre.

DJing

There are DJs and then there are DJs. Radio, club and mix tape DJs like Funkmaster Flex, Kid Capri, Tony Touch, DJ Clue, Ron G, Doo Wop, Eclipse and Tim Westwood serve their func-

Kid Capri

tion, but it's the logic of the cut and scratch that really separates hip-hop from disco. Of course, hip-hop DJing is more than just dragging a record back and forth across a stylus or segueing two tracks together nice and smooth. Hip-hop is a lot like the British class system: it's not so much what you say that matters, but how you say it. This is as true of the DJ as it is of the MC and graffiti tagger. Thus, great DJs recognize that the best music is a complete triumph of style over substance; everything's been said already, so why bother listening unless the speaker's got some serious moxie. In fact, the DJ's style is the very substance of turntablism. All of which serves to explain hip-hop's infatuation with kung-fu flicks: when everyone is using the same basic materials, style – whether it's drunken boxing and Shaolin shadow boxing or flaring and beat juggling – becomes all important.

Long before Kool DJ Herc started manipulating two copies of the same record to elongate the beat, the first piece of music to envision the turntable as a musical instrument was John Cage's **Imaginary Landscape No. 1** (1939), which was written to be performed in a studio by a pianist, a Chinese cymbal player and two turntablists playing Victor frequency records, taking advantage of the turntable's ability to switch gears from 33 1/3 to 78 in order to manipulate recordings of constant tones. While several composers took up Cage's challenge by scoring pieces for other apparatuses of electronic reproduction like the radio and microphone, the possibilities of the turntable as an instrument in its own right lay dormant until Kool Herc transplanted the Jamaican sound system to The Bronx in the early '70s.

Herc's breakbeat style laid the foundations for hip-hop, but it was another DJ, Grandwizard Theodore, who created its signature flourish in 1977 or 1978. Purely by accident, Theodore

→

stumbled across scratching when he was practising in his bedroom and had his attention diverted and rubbed the record across the stylus. You can hear Theodore scratching it up on "Can I Get a Soul Clap" (1988), but the two most vital documents of early hip-hop DJing are Grandmaster Flash's "The Adventures of Grandmaster Flash on the Wheels of Steel" (1981) and Afrika Bambaataa's **Death Mix** (1983) (see entries).

While Flash and Bamabaataa were using the turntable to explore repetition, alter rhythm and create the instrumental stabs and punch phasing that would come to characterize the sound of hip-hop, Grandmixer D.ST was busy cutting "real" musicians on their own turf. His scratching on Herbie Hancock's 1983 single, "Rockit", makes it perhaps the most influential DJ track of them all – even more than "Wheels of Steel", it established the DJ as the star of the record, even if he wasn't the frontman. Compared to "Rockit", West Street Mob's "Break Dancin' – Electric Boogie" (1983) was punk negation. Only DJ Code Money's brutalist record mangling on Schooly D's early records can match the cheese-grater note-shredding of "Break Dancin'". As great as "Break Dancin'" was, though, it also highlighted the limited tonal range of scratching, which was in danger of becoming a short-lived fad like human beat-boxing until the emergence of Code Money's DJ brethren from Philadelphia in the mid-'80s.

Despite New York's continued pre-eminence in the hip-hop world, scratch DJing was modernized 90 miles down the road in Philadelphia. Denizens of the City of Brotherly Love were creating the climate for the return of the DJ by inventing transformer

scratching. Developed by DJs Spinbad, Cash Money and DJ Jazzy Jeff, transform-
ing was basically click-
ing the fader on and off
while moving a block of
sound (a riff or a short
verbal phrase) across
the stylus. Expanding
the tonal as well as
rhythmic possibilities of
scratching, the trans-
former scratch epito-
mized the chopped-up
aesthetic of hip-hop
culture. The only prob-
lem with the Philly DJs
was their timing. Hip-
hop was starting to
become big money and
the cult of personality
started to take over.
Hip-hop became very
much at the service of

Mix Master Mike

the rapper and Cash Money and DJ Jazzy Jeff were saddled with
B-list rappers like Marvelous and the Fresh Prince and were
accorded maybe one track on an album to get busy (check
tracks like DJ Jazzy Jeff's "A Touch of Jazz" (1987) and "Jazzy's
in the House" (1988) and Cash Money's "The Music Maker"

➡

(1988)). Other crucial DJ tracks from this period include the Tuff Crew's DJ Detonator's "Behold the Detonator" and "Soul Food" (both 1989), Gang Starr's "DJ Premier in Deep Concentration" (1989) and 2 Live Crew's "Mr Mixx on the Mix!" (1986) and "Megamix 2" (1989).

With turntable chops so awesome that they've been banned from the competitions that are the lifeblood of the turntablist scene, Q-Bert and his Invisbl Skratch Piklz crew (Apollo, Mix Master Mike, Shortkut and DJ Disk) heralded the return of the DJ as a self-contained band. Emerging as a force in 1992 by taking the DMC World DJ Championship away from the odious DJ Dave from Germany (who, as John Carluccio's excellent film *Battle Sounds* showed, actually air-scratched and did hand-stands on a moving turntable), the Skratch Piklz brought turntablism back to the basics of scratching and cutting and away from the grandstanding showmanship that it had largely become. Where Flash and Herc created hip-hop out of the syn-cretic readymade of the breakbeat, on his **Demolition Pumpkin Squeeze Musik** mixtape (1994) Q-Bert colonized and infested the break with his scratches and blocks of viral noise, creating true adventures on the wheels of steel through fantastic George Lucas-style mindscapes where the scratches sounded like the shape-shifting video-game characters of Q-Bert's imagination.

The emergence of crews like the Skratch Piklz, the X-ecution-ers and the Beat Junkies dovetailed with the developing inde-pendent hip-hop movement to establish a flourishing "real" hip-hop culture that stood in opposition to the crass materialism, stu-pid violence and talentlessness of what they disparagingly

→

Babu/Beat Junkies

called "Rap". Originally released in 1995, **Return of the DJ Vol. 1**
was amazingly the first album to be devoted exclusively to the
hip-hop DJ. Picking up on an idea from Q-Bert (and John Cage),
who used to play tunes like "Mary Had a Little Lamb" on the
turntable by manipulating a recording of a pure tone with the
pitch control lever, X-ecutioner Rob Swift's "Rob Gets Busy"
used the pitch control adjustment on the Technics to mutate the
Moog riff from The J.B.'s "Blow Your Head" before embarking on
an exposition of the beat-juggling techniques developed by
Steve D in 1990. The Skratch Piklz showed off their battery of
flare and crab scratches on "Invasion of the Octopus People",
while Mixmaster Mike invoked the ghosts of Double Dee &
Steinski on "Terrorwrist". It wasn't all excitement and flash,
though. Peanut Butter Wolf's "The Chronicles (I Will Always Love

➡️

H.E.R.)" was a melancholic journey through hip-hop's short history that showed both how much had been gained and how much had been lost.

⊙ **Various Artists –**
Return of the DJ Vol.1 Bomb Hip-Hop, 1995

Although all three volumes of this groundbreaking series are worth picking up, this is the record that almost single-handedly resurrected the art of the DJ.

DMX/Ruff Ryders

long with Jay-Z, DMX and his Ruff Ryders crew ruled hip-hop at the end of the millennium. DMX may not be the best rapper in the world, but he's performed a feat that all sentient human beings have to respect: he's knocked Garth Brooks off the top of the American pop chart – twice – within a year. About as far away from Brooks' clean and corporate image as you could possibly be, DMX's satanic verses and over-the-top delivery remake hip-hop as heavy metal.

With his nuance-free pit bull bark that is as unsubtle as, and not all that different from, the growl from the bowels of hell of Napalm Death's Lee Dorian, the erstwhile Earl Simmons was a mix-tape legend in New York for years before he finally signed a record deal. Instead of metal's raging guitars, DMX's hellhound snarl is surrounded by the metallic polyrhythms of producer Swizz Beatz, who made the Casio futurism of Timbaland even shinier and sometimes wilder. It might seem like an odd match, but by making a hideous, amoral, no-hope vision of the world as catchy as the Spice Girls the pairing of DMX's brutal, future-gothic lyrics and Swizz's state-of-the-art pop craftsmanship is scarier than the blackest black metal.

Knocking hip-hop out of its Wu piano loop and Puffy karaoke machine stupor, DMX's debut album, **It's Dark and Hell Is Hot** (1998), was little short of a sensation. On the back of the street anthem "Get At Me Dog", it entered the US charts at #1 and went double platinum in a few weeks. Seven months later, **Flesh of My Flesh, Blood of My Blood** (1998) did the same. Like his metal brethren, DMX terror-ized motorists and pedestrians alike with his gang of motorcycle fiends in his videos and concerts (à la Judas Priest) and appeared on the sleeve of **Flesh of My Flesh, Blood of My Blood** covered in blood – Marilyn Manson even made an appearance on "The Omen".

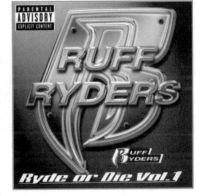

On his best tracks like "Get At Me Dog" (from **It's Dark**) and "What's My Name" (from 1999's **... And Then There Was X**), DMX is all bluster, like a wolf growling and panting at its cornered prey. With his asthmatic growl, Doberman tenacity when he attacks a beat, his collection of attack dogs and tales of death and pain, DMX tried to be hip-hop's Cerberus guarding the gates of hell. But where Cerberus had three heads (and presumably three different barks), DMX has only one voice, one flow and one gimmick.

The Ruff Ryders' posse album **Ryde or Die** (1999) attempted to remedy this with appearances from Eve, Drag-on, Bad Boy exiles The LOX and cameos from Jay-Z, Big Pun and Juvenile. Featuring the salsa-flavoured "What Ya Want" (which made Eve the biggest thing since striped toothpaste), the intense synth riffs of "Platinum Plus" and the impossibly weird "Bugout", **Ryde or Die** was really a production showcase for Swizz Beatz. Similarly, while Eve wasn't half bad on **Ruff Ryder's First Lady** (1999), it was the beats that made the record: the foghorn bombast of "Scenario 2000", the relentlessly catchy acoustic guitars of "Gotta Man", the Michael Nyman piano of "Philly, Philly" and the slip-sliding-away funk of "Ain't Got No Dough". The Ruff Ryders' biggest coup, however, was tempting The LOX away from an ailing Bad Boy for the **We Are the Streets** (2000) album. But, for all of The Ruff Ryders' commercial acumen, the two best beats came from ringers DJ Premier ("Recognize") and Timbaland ("Ryde or Die, Bitch").

⊙ **Ruff Ryders – Ryde or Die Vol.1**   Ruff Ryders/Interscope, 1999

DMX is pretty hard to take over the course of a whole album, so this collection of insane beats from Swizz Beatz is the one to go for. Just try not to listen to the lyrics.

The D.O.C.

Born Trey Curry in Dallas, Texas, The D.O.C. was poised to become one of hip-hop's biggest stars at the end of the '80s.

Signed to Eazy-E's Ruthless Records at the time of NWA's break-through, The D.O.C. was probably the best pure MC in the extended crew. Along with Masta Ace and Ice Cube, The D.O.C. could ride the fast beats prevalent at the time better than anyone, and at any tempo he had an authoritative voice and enunciation that would've made Rex Harrison proud.

His debut album, **No One Can Do It Better** (1989), was a huge hit and proved that the West Coast wasn't just about pulling gats and bitch-slapping hoes. Produced by Dr. Dre, **No One Can Do It Better** featured killer cuts like the intense "Portrait of a Master-piece", which taught the Chemical Brothers a trick or ten, the classic Cali roller "It's Funky Enough", which featured The D.O.C. dropping some Jamaican-flavoured rhymes, "The Formula" and the stellar "Grand Finale".

At the top of his game, though, The D.O.C. was in a car acci-dent that crushed his larynx. Despite this setback, he still managed to ghost-write lyrics for NWA's **Efil4Zaggin** (1991) and Dr. Dre's **The Chronic** (1992) and made brief cameos on **The Chronic** and Snoop Dogg's **Doggystyle**. Shortly afterwards, he split with Death Row in a dispute over money and recorded an ill-advised comeback album. Brave though it was, **Helter Skelter** (1996) was pretty awful. Over really tired beats, The D.O.C. rapped like '50s rock 'n' roll singer Clarence "Frogman" Henry, except that it wasn't meant to be funny.

Nonetheless, The D.O.C. continues to pen lyrics for other MCs and has worked with Tha Dogg Pound's Kurupt, Snoop and Dr. Dre.

⊙**No One Can Do It Better**   Ruthless, 1989

Even with appearances from most of NWA, The D.O.C.'s mic skills almost live up to the title.

Dr. Dre

"**S**even days a week, he's on call/To get the party people off the wall". He may not be the best or most consistent (that's DJ Premier), the most historically important (that's Marley Marl) or the most radical (that's the Bomb Squad), but **Dr. Dre** is certainly the most influential producer in hip-hop. From practically inventing high-energy, West Coast electro-funk with the **World Class Wreckin' Cru** (and starting the Cabbage Patch craze in the process) to creating the

blueprint for gangsta rap with NWA to birthing G-Funk as a solo artist, Dr. Dre has started more mini-epochs in popular music than anyone this side of James Brown.

Andre Young was born in Compton, California in 1965 and attended Centennial High, where he caught the music bug at block parties and all-ages clubs like Eve's After Dark. After wowing the crowd with a DJ set at Eve's, Dre was invited by the club's owner, Lonzo Williams, to join his crew of DJs and rappers, the World Class Wreckin' Cru. Along with DJ Yella, the Unknown DJ, Cli-N-Tel and Lonzo, Dre was responsible for such uptempo (125 bpm plus) electro-funk tracks as "World Class" (1984), "Juice" and Cli-N-Tel's ode to Dre, "Surgery" (both 1985). After one album, **Rapped in Silence** (1986), the WCWC disbanded and Dre and DJ Yella hooked up with Stereo Crew MC Ice Cube, MC Ren and Eazy-E to form Niggaz With Attitude.

With NWA, Dre produced some of the most powerful music ever made: **Straight Outta Compton** (1988) screamed out of the speakers with a sonic rage that matched the lyrics, while **Efil4zaggin** (1991) began the trend for whiny synths and P-Funk beats that Dre would perfect on **The Chronic**. During this time Dre also found time to produce records for The DOC and the "We're All in the Same Gang" (1990) single.

Extricated from his contract with Eazy-E's Ruthless label by Death Row CEO Suge Knight, Dre changed the world with what could have been a throwaway track from a movie soundtrack. Over a beat more menacing and askew than anything trip-hop would come up with in five years of ripping it off, "Deep Cover" (1992) introduced Snoop Doggy Dogg drawling "It's 1-8-7 on an undercover cop", in a Deep South accent that exuded a fearsome casual violence. **The Chronic** (1992) was even more frightening: with the fact that real gangsters listen to the smoothest music as its starting point, and exploring the tension between the two meanings of "chilling", **The Chronic**'s languid pace, lazy drawls and laidback beats surrounded tales of horrific, but matter-of-fact, violence and its insouciance was simultaneously bloodcurdling and seductive. The album dominated hip-hop: "Nuthin' But a G Thang" and "Dre Day" both went Top 10 and the album sold four million copies; it inspired more wiggas than Muddy Waters; and it ended the sampling era by emphasizing live basslines, Moog hooks and Leon Haywood, Isaac Hayes and Donny Hathaway interpolations.

After Death Row got itself into trouble, Dre formed his own label, Aftermath, and released the disappointing **Dr. Dre Presents ... The Aftermath**, (1996) which saw Dre backing away from G-Funk. The album's one great moment was actually the preposterous video for "Been There, Done That". After foisting Eminem on the world, Dre returned with **Dr. Dre 2001** (2000). Almost a decade after **The Chronic** Dre hadn't moved an inch. The misogyny was worse than ever; the mercenary capitalism, which was contextualised by the LA riots in 1991 on **The Chronic**, was now just grotesque and dumb, even if things haven't changed much; and the music was a garish imitation of past glories. Compared to producers like Swizz Beatz, who took Dre's ghetto symphonies to new levels of grandeur with shimmering synth lines, sleek beats and salsa touches, Dre's work on **2001** sounded as archaic as his World Class Wreckin' Cru records did when **Straight Outta Compton** dropped.

⊙ **The Chronic**   Death Row/Interscope, 1992

The most influential hip-hop album of the '90s.

Dungeon Family

Just as The Pharcyde and Freestyle Fellowship represented the avant garde response to G-Funk in LA, Atlanta's Dungeon Family (OutKast, Goodie MOb, Witchdoctor, Cool Breeze, Lil' Will and the Organized Noize production crew) were the Dirty South's arty alter ego. Unlike SoCal's commercial pariahs, however, these Southern alchemists working in their dungeon managed to turn their spiritual and semi-mystical vibes into gold and platinum.

A partnership that began at Tri-Cities High School (Atlanta's version of Juillard), OutKast (Antwan "Big Boi" Patton and Andre "Dre" Benjamin) is one of the most impressive acts in hip-hop. Without sacrificing hip-hop's main pleasure principle, Dre and Big Boi have managed to grow and shift directions over the course of their career – a unique feat in hip-hop. Their debut album, **Southernplayalisticadillacmuzik** (1994), sought to subvert the Southern stereotype of playa music. With gangsta-leaning production from Organized Noize (Rico Wade, Pat "Sleepy" Brown and Ray Murray) that was rich, deep and detailed, but never as seductive or crowd-pleasing as Dr. Dre's, **Southernplayalisticadillacmuzik** was a melancholy depiction of the game that never shied away from its consequences: the album's sonic trademark was a truncated, homunculus of the 808 clavé sound so characteristic of booty music; the chorus of "Crumblin' Erb" went, "There's only so much time left in this crazy world/I'm just crumblin' herb"; "Player's Ball" had a Curtis Mayfield-styled falsetto undercutting its depiction of "black man's heaven"; "Call of Da Wild" was the story of a G who had voices in his head like the Geto Boys; and the spoken "True Dat" had the brusque put-down: "If you think it's all about pimping hoes and slammin' Cadillac doors/You probably a cracker or a nigga who think you a cracker".

ATLiens (1996) was probably more "mature", but their acquired wisdom was never thrown in your face and it didn't shackle their vision, fun or grooves. With lines like "I live by the beat like you live cheque to cheque/If you don't move your feet, then I don't eat, so we like neck to neck", the amazing "Elevators (Me & You)" was one of the first Southern singles to go nationwide. Elsewhere, they got more explicitly political on tracks like "Babylon" and "Mainstream". Their masterwork, though, was **Aquemini** (1998). Opening with a song called "Return of the 'G'", **Aquemini** set you up for some big ballin' and shot callin', but then hit you with lyrics like "Return of the gangsta thanks to/Them niggas who got dem kids, who got enough to buy an ounce/But not enough to bounce dem kids to the zoo/Or to the park so they grow up never seein' the light/So they end up being like your sorry ass/Robbin' niggas in broad ass day light". Other highlights included the hoedown "Rosa Parks" (complete with harmonica break from Dre's pastor) and the mind-blowing "Liberation".

Comprising Carlito "Cee-lo" Green, Robert "T-Mo" Barrett, Willie "Khujo" Knighton and Cameron "Big Gipp" Gipp, Goodie MOb (Good Die Mostly Over Bullshit) make OutKast's allusions to the political realm explicit. Their debut album, **Soul Food** (1995), was released at the height of the murder music trend and its paranoia and brutal imagery fit in perfectly, except that they were dark like George Clinton. Dubbing Louis Armstrong into ghetto hell, the conspiracy-minded "Cell Therapy" sounded like an old plantation work chant with Casio drums replacing rhythmic handclaps. "Dirty South" was superficially an anthem of regional pride, but the video featured a girl drawing a Confederate flag, making obvious the real meaning of living in Dixie. **Still Standing** (1998) was similarly G-Funk in reverse: smooth guitars running backwards, synths that whimpered instead of whining and songs about people not dancing no more. On **World Party** (2000), however, their uncompromising vision had been replaced by a sharper, more current, electronic sound and lines like "The world would be a better place to live if there were less queers".

Disconcerting missteps aside, though, **World Party** maintained the Mob's playfulness on tracks like "What it Ain't (Ghetto Enuff)" (with labelmates TLC), "Get Rich to This" and "Chain Swang". With occasionally great, state-of-the-art production and a couple of great radio songs, **World Party** was the sort of compromise fans would have to settle for in an apolitical age.

Both Cool Breeze (Freddie Calhoun) and Witchdoctor are less compelling than their Dungeon brethren, but both, Breeze in particular, are excellent technical MCs. Breeze's **East Point's Greatest Hit** (1999) wasn't thematically interesting (mostly concerning itself with Freddie's ability on the cut-up; that's Southern for "fucking"), but it featured jumping production from Organized Noize, particularly on the hot posse cut "Watch Out for the Hook", which was based on a Neil Young cut-up (not that kind).

⊙ **OutKast – Aquemini**   LaFace, 1998

It's conflicted and drags in places, but this is nevertheless one of the most impressive hip-hop records in years.

Jermaine Dupri/ So So Def

Making hits is almost in Jermaine Dupri's blood: his father, Michael Mauldin, is an ex-musician who managed Arrested Development before he was appointed president of Sony's black music division. As a kid, Dupri danced with both UTFO and Whodini; by the age of fourteen he had produced his first record, Silk Tymes Leather's instantly forgettable debut.

Dupri made his name, though, as the Svengali behind Kriss Kross. Pulling the strings that made Daddy Mack and Mack Daddy "Jump", Dupri was behind the pop sensation of 1992, with their debut album, **Totally Krossed Out**, producing three Top 20 singles. When Kriss Kross's balls and voices dropped, however, Dupri shifted focus to another under-age R&B sensation, Usher, for whom he produced the enormous "You Make Me Wanna ... " (1997).

In the meantime, Dupri discovered Shawntae Harris (aka Da Brat) and signed her to his So So Def label. Her debut album, **Funkdafied** (1994), was the first album by a female rapper to go platinum. Featuring the title cut, **Funkdafied** was a more upwardly mobile take on Dr. Dre's G-Funk, with smoother synth riffs, bongo patterns stolen from cross-town producers Organized Noize, lusher production values, Da Brat's "Brat-a-tat-tat" flow and a more refined taste in product placements (Moët as opposed to Tanqueray).

Anuthatantrum (1996) was largely more of the same, except not as funky. While Da Brat cameoed on just about every single Dupri production, she wouldn't release another album until **Unrestricted** (2000), which saw her toss away her trademark baggy camouflage trousers in favour of make-up and cleavage. The music had a make-over too: with Timbaland triggers, flamenco guitar and R&B collaborations replacing rolling funk.

Dissatisfied with a large chink of the R&B and pop-rap markets, Dupri launched the So So Def Bass Allstars to bring the Atlanta Bass sound to the mainstream. He was also behind the Ghost Town DJs' summer hit, "My Boo" (1996). Dupri's real motivation, however, seemed to be imitating Bad Boy. He not only dragged in Notorious B.I.G. for "The Dirty B-Side" (1994), the flip of Da Brat's "Funkdafied", and gave shout-outs to Puffy's enterprise, he even rapped like Puffy on his debut album as an artist, **Life in 1472** (1998). On "Money Ain't a Thing" Dupri stumbled and mumbled just like Puff Daddy and Mase – he even pronounced his "r"s with a New York accent. Luckily, he called in Jay-Z to act as his Biggie-like crutch and the track blew up, with Jigga dropping gleaming jewels like "It's all basic/I've been spending 100s since they had small faces".

There were even rumours circulating that Dupri was trying to lure Mase away from Bad Boy before he retired from the rap game. With Bad Boy struggling, Dupri set about emulating that other high-profile ghettopreneur, Master P, when he started his own sports management agency. So So Def supermarkets can't be too far away.

⊙ **Da Brat – Funkdafied**   Columbia, 1994
Slick G-Funk retooled for a tomboy.

E-40 & The Click

Long before wannabe playas were sipping on Hennessey and champagne, gamers were chilling with jugs of cheap Burgundy. What Puffy is to Cristal, E-40 is to Carlos Rossi. The poet laureate of big ballin', shot callin' Yay Area hustlin', Earl Stevens is the Charlie Hustle of the Hall of Game: one of the great playas, but one who has never gotten the respect he deserves. E-40 is one of hip-hop's singular performers – he's brought more phrases into popular usage than anyone since Noah Webster (he's even published his own dictionary, *Dictionary Book of Slang*) and his phrasing and flow has influenced everyone from Outkast's Big Boi to Blackalicious' Gift of Gab – but due to his NoCal locale he has largely been ignored by the New York-centric hip-hop media. He's one of those MCs that you either smell or you don't.

E-40 first came to attention as part of The Click, a group made up of himself, his sister Suga-T, his brother D-Shot and his cousin B-Legit. Following the lead of Too $hort, they started their own company, Sick Wid' It, and hawked tapes out of the trunk of their car in the home turf of Vallejo, California. Before this, E-40, B-Legit and D-Shot started performing as students at Grambling State University in Louisiana and the transplanted Southern drawl became a large part of the group's charm. The **Less Side** EP (1990) was their first widely available release, but it was E-40's **Federal** (1992) album and his bizarre rhyming style on tracks like "Carlos Rossi", "Mr. Flamboyant", "Drought Season" and "Federal" that really got the clique noticed, and it officially sold 200,000 copies.

E-40's real breakthrough, though, was **The Mailman** EP (1993). "Practice Lookin' Hard" was a hilarious exposé of the playa poseur, while "Captain Save a Hoe" was the best example of his stuttering, drawling, light-speed combo-flow and Forty Fonzarelli's penchant for inventing words. As a result of the huge success of **The Mailman**, Jive licensed Sick Wid' It and distributed their product internationally.

In a Major Way (1995) went gold as E-40 tightened up his synth-funk and gave the people exactly what they wanted with the cheeky duet with Suga-T, "Sprinkle Me". The Click's **Game Related** (1995) followed with more expertly crafted street tales and the best drinking song since NWA's "Eightball" – "Hurricane". E-40's **Hall of Game** (1996) was a slight departure, featuring the hit "Rappers' Ball" with Too $hort and K-Ci from Jodeci, in which E-40 revealed his philosophy: "I don't freestyle, I don't rap for free".

The Element of Surprise (1998) was E-40's best since **The Mailman** and featured classic West Coast funk courtesy of producers Ant Banks and Tone Capone. "Hope I Don't Back" found 40 bragging about his success and praying he doesn't have to go back to hustling, while "Lieutenant Roastabotch" was a classic battle-of-the-sexes rhyme with Silk E. **Charlie Hustle: The Blueprint of a Self-Made Millionaire** (1999) found E-Freezy getting more autobiographical, but, instead of the hunger and humour that he used to sling, here he just sounded complacent and bloated.

⊙ **The Mailman**   Sick Wid' It, 1993

With its humour, slanguage and synth-funk, this is an absolute classic of Yay Area hip-hop.

Ed OG and the Bulldogs

Typically of Beantown's hip-hop scene, its most famous MC will permanently be associated with Brooklyn. While Guru had to leave Boston to gain fame with Gang Starr, Ed OG and the Bulldogs managed to garner a rep without ever having to set foot outside of Roxbury. That said, however, Ed OG and gang still owed their career to New York-based production team and radio DJs the Awesome Two (Special K and Teddy Ted), who produced their debut album and broke their hits on their influential show on WHBI.

Life of a Kid in the Ghetto (1991) probably couldn't have been made in any other year than 1991. Its naiveté was just about the last gasp of hip-hop's "golden age" before its wide-eyed optimism got blown away by Cypress Hill and Dr. Dre. On their biggest hit, "I Got to Have It", the erstwhile Edward Anderson told us that "the Bulldogs" was an acronym for "Black United Leaders Living Directly On Groovin' Sounds" – you can't get any more early '90s than that; actually you can't get any more late '80s than that. Despite such silliness, "I Got to Have It" was based on an irresistible, chopped-up loop of the human metronome Hamilton Bohannon and a killer horn riff that would be swiped by other producers and would later play a key role in X-Ecutioner Rob Swift's beat-juggling routine. **Life of a Kid in the Ghetto** also featured the irritatingly self-righteous "Be a Father to Your Child" (naturally a favourite of *Yo! MTV Raps* in its moralistic days) and "Bug-A-Boo", which would later be interpolated by Destiny's Child.

While they were behind the times when they released **Life of a Kid in the Ghetto**, they were hopelessly outdated on **Roxbury 02119**

(1994). Despite production by Diamond D and Prince Rakeem (aka the RZA), **Roxbury 02119** found Ed OG desperately trying to sound hard and failing miserably. Tracks like "Skinny Dip (Got it Goin' On)" were laughable, with Ed claiming his *nom de disque* was an acronym for "Every Day Other Girls". The only cut with any redeeming features was "Love Comes and Goes", a paean to victims of random street violence, including Ed's father.

After a few years laying really low, Ed OG returned with "Just Because" (1998) on the Mass In Action label. With production by DJ Spinna and Joe Mansefield, "Let's Be Realistic/Better Than Before" (1999) found Ed sounding comfortable with the sonics of the late '90s underground. His third album, **All Said and Done** (2000), followed a similar formula, with tracks from DJ Premier, Pete Rock, Spinna and Dialect.

⊙ **Life of a Kid in the Ghetto**   Mercury, 1991

It sounds impossibly corny now, but the production makes the album worthwhile.

Eightball & MJG

I f anyone made the Dirty South dirty it was Eightball & MJG. Before Eightball & MJG (aka Premro Smith and Marlon Jermaine Goodwin) hit the scene, Southern hip-hop was the source of endless laughs for heads from the two coasts. As soon as Eightball & MJG started telling their Southern-fried gangsta tales on top of the scatter-shot drum machine beats that characterized Memphis's Gangsta Walk dance, however, the South finally rose again and players from Atlanta to Winston-Salem got their swerve on and the entire US was bout it, bout it.

Smith and Goodwin are childhood friends from the crack-ravaged Orange Mound neighbourhood of Memphis who started rapping in high school. In 1991 they released the **Listen to the Lyrics** tape, which was a big hit in their hometown. They soon came to the attention of Suave House CEO, Tony Draper, who signed the duo and persuaded them to relocate to his homebase in Houston, where they recorded **Comin' Out Hard** (1993). Filled with brutal vignettes from the street like "9 Little Millimeta Boys" and rhyme after rhyme of pimp exploits like "Mr. Big", **Comin' Out Hard** proved that the South wasn't all Miami Bass soft porn and corny pre-teens who wore their clothes backwards.

On the Outside Looking In (1994) featured more tales of the M.E.M.P.H.I.S. (Making Easy Money Pimping Hoes In Style) lifestyle, with the anthemic "Lay It Down" being the highlight. They really made a virtue out of their Southern drawls on **On Top of the World** (1995), however. With no airplay whatsoever, the group did most of the promotion themselves, driving across the country below the Mason-Dixon Line and **On Top of the World** debuted in the Top 10 of *Billboard*'s album chart and at #2 on the R&B chart. The album's more sophisticated approach was epitomized by "Space Age Pimpin'", which housed their mackin' philosophy in the bluesy funk that the Organized Noize production crew would make their stock in trade.

MJG and Eightball reinforced their commercial clout with solo albums, **No More Glory** (1997) and **Lost** (1998) (a triple CD), which went gold and double platinum respectively. They re-emerged in 1999 with **In Our Lifetime Vol. 1**, which featured both reminiscing ("Dues Paid" with Cee-Lo from Goodie MOb) and crime-pays tales like "Armed Robbery", a version of the archetypal Southern beat,

"Triggerman" (taken from The Show Boys' "Drag Rap"), with a bit of *Mission Impossible* thrown in for good measure.

⊙ **In Our Lifetime Vol. 1**   Suave House, 1999

They sound like Compton's Most Wanted with exaggerated drawls, but these guys are Southern pioneers and this is their most well-produced album.

Electro

History is littered with "important" records, but few are truly as epochal as Afrika Bambaataa & Soulsonic Force's "Planet Rock" (1982). Testament to the most bizarre musical union since Hawaiian slide guitars found their way to the Mississippi Delta, "Planet Rock" was the ultimate result of the bizarre popularity among America's urban black communities of Kraftwerk's **Trans-Europe Express** and **Autobahn** albums. By taking the melody from "Trans-Europe Express" and welding it to the bottom end of "Numbers", Afrika Bambaataa imagined what the Teutonic man-machines would sound like if they had Afros and fat-laced Adidas shell-toes.

Teaching the world that drum machines and video games could be funky, "Planet Rock" single-handedly kick-started the electro movement of the early '80s. With Planet Patrol's "Play at Your Own Risk" (1982) and Jonzun Crew's "Pack Jam" (1982) and "Space Cowboy" (1983), Bam's label Tommy Boy fully jumped on the electro bandwagon. Sugar Hill managed briefly to keep pace with Reggie Griffin's Prince-meets-Cabaret Voltaire track, "Mirda Rock" (1982), but Sugar Hill was quickly supplanted by Tommy Boy as hip-hop's leading label.

→

Much of the best electro action, however, was happening on the margins.

Man Parrish's "Hip Hop Bee Bop (Don't Stop)" (1982) was Kraftwerk in dub. Probably the most original electro record after "Planet Rock" itself and a favourite of body-lockers the world over, the echoing synth shimmers and **Computer World**-era basslines of "Hip Hop Bee Bop" made it sound like an early Tears for Fears B-side being mercilessly cut to death by Grandmaster Flash. Even so, it affirmed Kraftwerk's glacial electronics as the new sound of urban cool and pointed the way for such dance-dub classics as The Peech Boys' "Don't Make Me Wait".

Tyrone Brunson capitalized on a bizarre dance craze with "The Smurf" (1982), while Hashim (Jerry Calliste and Aldo Marin) evoked some cyberdelic casbah on the amazing "Al-Naafiysh (The Soul)" (1983). Calliste was also part of the Imperial Brothers, whose "We Come to Dub" (1983) does for hiccups, sneezes and belches what "Planet Rock" did for drum machines. Calliste was a mainstay on New York's Cutting Records label and he also had a hand in cult classics by the Hi-Fidelity Three like "B-boys Breakdance" and "Never Satisfied" (both 1983).

Coming on like an old soul band that stumbled across one of their kid's vocoder, Newcleus made the girl go wikki-wikki with "Jam On Revenge" (1984). Whodini went with the new trend on "Magic's Wand" (1982), while real old-school cats like Bernie Worrell and Last Poet Jalal Nuriddin got electrified on records on the Celluloid label. Even soul collector Aaron Fuchs, who owned

the Tuff City label, got into the act with Davy DMX, who emphasized the sub-genre's debt to European ideas with a British
female rapper on classics like "One for the Treble" and "DMX Will
Rock" (both 1984).

With the ascendancy of Run DMC and their much harder
drum machine matrix, however, electro quickly died out on the
East Coast despite the best efforts of Mantronix and master
tape editors the Latin Rascals and Chep Nunez. On the West
Coast, though, things were different. With Egyptian Lover,
World Class Wreckin' Cru, Knights of the Turntable and The
Unknown DJ, electro-funk kept Californian poppers and lockers
rocking well into the mid-'80s.

Eminem

His views on bow hunting have yet to be recorded, but Eminem
is nevertheless the leading contender to inherit Ted Nugent's
title of "Motor City Madman". Born Marshall Mathers, Eminem grew
up on the east side of Detroit in a predominantly black neighbourhood. Of course, it's no small irony that the main contribution to hip-
hop of America's largest city with a predominantly African-American
population has been a string of melanin- and skills-deficient rappers.
Unlike Kid Rock and Insane Clown Posse, though, Eminem's got a lot
more going for him than some recycled Aerosmith riffs and second-
hand Kiss make-up.

Mathers began rapping in high school and he quickly acquired a rep for his freestyling abilities. In 1995 he released a single with fellow Detroit MC Proof on a tiny local label, which led to the **Infinite** (1996) album on the Web Entertainment label. While **Infinite** showcased Eminem's abundant wit and rhyming ability, it was a muddled effort in a far different, more positive style than has become his familiar approach.

On the **Slim Shady** EP (1997), however, Eminem got his licence to ill, and on the extraordinarily nihilistic "Just the Two of Us" (in which he talks to his daughter while her mother's corpse is in the trunk of the car they're driving) and "Just Don't Give a Fuck" he displayed the awesome skills and stoopidly mordant world-view that would make him multi-platinum on his next release.

After becoming a favourite on LA's *Wake Up Show*, Eminem signed to Aftermath and worked with Dr. Dre for **The Slim Shady LP**

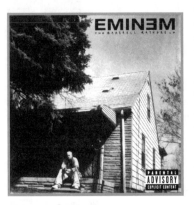

(1999). Built on a kiddie park calliope keyboard and a singsong bassline, "My Name Is" featured lines like "Got pissed off and ripped Pamela Lee's tits off/And smacked her so hard it knocked her clothes backwards like Kriss Kross" and "You know you blew up when women rush the stands and try to touch your hands like some scream-

ing Usher fans" and became one of the singles of the year. The second single, "Guilty Conscience", was based on that scene in *Animal*

House where Tom Hulce's conscience and id battle it out, with Dr. Dre playing the conscience, setting up Eminem's "You're gonna take advice from someone who slapped Dee Barnes?" line. Aside from the three Dre tracks, though, the production couldn't match Eminem's gratuitously offensive wordplay and made **The Slim Shady LP** feel too much like a novelty record.

Eminem was at his best, however, on indie singles like "Any Man" (1999), which featured on Rawkus' **Soundbombing II** compilation. Produced by Da Beatminerz, "Any Man"'s simple, raw and head-nodding beats suited Eminem's flow and rhymes ("I'll strike a still pose and hit you with some ill flows/That don't even make sense like dykes using dildos/So reach in your billfolds for ten ducats/To pick up this Slim Shady shit that's on Rawkus/Sumtin', sumtin', sumtin', sumtin', I get weeded/My daughter scribbled over that rhyme, I couldn't read it") far better than those on **The Slim Shady LP**.

With beats from Dre, 45 King, F.B.T. and Eminem himself, **The Marshall Mathers LP** (2000) didn't improve the production any (their cartoonish quality still deadened the impact of both his rhymes and his flow), but Eminem's growing self-consciousness made the album compellingly disturbing. There was a trend for rappers claiming that they weren't role models in the early '90s, but Eminem's response to the moral panic surrounding him and Marilyn Manson was to get both brooding and hurl invective at Middle America. He talks about raping his mother, he adopts the persona of an obsessed fan whose letters he doesn't respond to, and avers, "There's a Slim Shady in all of us". The first single, "The Real Slim Shady" was the only light relief: "I'm sick of you little girl and boy groups/All you do is annoy me/So I've been sent here to destroy you". If the beats were better, this would have been hip-hop's **There's a Riot Goin' On**.

⊙ **The Slim Shady LP**   Aftermath, 1999

Despite uneven production, the high points make this the most
cathartic, teenage angst cartoon since Slayer's *Reign in Blood*.

EPMD

hildhood friends Erick Sermon and Parrish Smith represent
hip-hop in its purest form: they're neighbourhood kids made
good, with no other aim than to find fresh beats and get paid. No
strict aesthetic sensibilities or political programmes for EPMD (Erick
and Parrish Making Dollars); instead they're "locksmiths with the key
to fame".

Their debut album, **Strictly Business** (1988), remains one of the
funkiest hip-hop albums ever made. Unlike the majority of MCs at the
time, who hyperventilated or yelled to get their words across, Erick
and Parrish (along with Rakim) originated the laidback rapping style.
EPMD relished in the sound of their plain speech – they made an art
out of their New York accents and Erick's cottonmouth flow. Making
Jeep beats for the booming car audio systems that dominated New
York's urban soundscape during the time, "You Gots 2 Chill" and "It's
My Thing" were grounded by woofer-destroying sub-bass and samples of Zapp's "More Bounce to the Ounce" and The Whole Darn
Family's "7 Minutes of Funk", while the title track sampled Eric
Clapton's "I Shot The Sheriff" to create a rhythmic juggernaut. The
album also introduced one of hip-hop's most enduring dick refer-
ences: "bozack".

Unfinished Business (1989) was slightly less accomplished, but followed the same formula to good effect. With its moody guitar sample and Funkadelic-inspired chorus, "So What Cha Sayin'" became their signature tune, while "Please Listen to My Demo" practically introduced back-in-the-day reminiscing to hip-hop. **Business As Usual** (1990) did just what it said on the cover, but, as Marx would surely have told them, business as usual leads to over-production. There were highlights, though: "Rampage", a collaboration with LL Cool J, which played the differences between Erick's mealy-mouthed style and Cool J's *My Fair Lady* elocution for all they were worth, and

"Hardcore", which featured a hot cameo from one of the members of EPMD's Hit Squad, Redman.

Business Never Personal (1992) built on the foundations of "So Whatcha Sayin'" and "Get the Bozack" by concentrating on a harder, darker, tenser music filled with hard-hitting guitar samples and brutal metaphors. Epitomizing the new approach was the awesome collaboration with

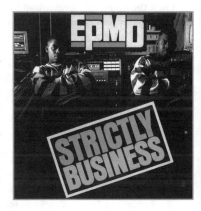

Redman and K-Solo, "Headbanger". After the album, however, Erick and Parrish split on extremely unfriendly terms. During their split, Parrish's PMD Records struggled while Erick's Def Squad crew included Redman and Keith Murray, who both appeared on his rather good, seriously blunted 1995 solo project, **Double or Nothing**.

In 1997 Erick and Parrish started making dollars together again

with a surprisingly decent comeback record, **Back In Business** (1997). Based on a killer loop from The Meters' "Just Kissed My Baby", "Never Seen Before" was the highlight and announced the duo's return with a raw take on the Jay-Z skitter style. Although they claimed that **Out of Business** (1999) referred to the end of the millennium, it was hard to shake the feeling that this was their final goodbye. Still, tracks like "Pioneers" and "Symphony 2000" showed that, unlike almost all of their contemporaries from the '80s, Erick and Parrish could cut it with the new style. Sermon's **Def Squad Presents Erick Onassis** (2000) emphasized the group's timelessness with a collaboration from beyond the grave with Eazy-E, trans-coastal cuts with DJ Quik and Xzibit, and who-cares-where-you're-from bangers.

⊙ **Strictly Business**   Priority, 1988

Their debut album probably introduced one of hip-hop's most enduring concerns – the dialectic between the rough and smooth.

Eric B & Rakim

Hip-hop may have been Run's House throughout most of the '80s, but Eric B & Rakim definitely jumped the fence and sprayed their musk around the backyard. When hip-hop made its artistic and commercial breakthrough in the mid- and late '80s, the genre's focus had shifted from New York's mean streets to the suburban enclave of Long Island. The duo of Eric Barrier (turntables) and William "Rakim" Griffin (vocals) heralded this paradigm shift in 1986 with their debut single, "Eric B Is President". With its stark minimalism and dub-like sound effects courtesy of producer Marley Marl, "Eric B Is President" was a staggering experiment in sound manipulation. It also introduced Rakim's thoroughly original and influential rapping style: calm, level, didn't miss a beat and incisive like a surgeon. Its opening lines – "I came in the door, I

said it before/I never let the mic magnetize me no more" – displayed Rakim's unique lyrical vision: almost "meta-rapping". The single was followed by the even more minimal "My Melody" (1986), which was little more than a kick drum beat, whomping sub-bass and Rakim's brutal sucker MC dis.

The landmark **Paid In Full** (1987) followed and became one of the two or three most influential hip-hop albums ever. On first listen, the album seemed like it was loaded with filler, but the instrumental tracks, which show off Eric B's fearsome turntable skills, were passionate defences of the concept of the DJ as a self-sufficient band. The album's austere minimalism was an expression of the duo's formalist rigour: hip-hop was now a science with its own internal logic. Aside from "Eric B Is President", the highlights were "I Know You Got Soul" and the title track. With a rhythm track sampled from James Brown, "I Know You Got Soul" was single-handedly responsible for hip-hop's cult of the Godfather of Soul. As Stetsasonic put it, "To tell

the truth, James Brown was old/'Til Eric and Rak came out with "I Know You Got Soul"". "Paid In Full" was the duo at their most melodic and introduced what has become hip-hop's central trope: "get[ting] some dead presidents". The track inspired a heap of remixes, with Coldcut's stunning "Seven Minutes of Madness" being the most notable. Although Eric and Rakim hated it, its sampling of Yemenite vocalist, Ofra Haza, was one of the boldest collages of sound and timbre ever committed to vinyl.

Follow the Leader (1988) saw the duo refine their ascetics, fleshing it out but retaining the music's raw ferocity. "Microphone Fiend" was based on Santa's sleigh bells and a guitar sample with an almost terrifying trebly quality, while "Lyrics of Fury"'s Eagles sample evidenced hip-hop's ability to redeem almost everything. Meanwhile, Rakim took over the "Chinese Arithmetic" from the first album with a series of cryptic axioms, bon mots, wordplay and pure flow that redefined the art of the MC. Eric B & Rakim did it the other way around from their sampladelic peers – all the complexity was in the lyrics, not the music.

Their next album, **Let the Rhythm Hit 'Em** (1990), was an attempt to rekindle the magical simplicity of their debut album. However, with the exception of "Let The Rhythm Hit 'Em", which did exactly that, the record was a fairly dull rehash of a style that was already an antique in hip-hop's world of hyper-speed stylistic innovations. Eric and Rak's final album, **Don't Sweat the Technique** (1992), managed to blend the high points of the first two plates. The hard rhythm, but smooth groove of the title track was representative of the scope of the entire album. The commercial failure of the album, however, suggested that hip-hop had left the duo behind and after a year of inactivity they split.

Eric B recorded a poorly received self-titled solo album in 1995 that went nowhere. Rakim waited until 1997 to drop his solo album, **The 18th Letter**, which was solid, if nowhere near his earlier brilliance. **The Master** (1999) was more of the same, but the dream-team collaborations with DJ Premier just about lived up to the names on the marquee.

⊙**Paid In Full – The Platinum Years**   4th & Broadway, 1999

The absolutely essential debut album, plus a bonus CD of remixes including Coldcut's awesome "Seven Minutes of Madness".

Esham/NATAS

On "Still Don't Give a ... " Eminem boasts that he's "a cross between Manson, Esham and Ozzy" – a claim that severely undersells Detroit legend Esham, the personification of evil on the microphone. The kind of guy that would make Cradle of Filth shit their bondage trousers, Esham Smith takes the funk out of hip-hop, remaking its pimp strut as the ominous, relentless march of Michael Myers. He calls his black metal schtick "acid rap" and his splatter patter has influenced everyone from horrorcore artists the Flatlinerz to Motown neighbours Kid Rock, Insane Clown Posse, Kottonmouth Kingz and Eminem. But whatever you think of his sales pitch, you've got to admire his energy: twelve albums and five EPs in ten years, making him the true extra prolific hip-hop artist.

Picking up on ideas from the Geto Boys, Esham released his first self-produced cassette, **Boomin 1990** (1990), which has since been reissued as **Boomin Words From Hell**. Picking up on ideas from Guns 'N Roses, he released the influential Black Sabbath-sampling **Judgement Day Vols 1 and 2** (1992). After the **Helterskkelter** EP (1992), Esham released the outrageous **KKKill the Fetus** (1993). On "Symptoms of Insanity" he talked about cutting the head off his dog and throwing it in a bucket, but, hey, at least he was pro-choice. Although it was the sonic equivalent of a grade-D Dario Argento rip-off, the cruddy sound and depressive metal samples made it somewhat compelling.

With TNT and Mastamind, Esham formed NATAS (which allegedly stands for "Nation Ahead of Time and Space") and released **Life After Death** (1993), an album that continued Esham's penchant for sampling the Beastie Boys, borrowing tricks from Slick Rick and really lame sex raps. Their **Blaz4me** (1994) album contained such acid-rap classics as "Boo Yah" and "Stay True to Your City". **Doubelievengod** (1995) was all doom-and-gloom oscillators, Biggie disses, a nice riff on Gil Scott-Heron ("We Almost Lost Detroit") and the unbelievable line, "I'm the nigger that raped the bitch that Tupac went to jail for", on "Torture".

Meanwhile, Esham had released **Closed Casket** (1994) on New York's Warlock label, but returned to his own Gothom-Overcore label for **Dead Flowerz** (1995), an altogether G-Funkier album than previous releases. **Bruce Wayne Gothom City 1987** (1996) found Esham flossing like it was 1998, with a sound not entirely dissimilar from Dr. Dre circa 1999, particularly on the shout-out to Michigan's favourite bank, "Comerica".

"BOOTLEG" (FROM THE LOST VAULT)-VOL.1

NATAS returned in 1997 with **Multikillionaire**, on which they "wrote their rhymes in blood" and quoted Sam Raimi's *Candyman*. Esham's **Mail Dominance** (1999) was slightly more tuneful, even sampling Walter Murphy's "A Fifth of Beethoven". NATAS's **Wicket World Wide.Com** (1999) was housed in an Hieronymus Bosch sleeve, took a hook from *Kojak* and tried to cast a black magic spell on you with "Levitation", but the production was grinding and irritating, highlighting just how bad their raps were.

⊙ **"Bootleg" (From the Lost Vault) – Vol. 1**   Overcore/TVT, 2000

Esham's gravest hits.

Fat Boys

Before they became the rotund court jesters of hip-hop, Prince Markie Dee, Kool Rock-ski and Darren "Buffy" Robinson (aka The Human Beatbox) were a trio of Brooklynites called the Disco 3. In 1983 they entered a rap contest at Radio City Music Hall and won first prize, a contract with Sutra Records, due in large part to Buffy's beat-boxing skills, which he started doing in 1981 while in junior high.

The Disco 3's first record was "Fat Boys/Human Beatbox" (1984), which was produced by Kurtis Blow. Other than setting up the microphones, it's unclear what Blow did on "Human Beatbox" because the record consists of Markie Dee and Kool Rock-ski dropping some invigorating old-school rhymes over the top of Buffy creating beats out of raspberries and Bronx cheers. "Human Beatbox" has since become one of the most sampled hip-hop records thanks to Buffy's trademark rhythmic hyperventilating. Aside from giving the group their future name, "Fat Boys" was notable for another stellar beat-boxing solo by Buffy and great mechano-dub production from Blow.

With a combined weight that would intimidate any WWF tag-team, it was inevitable that the Disco 3 would change their name to the Fat Boys. Mugging for the cameras with mountains of food in their publicity photos, the Fat Boys would soon make eating the subject of just about every one of their songs that wasn't a cover of a rock standard. Their first single under their new name, "Jailhouse Rap" (1984), again featured sublime early '80s production from Blow and a genius moment when Kool Rock-ski goes to jail for stiffing Burger King.

"The Fat Boys Are Back" (1985) was more of the same, but with less inspired production. "All You Can Eat" (1985) followed suit and their novelty image grew with their appearance in *Krush Groove* stuffing their faces to the track's dulcet tones. Somehow, the group managed to stay commercially viable and even starred in their own movie, the so-bad-it's-bad *Disorderlies*, in 1987. The film provided the group with a #12 hit, a shockingly awful cover of The Surfaris' "Wipeout" with The Beach Boys. **Crushin'** (1987), which included "Wipeout", went platinum and broke into the Top 10 of the album chart. As if that wasn't surreal enough, they collaborated with Chubby Checker on a version of "The Twist (Yo Twist)" (1988), which managed to reach #16. A version of "Louie Louie" (1988) managed to dent the lower reaches of the pop chart, but Prince Markie Dee soon left to pursue an ill-advised solo career. While his own records went nowhere, he did go on to work with Father MC and Mary J. Blige.

In 1995, Robinson died of a cardiac arrest. He was twenty-eight.

⊙ **All Meat, No Fillah! The Best of the Fat Boys**   Rhino, 1997

A collection of eighteen Fat Boys' songs is pure gluttony, but then they would've wanted it that way.

The 45 King

P referring these days to go by the name of The 45 King rather than DJ Mark The 45 King as he was once known, the erstwhile Mark James was one of the producers responsible for bringing hip-hop out of its drum machine doldrums in the late '80s. Looping up old James Brown and Kool and the Gang records for rappers like Queen Latifah, Lakim Shabazz and Chill Rob G, The 45 King, together with Marley Marl, was instrumental in leading hip-hop into its sampladelic age.

The 45 King began his journey through the intricacies of old-school funk at the dawn of hip-hop. As the record boy for the Funky Four (before they became Funky Four + 1), he had a rare insight into

the clandestine, arcane world of breakbeats where records like "Catch a Groove" by Juice and "Scratching" by the Disco Magic Machine – records that were rare to the point of nonexistence – acquired a mystical aura owing to their crowd-moving qualities. The 45 King's first production after a somewhat less than productive stint DJing was a demo for Marky Fresh that was picked up by DJ Red Alert.

It wouldn't be until 1986 and the arrival of the Flavor Unit, however, that The 45 King would get noticed. The Flavor Unit was a crew of Jersey-based MCs – Latee, Lakim Shabazz, Queen Latifah, Chill Rob G, Apache and Lord Alibaski – that had organized around The 45 King. Latee's bass-heavy, Lyn Collins-sampling "This Cut's Got Flavor" (1986) on the Wild Pitch label was the crew's break-out track. The sparseness of "This Cut's Got Flavor" gave way to the classically funky stylings of Latee's "No Tricks" (1987), Lakim Shabazz's under-rated **Pure Righteousness** (1988), Chill Rob G's "Court Is in Session" and "The Power" (1989, 1990) and Queen Latifah's **All Hail the Queen** (1989).

In 1990 The 45 King recorded a solo album for Aaron Fuchs' Tuff

City label that would yield the track that will be forever associated with his name. With a slowed-down horn riff from Marva Whitney's "Unwind Yourself" and an enormous drum loop, "The 900 Number" remains one of hip-hop's greatest, and funkiest, instrumental tracks. It has since become the unofficial theme song for *Yo! MTV Raps*, been in a beer commercial and pushed DJ Kool, who based his "Let Me Clear My Throat" on it, into the American pop charts. "The 900 Number" was the lead track on his first solo album, **45 Kingdom**, which also featured reconstructions of old-school beats from The Honey Drippers, The Soul Searchers and Kool & the Gang.

45 Kingdom was followed up by the almost as good **Lost Breakbeats** (1991), but afterwards The 45 King receded from public view because of an addiction to angel dust. With the re-release of **Lost Breakbeats** in 1997 by British label Ultimate Dilemma and DJ Kool's "Let Me Clear My Throat", though, The 45 King started his comeback which hit its apex in 1998 with his production of Jay-Z's *Annie*-sampling "Hard Knock Life". He even managed to make Craig Mack cool again with a beat based around Frank Sinatra's "High Hopes" on "Wooden Horse" (2000).

⊙ **45 Kingdom**   Tuff City, 1990

Featuring "The 900 Number", this is the best of The 45 King's breakbeat albums.

Foxy Brown

Taking her stage name from a '70s blaxploitation flick, Inga Fung Marchand has attracted as much notoriety and drooling admirers as Pam Grier's original Foxy Brown. She made a name for herself as a fourteen-year-old prodigy at the legendary Lyricist Lounge, calling herself Big Shorty, but really attracted attention on the remix of LL Cool J's "I Shot Ya" (1995). She exploded into the big time as Jay-Z's distaff foil on "Ain't No Nigga" (1996), pandering to Jigga's mercenary sexism with lines like "From Dolce & Gabbana to H. Bendel/I ring your bells/So who the player?/I still keep you in the illest gators". As a member of The Firm with Nas, AZ and Nature, Foxy Brown gave new meaning to the notion of standing by your man: "I'm married to The Firm, boo, you gotta understand I'll die for them/Give me a chair and I'll fry for them".

Calling herself "the ill na na with the slanted eyes", Foxy's debut album, **Ill Na Na** (1996), was the composite portrait of the hip-hop diva and promptly went platinum. Unsurprisingly, as is true of almost any woman in hip-hop and R&B who isn't Lauryn Hill, she attracted criticisms of materialism, being degrading to women with her overt sexuality and having her rhymes ghost-written by the likes of Jay-Z or Nas. While all of the above may or may not be true, **Ill Na Na** was state-of-the-art jigginess.

Beginning with the classic couplet, "Rhyme or crime, let's get it on/MCs want to eat me, but it's Ramadan", "Hot Spot" introduced her second album, **Chyna Doll** (1999). Although it wasn't quite the litany of designer apparel that **Ill Na Na** was, **Chyna Doll** was more of the same, except that she didn't sound as confident as on her debut.

⊙ **Ill Na Na**   Def Jam, 1996

Three words: attitude, attitude, attitude.

Freestyle Fellowship

Ever since LA producers stopped making silly little electro-funk tunes, the sound of Angeleno hip-hop has been the sound of glocks, drop-tops, smashing St. Ides bottles, sirens and whirring chopper blades. But, while the popular face of LA hip-hop was defined by nihilism, a group of aspiring MCs and poets dodged the crossfire at open-mic nights at a café fittingly called The Good Life.

Coming together as the Freestyle Fellowship, many of these MCs – Aceyalone, Mikah Nine, P.E.A.C.E., J Sumbi and Self Jupiter – released what many people consider the Holy Grail of underground hip-hop, **To Whom it May Concern** (1991). While A Tribe Called Quest and Gang Starr were remaking hip-hop in Donald Byrd's image and calling it "jazz", the Freestyle Fellowship were remaking the vocalese of Lambert, Hendricks and Ross as one of Ornette Coleman's harmolodic jams. Bionically scatting, creating narrative sequences with non-planar geometry, scattering syntax like ashes on the sea, the Freestyle Fellowship "took rap music to its threshold of enlightenment".

Of course, barely anyone was listening and J Sumbi left the fold before they recorded **Inner City Griots** (1993). Picking up where **To Whom it May Concern** left off, the group continued to shred text like Fawn Hall, but the experimentation was as tonal as it was verbal, allowing it to avoid sounding like a tongue-twisting cutting session. Aceyalone's showcase, "Cornbread", took hip-hop as far out into poetic realms as it had ever been, and it would take years for radical MCs like the Anti-Pop Consortium, Deep Puddle Dynamics and Mike Ladd to pick up its mantle.

→

Aside from a devoted cult following, most of the hip-hop community wanted to revoke their poetic licence and the group obliged by breaking up in 1994. Along with Abstract Rude, Aceyalone showed up at the Project Blowed nights, which replaced the Good Life as the headquarters of LA's freestylers. The **Project Blowed** (1994) album was another collection of skewed dynamics, scatted vocals and all manner of lyrical phantasmagoria. Acey's solo album, **All Balls Don't Bounce** (1995), paled next to the Fellowship's collective efforts, but still won over open hearts and minds on tracks like "Arhythmaticulas" and "Knownots". His **Accepted Eclectic** (2000) album was the most conventional album he ever made, but the melancholic "I Neva Knew" and the steamy "Bounce" prevented this from being a totally retrograde step.

In 1999 the Fellowship reunited with OD on "Can You Find the Level of Difficulty in This?", which, despite its title, was catchier than anything they had previously done, but still filled with potent, challenging imagery.

⊙**Inner City Griots**   4th & Broadway, 1993

If Ornette Coleman had been a wordsmith, he would've sounded like this.

French Hip-hop

Les banlieus may translate as "the suburbs", but the French have a very different understanding of the 'burbs than the English or Americans. Neighbourhoods like 93 Seine St Denis, Sarcelle and 92 Haut de Seine on the outskirts of Paris are characterized by bad housing, heavy-handed policing, lack of opportunity and a population of disillusioned immigrant families. In other words, prime hip-hop territory. With a large portion of France's urban populace living in *les banlieus*, France has the second largest hip-hop industry in the world. Of course, it also has the concommitant controversy: gangster business practices, run-ins with the police, the racist Front National and club owners, and a ban on hip-hop in the '80s. The French hip-hop industry is so well developed it even has its own Will Smith who raps over Elton John samples – Yannick.

The first French-language hip-hop record was "Une Sale Histoire" (1982) by Fab Five Freddy and B-Side. That same year graffiti took France by storm with exhibitions by Rammellzee and Jean-Michel Basquiat, and Dee Nasty set up the country's first hip-hop radio show. However, French hip-hop was largely imitative of American records and most MCs rapped in English. He may be *persona non grata* on the "real" hip-hop scene now, but MC Solaar was the person who changed French hip-hop from a tiny, specialized cult to the voice of French youth. His debut album, **Qui Sème le Vent Récolte le Tempo** (1991), was probably the biggest-selling and most important hip-hop album released outside the US. Riding Jimmy Jay and Boom Bass's jazzy beats, Solaar unleashed lines like "Ses hématomes étaient

→

plus grandes que le sein de Samantha Fox", and showed that French was hip-hop's second language. The album produced four French Top 10 singles, including the title track and "Victime de la Mode". Solaar's best single, however, was to be found on his second album, **Prose Combat** (1993). "Nouveau Western" rode a loop from Serge Gainsbourg's "Bonnie and Clyde" and had Solaar comparing the Wild West with America's cultural imperialism. Unfortunately, ever since, Solaar has become a pop

star and followed trends instead of setting them, but, even on his lame gangsta tracks like "Illico Presto", he still finds space to namecheck Umberto Eco.

Solaar was introduced on the legendary **Rapattitude** (1990) compilation. **Rapattitude** also launched the careers of Kool Shen and Joey Starr, who make up France's most potent act, NTM (Nique Ta Mère – "Screw Your Mother"). Their "Je Rappe" track on **Rapattitude** revealed very little of the controversy that would surround the band. On their debut album, **Authentik** (1991), they claimed they were committing "la sodomie verbale" and attracted more than a few raised eyebrows. However, worse was to come: after the release of

→

J'Appuie sur la Gâchette (1993) they were sent to jail for inciting their audience to kill cops. **Paris Sous les Bombes** (1995) was less aggressive and full of rage and sold 400,000 copies. **Supreme NTM** (1998) was even bigger with the ragga-tinged "Ma Benz" and the head-nodder "That's My People". Kool Shen and Joey Starr are both fine producers, responsible for outside projects like Sniper (Joey Starr) and the supergroup IV My People (Kool Shen, neighbour Busta Flex, the excellent lyricist Noxea and Serum).

From the Secteur A production house, Ministère A.M.E.R. introduced today's biggest stars in the early '90s: Doc Gynéco, Stomy Bugsy and Passi. All of the above have had platinum albums, with Stomy Bugsy being the French equivalent of Tupac. Other Secteur A stars include Ärsenik, Pit Baccardi and Hamed Daye. Tracks like Ärsenik's Sly Stone-interpolating "Affaires de Familles", Daye's "L'An D1000" and Bugsy's "Mon Papa à Moi Est un Gangster" may be little better than received G-Funk, but the Sectuer A live album, **Live at Olympia** (1998), could show their American brethren a thing or two about taking it to the stage.

From Marseille, IAM and their awesome MC/producer Akhenaton went double platinum in 1998 with their hit "Indepenza". Also from Marseille are Le 3ème Oeil, who have mastered the melancholy piano loop even better than RZA, and Fonky Family, who loop The Beatles on their hit, "Si Je les Avais Écoute" (1999).

Newcomers like 113, whose "Truc de Fou" (1998) sampled a Malian guitar band, and Bisso Na Bisso, who rocked on top of a groove fashioned out of Senegalese mbalax, Congolese soukous and Jamaican dancehall on their self-titled debut single (1998), have made compelling fusions of the traditions of the Maghreb and sub-Saharan Africa and modern technology. The purest hip-hop experience, however, may be offered by Saian Supa Crew. Their album, **KLR** (1999), sounded like Dadaists Tristan Tzara and Richard Huelsenback trading rhymes with Jurassic 5. They don't have a DJ; instead Sly and Leeroy beatbox all the scratches and sound effects, giving it that old open-mic night at the Cabaret Voltaire feel. The album's best moment was the amazing beatboxed version of Anita Ward's "Ring My Bell". French hip-hop: *toi-même, tu sais*.

⊙ **MC Solaar – Prose Combat**   Island, 1993

Perhaps the easiest to find of his albums, this features French hip-hop's greatest moment, "Nouveau Western".

⊙ **Saian Supa Crew – KLR**   Source, 1999

The cadences and the beats sound like everyone from Missy Elliott to Busta Rhymes to The Pharcyde, but as a distilation of every major sub-genre of '90s hip-hop, it's a lot of fun even if your French isn't sharp enough to keep pace.

Doug E Fresh

Although he once called himself "the world's greatest entertainer", the sad truth is that Doug E Fresh is a workmanlike rapper at best. His reputation basically rests on one truly inspired single, "The

Show/La-Di-Da-Di" (1985). While the former Douglas Davis claimed that he invented human beatboxing on his first single, "The Original Human Beat Box" (1984) (a claim refuted by both Biz Markie and the Fat Boys' Darren Robinson), one indisputable fact is that "The Show" might have been truly inspired, but it wasn't exactly original. "The Show"'s keyboard hook and beatboxing previously appeared on the Bad Boys' "Bad Boys", which was released a few months prior to "The Show".

"The Show", however, was the far superior record. Fresh's beatboxing was often mind-boggling, while the scratch of Cold Crush Brothers' "Punk Rock" (the "Oh my God!") became one of hip-hop's signature devices. "The Show" was that rarest of records: a disposable, novelty single with so much energy and sonic daring that it has remained a standard ever since. While "The Show" highlighted Fresh's beatboxing skills, the flip belonged to a guy called MC Ricky D even though he rapped over a

141

background made entirely of Fresh's raspberry percussion. "La-Di-Da-Di" was a dirty, braggadocious story about a guy wearing Gucci underwear and gold teeth filled with street-corner signifying and an ending that was absolutely scandalous at the time. With his British accent, MC Ricky D introduced at least three hip-hop stock phrases on "La-Di-Da-Di". Apparent that he was becoming a star in his own right, Ricky D went out on his own and became Slick Rick.

Fresh's debut album, **Oh My God!** (1986), failed to live up to his great single. Not only were his raps mediocre at best, but he had found God and couldn't resist singing about it. **The World's Greatest Entertainer** (1988) didn't even come close to living up to the title, but it did tone down the prosletysing. Paradoxically, however, the album's best track, "Keep Risin' to the Top", was a shout-out to the big guy that was a big hit.

Perhaps inevitably, Fresh faded from the limelight and made his comeback on Hammer's Bust It label with **Doin' What I Gotta Do** (1992) and tried one more time with Puff Daddy on the surprisingly bearable **Play** (1995).

⊙**Greatest Hits Vol. 1**   Bust It/Capitol, 1996

All you need to know is that it's got "The Show" and "La-Di-Da-Di".

Fugees

Aside from maybe Hootie & the Blowfish, the Fugees were the biggest pop group of the '90s. Forming in South Orange, New Jersey in 1989, vocalist Lauryn Hill, multi-instrumentalist Nel Wyclef

Jean and his cousin, keyboardist Prakazrel Michel, parlayed their warm grooves and gentle politics into a global market share even Michael Jackson would be envious of nowadays.

Their first album, **Blunted on Reality** (1994), was a frugged album that attempted to shed light on the political situation of Haiti, from where Wyclef and Pras are refugees (hence the name). It was a laudable album, except that it lacked personality, coming to life only on the remix of "Mona Lisa" and "Vocab".

The group took over production for the second album and the ensuing blend of Caribbean lilt, alterna-rap and supper-club soul became a worldwide phenomenon. Sporting a cover based on the posters for *The Godfather*, **The Score** (1996) got the kind of respect and success that John Gotti could only dream about. To date, the album has sold over eighteen million copies worldwide, which is fairly remarkable considering that, aside from the massive singles "Killing Me Softly", "Ready or Not" and "Fu-Gee-La", and the cover of Bob Marley's "No Woman, No Cry", **The Score** was a dark, downtempo album that talked about Newt Gingrich sucking dick comprised of sound bites from a Kingston dancehall, wafting vapour trails from an East Harlem air shaft and samples of doo-wop group The Flamingos.

While Hill stole the show with her rich vocals and not-bad mic skills, Wyclef's solo album, **The Carnival** (1997) showed that she did-n't have a monopoly on the group's talent. Nowhere near as good as **The Score**, **The Carnival** had Clef collaborating with the Neville Brothers and Celia Cruz and not embarrassing himself. He'd save that for his duet with Bono, "New Day" (1999). **Ecleftic: Two Sides of a Book** (2000), however, showed that **The Carnival** was a fluke: the cast of stars included Kenny Rogers, and "However You Want It" proves that Canibus was right about blaming him for the failure of his album.

Pras's **Ghetto Supastar** (1998) album had him living up to his Dirty Cash alias by including ten-plus minutes of celebrity endorsements from the likes of Elton John, Sting and, of course, Donald Trump. The real solo album action, however, was to be found on Hill's **The Miseducation of Lauryn Hill** (1998). Looking back to '60s and '70s soul's age-old virtues, referencing '70s sitcoms, reminiscing about mid-'80s hip-hop, dabbling in reggae and dancehall and digging in the crates like the best '90s beat-freaks, **The Miseducation of Lauryn Hill** was the black bohemian equivalent of a Beastie Boys album, but from a woman's point of view. Replacing the wisecracks and cheap laffs of the Beasties with a sense of personal triumph (that, granted, did occasionally creep into self-righteousness), Hill made the ultimate cross-over album of the hip-hop era.

⊙ **Lauryn Hill – The Miseducation of**
   Lauryn Hill   Ruffhouse/Columbia, 1998

It's not perfect, but, at its best, the soaring music – the string stabs, the upful drums, the motorvational scratches, the grain of her voice – transmits the album's message more potently than the lyrics, turning clichés into words that hit like the gospel truth.

Warren G

I f Dr. Dre is the mad scientist, Snoop Dogg the mischievous but lovable Dennis the Menace and Tupac the smooth-talking lothario, Dr. Dre's half-brother Warren Griffin III is G-Funk's boy next door. His subject matter doesn't stray that far from the gangsta blueprint, but where his compatriots relish the contradictions between their laid-back music and hard lyrics Warren G relaxes in his cushiony synths and takes being smooth as an end in itself.

Warren started rapping in a group called 213 with childhood friend Snoop and Nate Dogg in Long Beach, California. He produced a track for MC Breed, but really got noticed with Mista Grimm's "Indosmoke" (1993). Riding a similar groove to his half-brother, Warren crafted a jazzier version of the G-Thang, complete with keyboard noodling, for fellow LBC resident Grimm, who kept asking, "Are you high yet?" The track appeared on the *Poetic Justice* soundtrack and got Warren signed to Chris Lighty's new Violator label.

Warren's multi-platinum **Regulate ... G-Funk Era** (1994) album was announced with one of the singles of the decade, "Regulate". Using a big chunk of ex-Doobie Brother Michael McDonald's "I Keep Forgettin' (Every Time You're Near)", "Regulate" managed to combine G-Funk's bounce with an almost MOR quality, making it a sure-fire cross-over hit. It wasn't just a marketing strategy, though; "Regulate" had an affective, melancholy fatalism similar to Ice Cube's "Dead Homiez". The follow-up single, "This DJ", followed the same formula, but was a little more simplistic. The rest of the album didn't reach the same heights, but it was easy on the ears nevertheless.

Take a Look Over Your Shoulder (1997) tried to be a soundtrack for a summer jam in the LBC, but it was as airheaded and lazy as its

ambition. Even though he proved that he couldn't spell on **Regulate**'s
"What's Next", here his remedial rhyme skills were glaringly obvious.
The lo-lo beats were similarly smoothed out on **I Want it All** (1999).
Despite the presence of an all-star team of MCs including Snoop,
Slick Rick, Mack 10, Eve, Drag-On and Crucial Conflict, the closest **I
Want it All** came to rocking the streets was when its title track was
used as a warm-up song in football stadiums.

⊙ **Regulate ... G-Funk Era**   Violator/RAL, 1994

The perfect middle ground between Coolio and Dr. Dre.

Gang Starr

They've never had moments that shook the world like Run DMC or
Public Enemy, never really blown people's minds like De La Soul
or Eric B & Rakim, never transmuted their uncompromising vision into
platinum like A Tribe Called Quest or Wu-Tang Clan, but the duo of DJ
Premier (Christopher Martin) and Guru (Keith Elam) is unquestionably one of the greatest groups in hip-hop history. Unlike all of their
peers, Gang Starr are consistent: they've never made an unqualified
masterpiece of an album, but they've never made a duff one, either. As
Guru almost said, "They've got discipline and they use it a lot." Primo
and Guru aren't mere professionals, however. They might not have an
overarching vision that draws outsiders in, but they're the embodiment
of the hip-hop purist's creed – it's the skills, stupid.

Gang Starr started off life in Boston as a trio of Guru, Damo-D Ski
and DJ 12B Down. The group made a few singles like "Bust a Move"

(1987) and "Gusto" (1987) with The 45 King producing before the group split, leaving Guru in New York trying to maintain a career in the music biz. Guru hooked up with the Wild Pitch label, who passed him a demo of DJ Premier, who had previously been in a Houston, Texas crew called Inner Circle Posse. The two hit it off and in 1988 recorded "Manifest", an infectious combination of James Brown's "Bring it Up (Hipster's Avenue)", Dizzy Gillespie's "A Night in Tunisia" and Guru's ready-made battle rhymes. "Manifest" featured along with the trend-setting "Jazz Thing" on **No More Mr. Nice Guy** (1989). While the album is justly celebrated as the album that brought jazziness into hip-hop, it was a pure hip-hop track that stood out. "DJ Premier in Deep Concentration" was more than just a collection of Mach 1 scratches to display Premier's deck dexterity: it was an emotive sound assemblage that took in Kool & the Gang's "Summer Madness", Double Trouble's "Double Trouble", Billy Stewart's ululation from "Summertime" and the buzzing horn hook from Freda Payne's "Unhooked Generation". Of course, the scratching was pretty ace too, with one scratch sampled by Sonz of a Loop Da Loop Era at the beginning of the hardcore classic "Far Out". It was the loop of the piano intro from "Summer Madness", though, that made the track the best turntable montage since "Wheels of Steel". Undoubtedly influencing DJ Shadow and Peanut Butter

Wolf, Premier was able to incorporate a sense of melancholy into a genre normally associated with content-free thrills and spills.

No More Mr. Nice Guy had nice moments but it never quite came together. **Step in the Arena** (1990), however, was a major step forward, not just for the group but for all of hip-hop and beat-based music. With the background details of "Execution of a Chump", the smoking loops of "Who's Gonna Take the Weight", the string stabs of "Check the Technique", the keyboard peals of "Say Your Prayers" (which must have given Dr. Dre an idea or two) and the beat psyche-

MIKE LEWIS

delia of "Beyond Comprehension", Primo had dove head first into his Akai S950 and emerged on the other side as one of the best producers in hip-hop. Guru, too, had developed, combining book-smart battle rhymes with street-smart tales of the inner city to become one of hip-hop's best content-providers. The key track was "Just to Get a Rep":

Premier instantly became an object of cult fascination by sampling Jean-Jacques Perrey's then-obscure, Moog funk masterpiece "EVA", while Guru established himself as a street chronicler of rare sensitivity.

Daily Operation (1992) at first sounded like a retreat from the radicalism of **Step in the Arena**, but it was really just Premier redefining the sound of hip-hop. With the sampladelic-age ending, Premier threw out much of its sonic baggage, leaving his now trademark, neck-snapping kicks to do all of the damage, with some action going on in the mid-range and not much else (check "Take it Personal"). That said, the whirling strings of "Soliloquy of Chaos" filled the entire sound field and established a mini-genre of askew, orchestral hip-hop.

In 1993 Guru released his Jazzmatazz project, explicitly uniting live jazz and hip-hop, while Premier firmly established himself as the greatest producer in hip-hop with his work on Jeru the Damaja's **The Sun Rises in the East**, Nas's **Illmatic** and Notorious B.I.G.'s **Ready to Die**. Gang Starr returned in 1994 with **Hard to Earn**, which found Primo perfecting his symphonies of dissonance on "Speak Ya Clout" and giving a masterclass on the chopped beat on "Code of the Streets", which also featured Guru at his most eloquent.

With "You Know My Steez" (1997), Premier flipped the script once more, working magic with a guitar loop from Joe Simon's "Drowning in the Sea of Love". Simultaneously leaping from the speakers and wallowing in melancholy, "You Know My Steez" was a lesson in economy and the art of stabbing. **Moment of Truth** (1998) followed in a similar style, with clipped guitar phrases rocketing out from all angles. Amazingly, it was Gang Starr's first gold album.

⊙ **Full Clip – A Decade of Gang Starr**   Noo Trybe/Virgin, 1999

It's short on the group's weirder moments (where's "Deep Concentration"?), but this double CD collection offers conclusive proof that Primo and Guru are the finest exponents of pure hip-hop.

Geto Boys

Along with NWA and Ice-T, Houston, Texas's Geto Boys are hip-hop's OGs. Just like LA's original gangstas, the Geto Boys put not just Houston, but all of the US south of the Mason-Dixon Line on the rap map. But, where Cali's jheri curled MCs hid behind the "reality rap" label, the Geto Boys had no pretences about representing anything other than their own demented imaginations.

Under the auspices of James "Lil J" Smith's newly formed Rap-a-

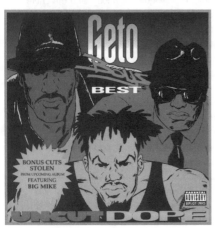

Lot label, the Ghetto Boys released "Car Freaks" (1987), a track about girls like L'Trimm sweating guys with nice rides. The Ghetto Boys – Juke Box, Ready Red, Johnny C, Raheem and dancer Bushwick Bill (Bushwick, Brooklyn raised Richard Shaw) – then released **Making Trouble** (1988), a lame rip-off of Run DMC (they even sported Homburgs, black clothing and gold medallions on the sleeve art).

With Lil J wanting the group to pursue a more violent direction, Juke Box, Johnny C and Raheem all left the group. Renaming themselves the Geto Boys, a new line-up of Bill, Red, DJ Akshen (aka

Scarface, Brad Jordan) and Willie D recorded **Grip It! On That Other Level** (1989) for a mere $2500. With tracks like the industry-bashing, Curtis Mayfield, "Apache"-sampling remake of "Do it Like a G.O." ("Mother fuck the KKK/Wearing dresses and shit, what the fuck, is they gay?"), which had previously appeared on Willie D's **Controversy** (1989) album and the over-the-top "Mind of a Lunatic" ("Had sex with the corpse before I left her/And drew my name on the wall like 'Helter Skelter'"), **Grip It! On That Other Level** eventually went gold and made the industry take note of regional rap.

Rick Rubin liked the album so much that he offered Rap-a-Lot a distribution deal, but Geffen balked at distributing an album that talked about necrophilia and **The Geto Boys** (1990) attracted a storm of controversy. Essentially an updated version of **Grip It!**, **The Geto Boys** added the splatter rap "Assassins" and Bill's savage solo turn, "Size Ain't", and attracted the full wrath of Tipper Gore's PMRC who, of course, missed the irony that tracks like "Do it Like a G.O." attacked the hypocritical, racist society whose values Gore was so stringently trying to uphold.

The cover of **We Can't Be Stopped** (1991) was the Geto Boys' most outrageous statement yet: it featured Bill on a hospital gurney with his eye shot out talking on a mobile phone. With production from John Bido, **We Can't Be Stopped** featured the stunning "Mind Playing Tricks on Me". Based on a moody guitar riff from Isaac Hayes' *Three Tough Guys* soundtrack, "Mind Playing Tricks on Me" was the paranoid flip-side to all the nut-grabbing gangsta poses and went platinum on the back of heavy MTV rotation. Elsewhere, on tracks like "Chuckie" and "Gota Let Your Nuts Hang" they were up to their usual shenanigans.

With the success going to his head, Willie D left the group to pursue a solo career and was replaced by Convicts' Big Mike on **Till**

Death Do Us Part (1993). Aside from the compelling "Six Feet Deep" and "Crooked Officer", **Till Death Do Us Part** was a sterile rip-off of **The Chronic** formula. The group then split and released mostly weak solo albums, with the exception of Scarface who shined on the Marvin Gaye-sampling "A Minute to Pray and a Second to Die" from **Mr. Scarface Is Back** (1991) and "I Seen a Man Die" from **The Diary** (1994).

The Geto Boys reconvened for the so-so **The Resurrection** (1996), but Bushwick Bill left amidst a suit with Rap-a-Lot and Willie D and Scarface carried on as a duo on the tired **Da Good, Da Bad & Da Ugly** (1998).

⊙ **Scarface – Mr Scarface Is Back**   Rap-a-Lot, 1991

Scarface is easily the best rapper in the group and he shines on his solo debut.

The Goats

With their left-wing politics, use of live musicians and multiracial make-up, Philadelphia's The Goats were probably doomed to be the hip-hop group that it was OK for indie kids to like. And, while it is true that their brand of hip-hop was focused more on jump-around than head-nod, Madd, Swayzack, OaTie Kato, Rucyl, Love and DJ 1Take Willie had enough skills to escape the backpack ghetto.

The Goats' first album, **Tricks of the Shade** (1992), was co-produced by Schooly D producer Joe "The Butcher" Nicolo, who ensured that there was plenty of boom and Code Money-style scratches to go along with the righteous politics. The lead track, "Typical American", was an explosion of enormous drum breaks, an undeniable sing-along chorus and high speed rhymes like "Pie à la mode/The ghettoes will explode/While you sit pigeon-toed at a diamond commode". With skits like "Columbus' Boat Ride", "Leonard Peltier in a Cage" and "Noriega's Coke Stand" set in a narrative that followed protagonists Chicken Little and Hangerhead around a freak show in search of the mother who abandoned them at birth, it became clear that **Tricks of the Shade** was a concept album about the state of the union. The politics might have been facile, but with the flowing deliveries of Madd, Swayzack and OaTie Kato and the chops of the live band, the album became something more than a funky feel-good session for self-righteous and complacent liberal white folk.

1994's **No Goats No Glory**, however, moved away from the lyrical flag-burning in an attempt to be accepted by the hardcore hip-hop market. While it wasn't just the politics that made them so enjoyable first time around, by excising the content in favour of style they lost a large part of their personality.

⊙ **Tricks of the Shade**   Columbia/Ruffhouse, 1992

A funny, scathing critique of Amerikkka that doesn't sacrifice beats and skills for the message.

Golden State Warriors

Like the basketball team from which this posse took its name, the Golden State Warriors have yet to fully realize their

potential. Ras Kass (John Austin), Saafir and Xzibit are all mic dev-
astators, but none of them have really made an album worthy of their
verbal talent.

Ras Kass and Saafir (who debuted on Digital Underground's **Body
Hat Syndrome** album), along with Ahmad, first appeared together on
wax on the underground favourite "Come Widdit" (1994), from the
Street Fighter soundtrack. Coming like a gangsta hip to Frantz Fanon,
Ras Kass's **Soul On Ice** (1996) had all the makings of a classic, until
you paid attention to the beats. While "Nature of the Threat" was a
scathing attack of racism and "Sonset" a clever dissection of the
East–West rivalry, the production was unfocused and couldn't match
his lyrical skills. It took Diamond D's David Axelrod-sampling "Soul On
Ice" remix (1997) for Ras Kass to find his metier.

As Ras Kass himself said, **Rasassination** (1998) was the "same
shit, different toi-
let". Although it
had some ghetto
fabulous *Sturm
und Drang* produc-
tion on a couple of
tracks and great
lines like "This one
girl tried to Billie
Jean me/But I was
wearing two rub-
bers, so name that
nigga Houdini", the
intro to "OohWee!"
summed it up: "I
don't give a fuck

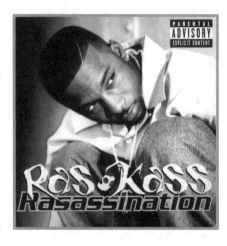

about a beat. I'm a lyricist, I just do my thing". The one element that had changed, though, was that Ras Kass didn't temper his West Coast party raps with intellectual trappings: this was pure game spitting that his team-mates would be proud of.

Like Ras Kass, Saafir has been caught in the no-man's land between drop-top anthems and backpackin' chin-strokers. **Boxcar Sessions** (1994) was impressively experimental, with both beats and syntax flying around at oblique angles, but you got the impression that his stridency was the result of a bullish aggression rather than a wish to be an MC Escher. **Hit List** (1998) confirmed this with a mixed-up collection of rhymes both clever ("The hustlers could peep all your flavour before the aftertaste") and dismal ("You ain't killed shit so I killed your little homey and fucked your bitch").

Xzibit's debut, **At the Speed of Life** (1997), featured the first full Golden State posse cut on "Plastic Surgery". The album, however, was more notable for killer cuts like "Paparazzi" and the moody, flute-driven "Los Angeles Times". Unlike most West Coast albums, **At the Speed of Life** was introspective, suggesting menace rather than shoving it down your throat. **40 Dayz & 40 Nightz** (1998), on the other hand, was a lyrical tempest with his "Olde English leav[ing] you broken with a Crooked I". Even though "Three Card Molly" had lines like "Picture yourself crushin' Xzibit with your tough talk/That's like Christopher Reeves doin' the Crip walk", Xzibit didn't really break through until his show-stealing verse on Snoop Dogg's "B Please" (1999) and his Dr. Dre-produced **Restless** (2000) album.

⊙ **Xzibit – At the Speed of Life**   Loud, 1997

The production was closer to the East, but Xzibit's lyrics and flow let you know where the sun sets.

Graffiti

Although humans have been painting walls since the beginning of time, in New York and Philadelphia in the late '60s and early '70s the word was made fresh. These kids knew their Bible and knew that if the Word made the world, then the word could change it. Dreaming bigger than the guys who wrote "Joey-n-Stacy 2gether 4ever" or "For a good time, call Vicki ... " in the stalls of the men's room at Howard Johnson's, early graff heroes like Top Cat, Cornbread, Tracy 168 and Taki 183 imagined what their names would be like up in lights and proceeded to make that dream a reality on concrete with Rust-Oleum and magic marker.

While gangs in Chicago had scrawled territorial messages in the early '60s and Philly's Top Cat and Cornbread had most likely invented the idea of the tag and the manifest-destiny will to get bigger, broader and farther out than anyone else, it was in New York that graffiti really took off. The arrogance of New Yorkers (the world is a microcosm of Gotham, not the other way around) who believe that the city is a universe onto itself combined with the inter-borough transit system to make graffiti the ticket to fame. Take your name or your nickname, add the number of the street you live on, bomb the number 4 IRT and boom, you're name is known from Van Cortlandt Park to Flatbush. Graff may have predated hip-hop as a musical form by a few years, but writing was the essence of hip-hop culture: Who with the most limited of materials could make the most ghetto-fabulous style? Who could go all-city with the flyest colours and the deffest style? Who could make the letters flow like a fountain?

The earliest tags were basic block letters with the scantest of flourishes. Writers soon progressed to bubble letters and then to what Tracy 168 dubbed "Wildstyle": mad abstract geometry that would have MC Escher and Kasimir Malevich scratching their heads, Jackson Pollock drips, crazy calligraphy to shame both fourteenth-century monks and Japanese Kenji artists. With New York a lawless, financial ruin in the mid-'70s, writers like Dondi, Futura 2000, Daze, Blade, Lee, Zephyr, Rammellzee, Crash, Kel, NOC 167 and Lady Pink became public enemies number

MIKE LEWIS

→

one, and the Mass Transit Authority (MTA) spent the equivalent of the gross domestic product of many Third World countries trying to halt the menace.

Eventually, though, graff became both mainstream (among the '80s art set who were after a bit of authentic rough) and marginalized (in its original milieu). Jean-Michel Basquiat and his "SAMO" tag soon became the darling of the art world, *Beat Street* brought writing, breakdancing and rapping to Hollywood, and the subway burner soon became less important, less meaningful. Hip-hop was big money by the mid-'80s, and who cared about pissing off the MTA and getting known in Far Rockaway when you could make a record and have the whole world sing your name. With 'zines like the *International Graffiti Times* and *Can Control* and eventually videotapes, Web sites and Mo' Wax album covers, graffiti became domesticated, a thing, not a process. Nevertheless, the art of eye-shocking still gives people a buzz and, whether they're bombing a freight train in Kansas, a highway underpass in Tokyo or a canvas in some highfalutin art college in London, Krylon will always have a certain frisson.

For burners on chromium oxide, check the Artifacts' "Wrong Side of Da Tracks" and Company Flow's "Lune TNS".

Grandmaster Flash & the Furious Five

Grandwizard Theodore may have invented scratching, but it wouldn't mean a thing without the swing developed by Grandmaster Flash (Joseph Saddler). The sound of a record being rubbed across a stylus is hip-hop's equivalent of the guitar solo (the climactic moment of intensity that everyone wants to emulate) but the techniques developed by Grandmaster Flash are hip-hop's riffs – the less obvious facets, yet the genre's very foundation. Inspired by Pete DJ Jones, Flash brought DJing to a new level of sophistication by introducing the techniques of backspinning and cutting. Flash was the pioneer of the cross-fader, cutting back and forth between records, slicing and dicing them and overloading the mixer's channels with brilliant, arrogant noise. With his phonographic flights of fancy, Flash truly made DJing something other than just spinning records and proved that the audio montage could amount to more than the smart-ass shenanigans of the Dickie Goodmans and Bill Buchanans of this world.

Of course, Flash had more than mere turntable skills going for him; he had the Furious Five, one of the best of the old-school MC troupes. With Melle Mel (Melvin Glover), Cowboy (Keith Wiggins), Kidd Creole (Danny Glover), Rahiem (Guy WIlliams) and Mr. Ness (Eddie Morris), Flash signed to Enjoy in 1979 and released "Superappin'" (1979). Although it blew "Rapper's Delight" out of the water and featured a verse that would later show up on the epochal "The Message", "Superappin'" and its follow-up, "Super Rappin' No 2" (1980), didn't get anywhere near the attention that those interlopers of the Sugar Hill Gang received, and Flash and the Five defected to Sugar Hill. Their first release for their new label was the effervescent party jam "Freedom" (1980), which looped the kazoo intro and the trumpet bridge of Freedom's "Get Up and Dance".

The group's early records had emphasized the MCs at the expense of Flash's deck skills, but "The Adventures of Grandmaster Flash on the Wheels of Steel" (1981) redressed the balance and exposed the world outside of the Bronx to the art of the DJ. A collage of the Sugar Hill Gang's "8th Wonder", Queen's "Another One Bites the Dust", Blondie's "Rapture", Chic's "Good Times", The Sequence &

Spoonie Gee's "Monster Jam", Grandmaster Flash & the Furious Five's "Birthday Party", The Incredible Bongo Band's "Apache", a *Flash Gordon* record and a mock children's story from an album called **Singers, Talkers, Players, Swingers & Doers** by The Hellers, "Wheels of Steel" was done live on the decks; if Flash messed up, he erased everything and started from scratch. He nailed it on the fourth or fifth take. Of course, "Wheels of Steel" was more than just a simple collage – it was a cut-up that was *on beat* for the track's full seven minutes. Flash showed that, despite its normal usage, the turntable was really a percussion instrument with a tonal range and expressive capability far beyond that of drums, wood blocks and marimbas. As audacious, assertive and aggressive as anything coming from downtown New York's art-punk fringe (check the vicious scratch that served as the bridge from the children's story to "Birthday Party"), "Wheels of Steel" was (and remains) hip-hop's greatest feat of der-ring-do.

Flash had changed the face of music with "Wheels of Steel", but the Furious Five, without Flash (who hated the record), changed the face of hip-hop with "The Message" (1982). Before "The Message" hip-hop rhymes had been all about partying, yes-yes y'alling and bat-tling fellow MCs, but "The Message" (written by Melle Mel and Duke Bootee) was a devastating blast of social realism filled with rage ("Don't push me 'cause I'm close to the edge") and dislocation (the otherworldly space age synth-dub production).

While the group continued to release landmarks like "Flash to the Beat", "It's Nasty (Genius of Love)" and "Scorpio" (all 1982), "The Message" had driven a rift into the Furious Five. After recording the awesome "White Lines (Don't Do It)" (1983), which was really a Melle Mel solo turn, the group split, with Rahiem and Kidd Creole staying with Flash and Melle Mel, Ness and Cowboy going out on their own.

Melle Mel's group stayed with Sugar Hill, Flash signed to Elektra, but neither troupe could survive in Run DMC's new school. They reunited in 1988 and proved how old they were by recording a version of "Magic Carpet Ride" with Steppenwolf's John Kay.

⊙**Adventures on the Wheels of Steel**   Sequel/Sugar Hill, 1999

An essential three-CD collection of all of Flash & the Furious Five's work for Sugar Hill.

Grandmixer D.ST

Born Derek Showard, Grandmixer D.ST is one of the greatest DJs in the history of hip-hop. Building on the innovations of Grandmaster Flash and Grand Wizard Theodore, D.ST (his name comes from his graffiti tag which is short for "Delancey Street") basically helped make turntablism what it is today. D.ST elevated scratch DJing from a rather primitive technique to a rhythmic artform as complex as a school of octopuses playing Latin polyrhythms.

D.ST was originally one of the Zulu Nation DJs with Bambaataa and Whiz Kid in the late '70s. He really came to prominence, however, in 1982, when he won the New Music Seminar DJ battle in 1982. This led to him working with producer/bassist/agent provocateur Bill Laswell, who had been commissioned by French label Celluloid to produce five hip-hop records. His first single, "Grandmixer Cuts It Up" (1982), didn't highlight his deck skills, but it was a pretty amazing example of the early '80s video-game soundscape metamorphosing on to vinyl.

Becoming the Dizzy Gillespie to Grandwizard Theodore's Louis

Armstrong, D.ST made the turntable the electric guitar of the next decade with his scratching on Herbie Hancock's 1983 single, "Rockit". "Rockit" only reached #71 on the American charts, but its moderate cross-over success (and heavy airplay on MTV) meant that it is one of the most influential hip-hop tracks ever. Cited by nearly every turntablist as the reason they started DJing, "Rockit", even more than Grandmaster Flash's "Wheels of Steel", established the DJ as the star of the record, even if he wasn't the frontman. Produced by Laswell, "Rockit" was a dense assemblage of Fairlight keyboards, Oberheim DMX drum machines and vocoders that managed to move with a dexterity that belied its rump of steel skin. However much detail might be packed into it, everything was superfluous aside from D.ST's scratching – it's what you listened to and what you listened for. Epitomizing the hip-hop-jazz metaphor far more than any Roy Ayers-sampling Pete Rock track, D.ST approached his solo as if he was playing at a cutting session at Minton's Playhouse in the '40s. Nearly as in-your-face as "Wheels of Steel", D.ST's scratching (according to David Toop, he was using a record of Balinese gamelan) trashes Hancock and tells him to go back to the '70s because "this is our time now".

While Flash and Bambaataa were using the turntable to explore repetition, alter rhythm and create the instrumental stabs and punch phasing that would come to characterize the sound of hip-hop, Grandmixer D.ST was continuing to explore the furthest reaches of turntable science. "Crazy Cuts" (1984) may have reprised a lot of his scratching from "Rockit", but the new passages showed just how rhythmically inventive he was. "Mega-Mix II (Why Is it Fresh?)" (1984) was the kind of turntable throwdown that wouldn't be heard until DJs like Cash Money and Spinbad invented transforming. D.ST was also featured on records like Time Zone's "The Wildstyle", Last Poet

Jalaluddin Mansur Nuriddin's "Mean Machine" and records by
Material and Manu Dibango.

D.ST (now renamed DXT) has continued to work with Laswell and
appears on many of his nefarious projects – particularly noteworthy
are his contributions to 1996's **Altered Beats** compilation.

⊙**Herbie Hancock – "Rockit"**   Columbia, 1983

Probably the most influential DJ track of them all, this showcases D.ST's
jaw-dropping turntable skills years before this kind of scratching
became commonplace.

Hammer

Stanley Kirk Burrell was an entertainer first and foremost, a
businessman second and a hip-hop artist somewhere down on
the list below dancer and corporate shill – if Berry Gordy had still been
around, he would have signed him on the spot. A former batboy for
the Oakland A's baseball team, Burrell earned his mic name because
of his resemblance to baseball legend "Hammerin'" Hank Aaron. With
money he borrowed from some of the A's, MC Hammer started his
own record label, Bust It, and released a couple of records by himself
and Oaktown's 3-5-7 that garnered enough local attention to get him
signed to Capitol.

Let's Get It Started (1988) was his major-label debut. With production by Felton Pilate from Con Funk Shun, **Let's Get It Started**
inaugurated the formula that would make Hammer the biggest rap
star in the world: lots of obvious, pre-digested samples from P-Funk,
James Brown and The Jacksons, simple rhythms that your grand-

mother could rap over without stumbling and plenty of "Hammer time" breaks so that he could show off his footwork and balloon trousers during live shows and videos.

Please Hammer Don't Hurt 'Em (1990) picked up on the momentum that his debut generated and became the biggest-selling rap album ever. The Rick James-sampling "U Can't Touch This" is the single everyone remembers, but the Chi-Lites cover, "Have You Seen Her", and the Prince-sampling "Pray" were bigger hits. Twenty-one weeks on top of *Billboard*'s album chart later, Hammer was everywhere: ads for Taco Bell, Pepsi and Kentucky Fried Chicken, a Saturday-morning cartoon show called *Hammerman* and even a Mattel doll.

Too Legit to Quit (1991) was typical music-biz overkill: even if people weren't already sick of the guy, the corporate hype machine ensured that the album wouldn't live up to expectations. The album was as lame as ever, but you had to admire the gargantuan proportions of the title track (maybe he should've hooked up with Keith Emerson) and, admit it, you still remember the hand signals from the "Too Legit to Quit" video.

With Dr. Dre ruling the charts, Hammer went gangsta on **The Funky Headhunter** (1994) and, remarkably, people bought the damn thing. The album went gold and the George Clinton-sampling "Pumps and a Bump" made the Top 40, but the sight of a former Christian rap artist (he was in a group called the Holy Ghost Boys) dropping the G-Funk was laughable. Although he has released a couple of albums since, the only time his name crops up is when his bankruptcy saga blows up enough to reach the press.

⊙ **Please Hammer Don't Hurt 'Em**   Capitol, 1990

Hey kid, you wanna hear where Puff Daddy got all his ideas?

Heavy D

Heavy D (Dwight Myers) is probably the only rapper who has been able to maintain a resolutely pop career without being hounded out of the industry by either fickle tastes or hip-hop's hard-core element. Perhaps it's because Dwight Myers *is* the industry – he replaced Andre Harrell as the boss of Uptown Records and is currently a vice president at Universal – and no one wants to front on someone with so much power, but more likely it's that the "overweight lover" has an engaging microphone personality that manages to stay on just the right side of novelty.

Havey D formed Heavy D & the Boyz in the mid-'80s in Mount Vernon, New York with schoolmates Trouble T-Roy, Eddie F and G-Whiz. Harrell, who was working at Def Jam at the time, wanted to sign the group, but Russell Simmons thought the group would go nowhere and passed. When Harrell formed Uptown in 1987, though, he signed the group and **Living Large** (1987) went gold on the strength of a string of hits produced by Marley Marl and Harrell that blended easy pop appeal, playfulness and surprisingly on point mic skills: "Mr. Big Stuff", "The Overweight Lover's in the House" and "Chunky But Funky".

Big Tyme (1989) featured an all-star cast (Marley Marl, Q-Tip, Big Daddy Kane) and another hit in the form of "We Got Our Own Thang" and an OK reworking of Zapp's "More Bounce to the Ounce" in the form of "More Bounce". Heavy's breakthrough, however, was 1991's cover of the O'Jays/Third World classic, "Now That We Found Love". With Aaron Hall singing the chorus with unbearable, overwrought melisma, Heav's version combined just about every form of black music that was selling at the time – hip-hop, swingbeat, house and Jamaican dancehall – in an undeniable assault on the pop charts.

"Now That We Found Love" anchored **Peaceful Journey** (1991) along with his other hit, "Is it Good to You".

Blue Funk (1993) saw Heavy moving in a more hardcore direction with darker, more menacing production, although his subject matter would always stay focused on girls. "Who's the Man?" found the Heavster brushing off his critics and playa haters to the refrains of Steve Miller's "Fly Like an Eagle" and Cypress Hill's "How I Could Just Kill a Man". **Nuttin' But Love** (1994) returned Heav to his playful pop roots. "Got Me Waiting" rode a Luther Vandross sample into the US Top 30, while the title track found the unlikely loveman convincing enough people to reach the lower reaches of the Top 40.

Waterbed Hev (1997) was overinflated with too much R&B, and was as lame as its title's reference to the original genius of love, Waterbed Kev. **Heavy** (1999), though, was a more prepossessing blend of the latest sounds. "You Know" featured Cee-Lo from the Goodie Mob and was a decent blend of the Big Apple with the Dirty South, while "On Point", with Big Pun and Eightball, was produced by Erick Sermon and had so much weight it crushed you into submission.

⊙**Living Large**   Uptown, 1987

One of the blueprints of all subsequent pop rap, this has a charming innocence that overcomes its lightweightedness.

Hieroglyphics

O ne of the underground's most beloved crews, the Hieroglyphics' story could be the blueprint of hip-hop's standard caution-ary tale if it wasn't for the legions of groups who preceded them down the same path. From offering a bright and breezy alternative to the doom and gloom of G-Funk to retreating to a dark, paranoid, interior pose, to learning lessons from their Bay Area forbears and introducing their music directly to the people and taking the means of production into their own hands, the Hiero- 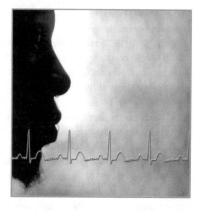 glyphics represent what seems to be the only path available to hip-hop crews who don't make records that get played on Hot 97.

The Hieroglyphics first gained attention when Ice Cube's cousin made a phone-in appearance on *Amerikkka's Most Wanted*, saying, "Fuck radio", and ghost-wrote some rhymes for Cube associate Yo-Yo. It was his debut single, **Del tha Funkée Homosapien**'s "Mistadobalina" (1991), however, that was the real breakthrough. With its samples of Parliament and James Brown, "Mistadobalina" was an infectious, crowd-pleasing, sing-along tale of hip-hop fakes. **I Wish My Brother George Was Here** (1991) continued in the same vein with bubbly funk underpinning eccentric rhymes on tracks like "Dr. Bombay" and "Ahonetwo, Ahonetwo".

The East Oakland-based **Souls of Mischief** (**Tajai, Opio, Phesto** and **A Plus**) made their debut on Del's "Burnt", which was the B-side of "Mistadobalina". According to legend, however, it was a Hieroglyphics showcase at an industry convention that got SOM,

Extra Prolific and Casual signed to Jive. SOM's debut, **'93 'Til Infinity** (1993), was an absolute classic: hazy like a sweet daydream, but with torrents of words that proved they weren't just hiding behind their Freddie Hubbard samples. Casual's **Fear Itself** (1993) was more spotty, but tracks like "This Is How We Rip Shit" and "Thoughts of the Thoughtful" proved that West Coast MCs could battle as well as drawl gangsta fantasies.

By the time of Del's **No Need For Alarm** (1993), however, things were looking bleak. Plagued with hip-hop's number one killer – crossing over to white critics and indie kids – the Hieroglyphics grew darker and more insular. Extra Prolifics' **Like It Should Be** (1994) was just plain tedious, while SOM's **No Man's Land** (1995) found them wrestling with their image and trying to prove that they were hard.

Unsurprisingly, the Hieros found themselves without contracts and, taking after Too $hort and E-40, they launched their own Web site (*www.hieroglyphics.com*) and their own label, Hieroglyphic Imperium. Long before MP3 became the biggest thing since coloured vinyl, the Hieros were attracting ridiculous numbers of hits and sold crazy units through the Internet. The Hieroglyphics' **Third Eye Vision** (1998) was a huge underground hit and announced the crew's re-emergence after Del had devoted himself to studying Japanese and Tajai graduated from Stanford with a degree in Anthropology.

SOM's **Focus** (1999) didn't create the buzz **Third Eye Vision** did, but it proved that they were as tight as ever. Del's **Both Sides of the Brain** (2000) showed that he was the only rapper who could out-weird Kool Keith. With strings of bizarre images and gruesome metaphors, Del "eviscerates your mental state" as he "spits the wickedness" and "surgically removes you from his testes". Light years away from the crowd-pleasing funk of "Mistadobalina", Del and guest producers Casual, Domino, El-P, Prince Paul, Khaos Unique and A-Plus surrounded his brutal science fiction with the crazy, Company Flow-influenced beats his new world-view demanded.

⊙ **Souls of Mischief – '93 'Til Infinity**   Jive, 1993

That rarest of things: a jazzy, bohemian album that didn't sound like it was infatuated with its own magnificence.

House of Pain

A lthough they are known primarily for the greatest frat party anthem since "Louie Louie", Erik "Everlast" Schrody, Leor "DJ Lethal" Dimant and Danny Boy O'Connor had a rep on the LA hip-hop underground before "Jump Around" ever got backwards-baseball-cap-wearing future bankers to do just that. While attending Taft High School with some guy who would eventually become Ice Cube, Everlast became a graffiti artist and started hanging out with Divine Styler and DJ/producer Bilal Bashir. Soon enough he was a member of Ice-T's Rhyme Syndicate crew and released **Forever Everlasting** (1990) for Warner Brothers. With a single called "I Got the Knack" that sampled The Knack's "My Sharona", the album under-standably stiffed even though it was real close to Vanilla Ice territory.

With House of Pain, though, Everlast found an image that res-onated. With the goatee, Boston Celtics gear and drunken thuggish-ness, the "shit-kickin' Irish beat jacker" embodied a certain kind of Northeast white boy just as DJ Quik and Dr. Dre represented Compton. Beginning with the timeless horn intro from Bob & Earl's "Harlem Shuffle", "Jump Around" from **House of Pain** (1992) was one of those records that you knew would be a hit from the second you heard it. The sax squall, bagpipe drones and damningly catchy lyrics only reinforced that impression. "Top o' the Morning to Ya" followed with more shillelagh pounding, as did "Shamrocks and Shenanigans", although the original paled in comparison to Butch Vig's rock reconstruction.

Same As it Ever Was (1994) was exactly as its title said, only less catchy and without a hit. **Truth Crushed to Earth Will Rise Again** (1996) followed suit and House of Pain broke up amidst problems with the IRS and substance abuse. Just when you thought you would never hear from them again, DJ Lethal showed up as a member of rock-rap nightmare Limp Bizkit and Everlast released the surprise hit, **Whitey Ford Sings the Blues** (1999). Trying to remake hip-hop as folk and blues, **Whitey Ford Sings the Blues** found Everlast playing a beat-literate troubadour, cataloguing urban ills on "The Ends" and "What it's Like" like a Woody Guthrie hip to Rakim.

⊙ **House of Pain**   Tommy Boy, 1992

It's not exactly Proust, but you couldn't ask for a better soundtrack to a beer-bust.

Ice Cube

W hen Ice Cube walked out of NWA in 1989 after a dispute over royalties, it quickly became clear who the real talent was among the gangsta godfathers. Although NWA still had Dr. Dre (who wouldn't find his Midas touch until he left the group), Eazy and Ren (without Cube's ghostwriting skills) rapidly descended into straight-up sleaze peddling. Cube, on the other hand, went to New York to work with Public Enemy producers the Bomb Squad and produced one of the most powerful hip-hop records ever.

It may have lacked the visceral force of the best tracks from **Straight Outta Compton**, but **AmeriKKKa's Most Wanted** (1990) was nevertheless a thunderous album of alienation and rage. There was plenty of misogyny, to be sure ("I'm Only Out For One Thing", "You Can't Fade Me"), but it was situated within a riotous, feverish

MARIO CASTELLAMOS

rant about life in black Amerikkka that separated it from his old partners' exploitation. Daring to ask questions like, "Why more niggas in the pens than in college?", over a hyped-up, funkier version of the trademark Bomb Squad sound, Cube managed to blend sound and fury like very few before or after. The **Kill At Will** EP (1990) may have been intended as a commercial stopgap, but it included the remark-

able "Dead Homiez", a haunting track dealing with the consequences of the gangsta lifestyle that started an entire sub-genre of
"dead homie" tracks, and the great "Jackin' For Beats", which
swipes rhythms from Digital Underground, Public Enemy, EPMD and
LL Cool J.

Cube's jheri curl was gone for **Death Certificate** (1991) as he
came under the sway of the Nation of Islam. Unfortunately, he also
embraced their bigotry and "No Vaseline" (a scathing dis of NWA featuring choice epithets for their Jewish manager), "Look Who's
Burnin'" and "Black Korea" all suffered from it. Nonetheless, it was
still incredibly powerful stuff as Cube introduces the oft-stolen line,
"Rather be judged by 12 than carried by six", into hip-hop's lexicon,
although the more subdued production slightly deadened the impact
of his rhymes.

The Predator (1992) continued the more streetwise, soul-based
production of **Death Certificate**. Anchored by a sample of the Isley
Brothers' "Footsteps in the Dark", "It Was a Good Day" was a stunning track that derived its stark power from what didn't happen ("I
didn't even have to use my AK") rather than a cataloguing of gruesome events. "Check Yo Self" and "Wicked", meanwhile, found Cube
collaborating with Das EFX to surprisingly good effect. The cinematic
sweep of Cube's storytelling was matched by his appearance in *Boyz
'N the Hood*. His flirtation with Hollywood, however, would eventually
make his recording career increasingly irrelevant.

In between albums with his Da Lench Mob crew, **Guerillas in tha
Mist** (1992) and **Planet of da Apes** (1994), Cube found time to record
Lethal Injection (1993). The work rate, not to mention the re-
emergence of Dr. Dre, seemed to drain his creative wellsprings and
Lethal Injection was little more than a rehash of Dre's beats, with the
most grotesque gynophobia of his career ("Cave Bitch").

After a pointless collection of obscurities and remixes and another movie (*Friday*), Cube formed Westside Connection with WC and Mack 10. Despite, or maybe because of, the supergroup status, **Bow Down** (1996) wasn't notable other than as a firestarter: it did its share of East Coast baiting, and tracks like "Hoo Bangin'" and "King of the Hill" continued beefs with Common and Cypress Hill. That Cube lost both of these vinyl wars proved that the fire was gone and his **War & Peace – Vol. 1 (War)** (1998) and **War & Peace – Vol. 2 (Peace)** (2000) were complete duds.

⊙ **AmeriKKKa's Most Wanted**   Priority, 1990

Hurling invective at everyone within earshot on top of beats that raged equally hard, this remains Ice Cube's most potent album.

Ice-T

I ce-T (Tracy Morrow) is hip-hop's version of Motörhead's Lemmy Kilmister: despite the fact that he's an average rapper, has dodgy politics and has catalysed some of the worst aspects of hip-hop culture, you've got to love him. His unrepetance about his scabrous obsessions is disarming and, coupled with a fierce intelligence and bullshit detector – when Charlton Heston crawled out of the mothballs to denounce "Cop Killer" by Ice-T's metal band, Body Count, he responded by pointing out Heston's hypocrisy (as the chairman of the NRA, Heston had fought to keep legal a bullet called "the cop killer") – it makes Ice-T one of hip-hop's biggest icons and its most effective spokesperson.

Morrow was born in 1959 in Newark, New Jersey but moved to LA
to live with relatives as a teenager when his parents died in a car acci-
dent. His first encounters with hip-hop culture were as a dancer (with
the Radio Crew and West Coast Locksmiths) and as a graffiti artist.
Running with the Crips, Morrow was introduced to toastin' and the
ghetto fiction of Iceberg Slim. Taking the name Ice-T as a tribute to
Iceberg Slim, he released "The Coldest Rap/Cold Wind Madness"
(1983) on Cletus Anderson's Saturn label, which had previously
released the LA classic, "Bad Times" by Captain Rapp. Over an electro-shocked beat from Terry Lewis and Jimmy Jam, Ice-T rapped
about being "the virgin's wet dream" and wove a hustler's tale that
hadn't been heard since Lightnin' Rod's *Hustler's Convention*.

"Killers" (1984) was an even starker tale of street life, but its flip,
"Body Rock", was a pretty lame recitation of the elements of hip-hop
culture. Around this time Ice appeared in *Breakin'* and met the New
York City Spinmasters, Hen G and Evil E, who would become his col-

laborators. "Ya Don't Quit"
(1985) was filled with energy
(particularly Evil E's stunning
scratches), but was too imitative of New York. The
breakthrough was "6 'N the
Mornin'" (1986) (the flip-side
of the murderous battle rap
"Dog 'N the Wax"), a slow
and menacing track that,
despite Ice sounding a lot
like Schooly D, was the
beginning of a distinctive
Californian hip-hop style.

A new version of "6 'N the Mornin'" appeared on Ice's debut album, **Rhyme Pays** (1987). Although the album continued Ice's street narratives, it introduced his abundant sense of humour with rhymes like "Five freaks just to comb my hair/Monograms on my underwear" and the sample from Black Sabbath's "War Pigs" on the title track. Featuring a rather scandalous cover with Ice's wife Darlene in a V-shaped swimsuit holding a pump-action shotgun, **Power** (1988) offered more of Ice-T's gripping chronicles with his rewrite of Curtis Mayfield's "Pusherman", "I'm Your Pusher", a particularly thorny standout.

After running into trouble with the PMRC over "Girls LGBNAF" (i.e. "Let's Get Butt Naked And Fuck"), **Iceberg/Freedom of Speech ... Just Watch What You Say** (1989) was an assault on the hypocrisy surrounding the First Amendment. "Shut Up, Be Happy" featured the Dead Kennedys' Jello Biafra doing one of his spoken-word routines, there was plenty of gratuitous titty jokes, f-words and *Driller Killer* references, but more effective was the straight-up gangsta shit like the harrowing "Peel Their Caps Back". While Ice's intentions were laudable, it was the sound world created by his Rhyme Syndicate posse – Evil E, Afrika Islam, DJ Aladdin, DJ SLJ and Bilal Bashir – that really stood out.

This was perfected on Ice-T's best album, **OG Original Gangster** (1991). Ice's misogyny had largely been toned down in favour of no-nonsense, bone-rattling ghetto reportage. The relentless, jarring guitars of "New Jack Hustler", the punishing bassline of "Straight Up Nigga", the hard-hitting drums of the title track – all matched Ice's unblinking lyrics and virtuoso delivery.

Unfortunately, Ice has been unable to follow up this undeniable classic. His two Body Count albums would be instantly forgettable were it not for the "Cop Killer" controversy. **Home Invasion** (1993), a putative concept album about the possible implications of white, sub-urban kids listening to hip-hop, couldn't live up to its premise. While Ice was pursuing careers as an author, actor and TV presenter, he released **VI: Return of the Real** (1996) as an afterthought and it felt like it, especially with Ice trying to sing. **7th Deadly Sin** (1999) found Ice hooking up with Web impresarios Atomic Pop and delivering a tired, lazy album about envious rappers, but with his post-"Cop Killer" commerical exile and taking on acting roles like the kangaroo in *Tank Girl*, it's hard to imagine too many rappers being jealous of his current status.

⊙ **OG Original Gangster**   Sire, 1991

The best album ever made by a Black Sabbath-loving ex-Crip, with a stand-up's sense of timing and James Ellroy's eye for detail.

Intelligent Hoodlum/Tragedy

Percy Chapman (aka Percy Coles) is the original Queensbridge thug. As a tangential member of the Juice Crew, Tragedy contributed "Live Motivator" to Marley Marl's **In Control Volume One** (1988) compilation, but after serving time in a correctional facility for robbery Chapman converted to Islam and renamed himself Intelligent Hoodlum.

With Marley Marl in the production seat, his debut album, **Intelligent Hoodlum** (1990), featured underground classics like "Arrest the President", "Black and Proud" and "Party Pack". The streetwise Afrocentrism continued on **Tragedy: Saga of a Hoodlum** (1993). Again Marley Marl was producing, but now some years past his prime, the album struggled to find its feet in a rapidly shifting hip-hop climate. "Grand Groove" and "Street Life" were both lyrical gems worthy of his first album, but the overproduction dragged the rest of the album down.

In 1995 he hooked up with fellow Queensbridge resident Capone and with Noreaga and Mobb Deep. As Tragedy Khadafi he recorded "LA, LA" (1995), a dark retort to Tha Dogg Pound's "NY, NY", and released it on his own 25 To Life label. Capone-N-Noreaga released their debut album, **The War Report**, on his label, but after Capone went back to prison, Noreaga severed ties with Tragedy. Trag responded on the **Iron Sheiks** EP (1998). On tracks like "NORE-Faker" and "Blood Type", Trag mixed wrestling metaphors to denigrate Noreaga's name and accused him of stealing his style.

Noreaga responded with "Halfway Thugs Pt. II" (1998), saying, "I used to write his rhymes and let him shine/Knowing that he old school and out of time". Tragedy attempted to turn back the clock with **Against All Odds**, but the album was much delayed and, despite some fine jail-door-slamming, work-gang-style production, singles like "Bing Monsters" (2000) sounded like they were only going to convince fans that Noreaga was right.

⊙ **Intelligent Hoodlum**   A&M, 1990

There are a few severely wack tracks, but overall the production from Marley Marl and the Hoodlum's lyrical finesse on "Arrest the President" eventually win out.

Jay-Z

Replacing Biggie, Nas and Christopher Walken as the king of New York, Shawn Carter's status is such that both the streets and the charts call him "Jayhova". Like Tupac, Jay-Z is a hip-hop John Woo: chronicling violence and drug dealing with often breathtakingly vivid detail one minute, then sobbing uncontrollably about his moms the very next moment. He's not exactly an original stylist, but his relaxed flow and attention to hip-hop punctilios make Jay-Z the most influential, if not the best, MC around. If his records don't convince you, then his ghostwriting business for the likes of Foxy Brown, Puffy and Dr. Dre should.

The former dealer from Brooklyn's Marcy Projects debuted on Big Jaz's "The Originators" (1990) with a high-top fade and a tongue-twisting style radically different from that which he would become known for. After spending a few years establishing a rep on his own, he hooked up with Damon Dash and Kareem Burke and set up Roc-A-Fella Records. The new label released "Can't Get With That/In My Lifetime" (1995), which created an underground buzz in New York. Jay-Z blew up with his next single, "Ain't No Nigga/Dead Presidents" (1996). "Ain't No Nigga" was a hip-hop remake of the Four Tops' "Ain't No Woman (Like the One I've Got)" set to the Whole Darn Family's "Seven Minutes of Funk" break with production by his old mentor, Big Jaz. Introducing Foxy Brown, "Ain't No Nigga" was a pretty grotesque take on the battle of the sexes theme, but Jay-Z was simply awesome on the mic.

"Ain't No Nigga" and "Dead Presidents" both featured on Jigga's debut album, **Reasonable Doubt** (1996). Filled with tales of hustling and label fetishism, **Reasonable Doubt** dominated New York by carefully

balancing underground concerns with the garish livin'-large fantasies that were beginning to dominate the mainstream: "Can't Knock the Hustle" had Mary J. Blige belting out the hook, while "Brooklyn's Finest" had Biggie going one on one with Jigga. **In My Lifetime, Vol. 1** (1997) wasn't as striking, but on the remarkable "You Must Love Me" he created a gangsta tear-jerker out of a tale of him selling crack to his mother.

Vol. 2 ... Hard Knock Life (1998) had more tales of mercenary capitalism like "Can I Get A ..." set to futuristic beats from Timbaland and Irv Gotti and party-rockers like "It's Alright" set to Talking Heads samples and featuring guest verses from Roc-A-Fella up-and-comers like Memphis Bleek. Once again, though, the pivotal track was another tear-jerker, the 45 King's *Annie*-sampling "Hard Knock Life". On one level sampling *Annie* was the crassest commercial gesture hip-hop had yet conceived of; on the other hand, however, combining Broadway's saccharine sentimentalizing of poverty with hip-hop's reality tales was a stroke of genius.

Vol. 3 ... Life and Times of S. Carter (1999) contained the awful sequel to "Hard Knock Life", the *Oliver*-sampling "Anything", but featured some choice Timbaland and DJ Premier beats to compensate. However, Jay-Z's work rate and his cul-de-sac themes meant that, despite his undoubted presence and charisma, he was getting tired.

⊙**Reasonable Doubt**   Roc-A-Fella, 1996

Back when Jay-Z was a hungry MC and not a bloated corporate mogul living out his own raps, he was one of the most forceful mic personas in hip-hop.

Jeru the Damaja

I n the mid-'90s Jeru the Damaja (aka Kendrick Jeru Davis) was hailed as one of hip-hop's most innovative MCs. Although the truth is that Jeru's unorthodox flow and gruff, stentorian vocals allowed producer DJ Premier to be his most radical, creating some of hip-hop's wildest sonic experiments. With his help Jeru was at least partially responsible for two of the more compelling hip-hop albums of the decade.

Jeru first appeared on Gang Starr's "I'm the Man" (1992) from their **Daily Oper-**

ation album. Riding a really screwed-up Premier jazz deconstruction (a harbinger of things to come), Jeru dominated the track and made both Guru and Lil' Dap (less of a feat) sound like street-corner cipher amateurs. The following year, Jeru proved his status with one of the all-time classics and certainly the '90s' most outrageous single, "Come Clean". Over a beat culled from a Shelley Manne record that sounded like Chinese water torture gamelan and ran counter to Dre's facile, all-conquering G-Funk, Jeru reminded that the West Coast was about metaphor, not "reality".

Nothing on **The Sun Rises in the East** (1994) could match "Come Clean", but a lot of it came close. Premier's was making beats out of out-of-tune pianos, Stockhausen samples, backwards Tom Scott loops, scything horror movie strings and, most unbelievably, static. Jeru never regained the absolute authority he had on "I'm the Man" or "Come Clean", but on "Statik", "Ain't the Devil Happy" and "D. Origi-

nal" he was imposing and managed to ride Premier's beats without sounding too awkward.

Wrath of the Math (1996) was a slight disappointment. Instead of trying to boggle the mind, Premier tried to ruffle feathers: "Ya Playin' Ya Self" flipped (cleverly, granted) the beat from Junior M.A.F.I.A.'s "Player's Anthem" to accompany Jeru's wax war with Cream Puff and his ilk. Although he aimed at the right targets, Jeru's lyrics didn't move much beyond standard battle rhymes. When things did work, though, like on "Black Cowboy" and "Invasion", it really did sound like Jeru could save hip-hop from its worst instincts.

After four years of silence, Jeru returned with a self-produced album, **Heroz4hire** (2000), on his own KnowSavage label. Jeru's consciousness was a bit dated, but he learned enough lessons from Preemo to make the production pleasantly rootsy in a climate dominated by slip-sliding, futuristic drum machines.

⊙ **The Sun Rises in the East**   Payday, 1994

Jeru's focus on the mental side was honourable at the crux of the G-Funk/Bad Boy era, but it was Premier who was the real hero.

JJ Fad

ike their name, Just Jammin' Fresh and Def epitomized a long-lost era of hip-hop history. Like most girl groups from any era of pop history, JB, Sassy C and Baby D, with Lady Anna on the ones and twos, were all about an infectious camaraderie and a bubbly innocence. They rocked spandex biker shorts, oversized sunglasses and sweats and were entertainers at a time when you didn't have to be hardcore to get radio play.

With simple, but effective production from Dr. Dre, their one hit, "Supersonic" (1988), went gold and peaked at #30 on the US pop chart. It may have been a novelty dance hit, but "Supersonic" made **Supersonic** (1988) Ruthless Records' first platinum album. "Way Out" was the second single, but it failed to capture listeners' imaginations the way that "Supersonic" did. Far more notable was the nasty dis track, "Anotha Hoe", which used dirty nursery rhymes to savage Roxanne Shanté, Salt'n'Pepa, the Real Roxanne and Sparky D.

Fully engaged in a cat fight with Shanté after her "Wack It" thoroughly disrespected LA's finest, JJ Fad retaliated with "Ya Goin' Down" (1990), a title which questioned Shanté's sexuality. Unfortunately, "Ya Goin' Down" was the only decent track on **Not Just a Fad** (1990) that failed to live up to the title and the group quickly faded into obscurity as Ruthless became more successful and paid more attention to the likes of Michel'le.

⊙ **Supersonic**   Ruthless, 1988

This has all the JJ Fad anyone could ever need or want.

Juice Crew

I n the mid-'80s Queens ruled hip-hop: Run DMC, LL Cool J, Salt'n' Pepa and Def Jam's Russell Simmons. Although the Juice Crew didn't achieve anywhere near the success of their neighbours, they were perhaps the best and most important of the Queens rappers. A measure of their status was that no one has been involved in more wax wars than the Juice Crew.

In fact, the Juice Crew has its roots in an answer record, Dimples D's "Sucker DJs" (1983), a response to Run DMC's "Sucker MCs". "Sucker DJs" was the first record produced by Queensbridge native Marley Marl (Marlon Williams), who had previously worked as an intern under "Planet Rock" producer Arthur Baker. While Marley Marl produced other old-school landmarks like Just Four's "Games of Life" (1983), he would have to wait for another answer record and another female MC to really make a name for himself.

Marley Marl had landed a gig as engineer for Mr. Magic's hip-hop show on WBLS. When UTFO reneged on a promise to record a promo for Mr. Magic and did for his arch-rival Red Alert instead, Marley Marl teamed up with fourteen-year-old Roxanne Shanté to record "Roxanne's Revenge" (1985), which answered UTFO's "Roxanne, Roxanne" with gum-snapping sass. Kicking off the biggest answer-record craze in pop history, "Roxanne's Revenge" rather than "Roxanne, Roxanne" inspired over a hundred records that ripped on Shanté. While the rap community was obsessed with the Roxanne saga, Shanté moved on, dropping (admittedly lame) social commentary on "Runaway" (1985), but returning to what she did best – remorseless disses – on "Bite This" and "Queen of Rox" (both 1985). While her "The Def Fresh Crew" (1986) introduced the Juice Crew's clown prince Biz Markie, "Payback" (1987) featured Shanté "getting wild" and spitting harder rhymes than just about anyone, male or female. While Shanté had more spunk than a fertility clinic, it took the rhymes of the Juice Crew's poet laureate Big Daddy Kane to produce her greatest record, "Have a Nice Day" (1987). Quite simply, records, hip-hop or otherwise, just don't get any better: Shanté was "a pioneer like Lola Folana/With a name that stands big like Madonna", "like Hurricane Annie she [blew] you away" with lines like "Now KRS-One you should go on vacation/With a name sounding like a wack radio station/And as for Scott La Rock you should be ashamed/When T La Rock said, 'It's Yours', he didn't mean his name".

The Juice Crew was blessed with awesome mic talents, but Marley Marl was still the ringleader. Marley was perhaps the greatest producer in hip-hop history, almost single-handedly responsible for bringing the sampler into hip-hop with his production on Eric B & Rakim's "Eric B Is President" (1986). But even when he was still using Linn drums, as he did on "Marley Marl Scratch" (1985), he brought it harder and funkier than anyone else.

The MC on "Marley Marl Scratch" was MC Shan, whose "The Bridge" (1986) started the second most famous battle saga in hip-hop. Rocking the beat from the Honey Drippers' "Impeach the President" and a loop of fearsome dissonance, Shan bragged about Queensbridge being the home of hip-hop, infuriating a crew from The Bronx calling themselves Boogie Down Productions who shot back with "South Bronx", thus inspiring Shan's "Kill That Noise" (1987).

Ducking the inter-borough crossfire, Marley introduced the "Funky

Drummer" into hip-hop on Kool G Rap & DJ Polo's "It's a Demo"
(1986). Although he was perhaps overshadowed in the crew by Big
Daddy Kane (whom Kool G Rap accused of biting his style on "Ain't
No Half Steppin'"), Kool G Rap was one of the great MCs of all time.
With an awesome, multi-syllabic, intensely rhythmic flow, his mic skills
were on a par with Kane and Rakim, and the darkside tales he rapped
helped usher in hip-hop's hardcore age. Featuring "It's a Demo", the
ferocious battle rhymes of "Poison" and the prototypical criminology
rap "Road to the Riches" made the duo's debut album, **Road to the
Riches** (1988), one of the best of that landmark year. **Wanted: Dead
or Alive** (1990), meanwhile, included such vivid narratives as "Streets
of New York", "Money in the Bank" and "Rikers Island". **Live and Let
Live** (1992), with the title track and "Ill Street Blues", completed a
staggering triptych of albums that revelled in the dark demimonde of
New York.

Based on a piano loop from Otis Redding's "Hard to Handle",
Marley Marl's "The Symphony" (1988), featuring Kool G Rap, Big
Daddy Kane, Masta Ace and Craig G, was most likely the greatest
posse cut ever. "The Symphony" was the best track on Marley's **In
Control** (1988), making Marley Marl the first hip-hop producer to
release an album under his own name. However, the album's title was
a misnomer. Despite orchestrating LL Cool J's comeback on **Mama
Said Knock You Out** (1990), Marley was becoming the victim of the
more sophisticated production techniques that he pretty much originated and the name of his House of Hits studio was more optimism
than undeniable fact as it had been a few years earlier.

⊙ **Various Artists –**
Droppin' Science: The Best of Cold Chillin'   BBE, 1999

There are many Marley Marl compilations floating around, but this fine
collection was compiled by the man himself.

Jungle Brothers

With their first three albums, the Jungle Brothers probably did as much as any other crew to expand the language of hip-hop. While using classic old-school breakbeats to maintain connections to the block parties that nurtured the hip-hop aesthetic in the early days, Afrika Baby Bambaataa delved in the depths of the sampler and Sammy B played Twister on the turntables to create a more musical hip-hop. At a time when rap was ruled by fierce regional feuds, the rhymes and delivery of Mike G and Afrika suggested an open-ended camaraderie that hadn't existed since the Treacherous Three and Funky Four + 1. Unlike the verbal virtuosity of Rakim and the clinical turntable precision of Mantronix, the Jungle Brothers made rich, numinous music that was connected to the world outside the hip-hop community. Of course, in a genre whose hardcore underground protects itself with an armour every bit as arcane as free improv, this broad outlook is heresy and the Jungle Brothers have never seen their innovations translate into sales.

Their debut, **Straight Out The Jungle** (1988), was a strikingly original album that grafted loose-limbed funk on to the angular geometry of mid-'80s hip-hop beats. The single, "I'll House You", was the foundation for the short-lived hip-house craze; elsewhere, Marvin Gaye and Charles Mingus samples crept into the mix. Like their music, the Jungle Brothers' raps were rare examples of political and sexual democracy. "Jimbrowski" poked fun at macho posturing about sexual prowess, while "Black Is Black" slayed racism and black-on-black violence.

Done By The Forces Of Nature (1989) was even better. The spirituality and fraternity of the first album remained and were bolstered by

fatter bass and better hooks. Samples ranged from The Coasters to Bob Marley to South African township jive, and the funkier feel created an album that married hip-hop's oblique verbal dexterity to pop's more demotic language. With big-budget, but never too slick, production values, jokes that were actually funny and an overall feel that was almost sweet, **Done By The Forces Of Nature** was (and still is) hip-hop's most inclusive album.

In a genre obsessed with being hard, the JBs' unthreatening masculinity made them relative outcasts outside their Native Tongue posse (De La Soul, A Tribe Called Quest, Queen Latifah). Aside from a brilliantly bleak re-reading of Cole Porter's "I Get a Kick Out of You" on the **Red, Hot And Blue** (1990) AIDS benefit album, the JBs kept a low profile until **J. Beez Wit The Remedy** (1993). The Afrocentricity and embrace of pop were gone. In their place a hazed and phased experimentalism had developed. Drowned in a narcotic fog, **J. Beez** was far from the generous, funky jam of old, but no less brilliant. Radically different from the blunted hip-hop of Cypress Hill or the grim mysticism of the Wu-Tang Clan, **J. Beez** was obscurantist, black psychedelia at its best.

Of course, this couldn't have been further from the hip-hop mainstream if it was made by Amy Grant, and the Jungle Brothers disappeared for another four years. **Raw Deluxe** (1997) was stripped-down, yet still overproduced, and showed that while hip-hop had been moving on the Jungle Brothers had been treading water. At around the same time as New York label Black

Hoodz was releasing the **Crazy Wisdom Masters** EP of outtakes from **J. Beez Wit The Remedy**, the group was bizarrely aiming for the British pop market with the appalling **VIP** (1999). The ultimate indignity, however, was when the group opened up for the, wait for it, Backstreet Boys.

⊙ **Done By The Forces Of Nature**   Warner Brothers, 1989

A spectacular pop album and a great hip-hop record, this should have been as big as De La Soul's *Three Feet High And Rising*. Less self-conscious and less oblique than their Native Tongue brethren, this contains the most all-embracing hip-hop ever made.

⊙ **J. Beez Wit The Remedy**   Warner Brothers, 1993

A hip-hop record that samples The Stooges? Taking a snippet of offhand noise from Iggy and turning it into a hook, the Jungle Brothers manage to create a whirling, disjunctive sound from a conglomeration of infinitesimal details.

Jurassic 5

It doesn't sound like anyone in hip-hop has more fun than LA's Jurassic 5. Formed from the fusion of two SoCal crews, Unity Committee and Rebels of Rhythm, Jurassic 5 (DJs Cut Chemist and Numark and MCs Chali 2na, Zaakir, Akil and Mark 7even) are all about recreating the inclusive, joyous vibe of the first Sugar Hill and Enjoy records. Their vinyl debut was the "Unified Rebelution" 12" (1995), which was a combination of the Harlem Underground Band's "Cheeba Cheeba", Kraftwerk's "Trans-Europe Express" and the theme to *Different Strokes*. The flip featured Cut Chemist's old-school throw-down, "Lesson 4", which later appeared on **Return of the DJ**. Encompassing snippets of radio station IDs, Indeep, Harlem Underground Band, Bob James, Dan Ackroyd and Spoonie Gee jig-sawed together, "Lesson 4" was a tribute to both Double Dee & Steinski's pioneering cut 'n' paste records "Lessons 1, 2 and 3" and to the days when hip-hop was about the simple pleasures of finding a new sound and grooving to it.

1997's **Jurassic 5** EP, released on their own Rumble/Pickaninny label, perfected their back-to-the-future sound. Tracks like "Concrete Schoolyard" and "Action Satisfaction" were similar in vibe to the first two Jungle Brothers albums, but the highlight was Cut Chemist's follow-up to "Lesson 4", "Lesson 6", which sounded like Magnus Pike caught in a breakbeat tape loop. When the **Jurassic 5** EP was released in Europe in 1998 with the inclusion of "Jayou" (a flute-driven groove with the sterling couplet, "With malignant metaphors and ganja-stained herbs/We conjugate verbs and constipate nerds like you") as an album, the group blew up and they became stars in Europe.

Following this success, Jurassic 5 signed to Interscope in the US and released the **Improvise** EP (1999). With the excellent title track

and a brilliant remix of "Concrete Schoolyard", "Concrete and Clay", **Improvise** didn't exactly break any boundaries, but it did reaffirm them as prime exponents of underground hip-hop. **Quality Control** (2000) suffered a bit from the typical underground trap: they spent too much time trying to answer their critics and not enough just doing their thing. There was an odd line here and there that slapped you upside the head like a can of Tango, but their interaction wasn't as joyous as on their EP. Perhaps they ran out of Cold Crush Brothers routines to borrow.

⊙ **Jurassic 5**   Pan, 1998

In terms of quantity, it's a bit skimpy to be called an album, but the breezy vibe, old-school reminiscing and easy grooves are joyous enough that you don't mind.

Just Ice

Calling himself "the original gangster of hip-hop", Joseph Williams was bound to court controversy. In 1987 he was the victim of lazy reporting and was accused of murder in sensationalized newspaper and television coverage, which meant he wasn't accorded the right his mic name demanded. Just Ice was more than just tabloid fodder, however. He was one of the best old-school MCs and his gruff voice was a perfect match for the booming drum machines of the day.

Recorded with Mantronix, Just Ice's first album, **Back to the Old School** (1986), was a perfect example of the sound that made unprepared New Yorkers fear for their lives. Filled with the kind of drums that seemed like they could make skyscrapers crumble at 30 yards and Just Ice's fierce lyrics and violent cadences, **Back to the Old School** was hip-hop made with punk rock attitude. The key track was the stunning "Cold Gettin' Dumb". Filled with plain-speech lines like, "So try to make me believe all of your stupid nonsense", and chest-puncturing beats, "Cold Gettin' Dumb" was the record Slayer wish they could've made.

Kool and Deadly (Justicizms) (1987) saw Just Ice team up with KRS-One for an equally devastating album. Simply put, Just Ice and KRS-One tear shit up. "Going Way Back" was an old school history lesson, but with the drum-machine thunder and Just's breathless rasping, it became a threat, a self-actualisation exercise and a subtle dis of the Juice Crew all rolled into one. "Moshitup" featured KRS and Just trading lyrics and it did exactly what it said on the label.

While it had the savage "Welfare Recipient", **The Desolate One** (1988) was most notable for Just's version of Jamaica's "Sleng Teng" beat, "Na Touch Da Just". With production that imitated a Kingston selector constantly rewinding, "Na Touch Da Just" was part of hip-hop's burgeoning love affair with dancehall.

By the time of **Masterpiece** (1990), hip-hop had matured considerably and Just's old school disses and boasts sounded decidedly behind the times. Neither **Gun Talk** (1993) nor **Kill the Rhythm (Like a Homicide)** (1995) could bring Just's vision of hardcore up to date either.

◉ Kool and Deadly (Justicizms)   Sleeping Bag/Fresh, 1987

Officially out of print, this stunning record of old-fashioned b-boy attitude does occasionally show up on bootleg versions.

Kid 'N Play

Although they were decent pop rappers, Christopher Reid (Kid) and Christopher Martin (Play) will not be remembered for their music. Far more crucial to the development of hip-hop were their contributions both sartorial (Kid's skyscraping high-top fade, the leather jackets that Play designed for Salt 'n'Pepa) and cinematic (their starring roles in the *House Party* flicks).

Kid 'N Play first came to attention with "Last Night" (1987). Based on Esther Williams' "Last Night Changed it All (I Really Had a Ball)", "Last Night" was a corny tale of a double date gone wrong. Produced by Hurby "Luv Bug" Azor, the duo's debut album, **2 Hype** (1988), featured more innocuous, wholesome raps like the title track, "Gittin' Funky" and "Do This My Way". Inevitably, there were also parent-placating messages like "Don't Do Drugs". The best track, however, was probably the go-go-esque "Rollin' With Kid 'N Play", which gave Kid and Play plenty of room to rock their dance moves. Needless to say, **2 Hype** didn't move many units on the street.

After starring in *House Party*, Kid 'N Play tried to up their street cred slightly with **Kid 'N Play's Funhouse** (1990), which featured "harder" raps, but it was peppered with dialogue from *House Party* and just served to prove that these guys were nothing but slumming showbiz types. Far better was the **House Party OST** (1990), which had the good sense to include other rappers alongside Kid 'N Play's "Funhouse" and "Kid vs. Play". By the time **Face the Nation** (1991) came out, it was clear that the duo's future lay squarely with *House Party 2, House Party 3*, etc.

⊙ **2 Hype**   Select, 1988

Cornier than a big plate of succotash, though an enjoyable piece of pop fluff nonetheless.

Kid Frost

Kid Frost (aka Arturo Molina, Jr.) will always be known more for the novelty aspects of rapping in Spanish and bringing an Hispanic perspective to hip-hop than for the quality of his music. While this pigeonholing may be a little unfair to Frost, who is more than a competent rapper and producer, it is also testament to the fact that he has yet to make a record that's solid all the way through.

Frost spent the early part of his career hanging out with Ice-T and performing at low-rider car shows throughout LA. He wouldn't come to prominence until 1990, with "La Raza". Understated but unmissable, "La Raza" might not have been the first hip-hop track about Hispanic pride, but it was certainly the best. Frost's subtle rap style evaded the pop novelty territory of someone like, ulp, Gerardo, while the congas, bongos and the weird synth break that sounded a bit like an Andean panpipe group made his Latin roots just as clear as his words. "La Raza" was so good that it both opened and closed **Hispanic Causing Panic** (1990). Unfortunately, what came in between – with the exceptions of the unity call "Come Together" and the Spanish lesson "Ya Estuvo" – couldn't live up to it.

In 1991 Frost founded the Latin Alliance with fellow Hispanic hip-hoppers ALT, Lyrical Engineer, Astronaut, Mellow Man Ace and Markski. Their self-titled album produced a hit in the form of the inevitable cover of War's "Low Rider", but more original were "Latinos Unidos" and "Valla En Paz".

Frost's **East Side Story** (1992) was a loose narrative about a Chicano victim of Darryl Gates' policing policies. Its *mise-en-scène* was strictly old soul samples (Bill Withers, The Persuaders) and wasn't terribly original, but like, say, Michael Mann, Frost managed to make the utterly generic seem insightful. Tracks like "Mi Vida Loca", "Another Firme Rola (Bad 'Cause I'm Brown)" and "Raza Unite" make this Frost's best album.

Signing to Eazy-E's Ruthless label, however, seemed to bring out the worst in Frost. **Smile Now, Die Later** (1995) was his attempt at going hardcore and was filled with the same gangsta clichés (both musically and lyrically) that the label boss had been trying to peddle for the past several years. **When Hell. A. Freezes Over** (1997) was more of the same and pushed Frost's 2Pac fetishism to the fore. There was more Tuplacation on **That Was Then, This Is Now** (1999), but there was plenty of low-ridin' funk and guest appearances from the likes of Rappin' 4-Tay, Kurupt, Jayo Felony and Roger Troutman.

⊙ **East Side Story**   Virgin, 1992

Tackling racism, prison life and what it means to be Hispanic, this is Frost's most conceptually satisfying and well-executed album.

King Tee

While his peers catalogued the ills of their Compton surroundings to multi-platinum success, South Central's King Tee attempted to blunt the reality of his environment with wine, women and song, but no one was interested. Despite having one of the purest flows on the Left Coast, "Tila" has been unable to translate his skills into ducats.

Tee started out as a radio DJ in the early '80s and he soon hooked up with LA impresario Greg Mack, who released Tee's fine debut single and West Coast classic, "Payback's a Mutha" (1987) with DJ

Keith Cooley on the ones and twos cutting up the James Brown breaks, on his Techno-Hop label. Tee then bragged about being "the cool Wop dancer" over a Meters sample on "The Coolest" (1987). The wall-quaking and rump-shaking collaboration with DJ Pooh, "Bass" (1988), followed and Tee landed a contract with Capitol.

Although "Bass" and "Payback's a Mutha" both appeared on **Act a Fool** (1988), Tee's lyrics about 30-inch dukeys and Casanova fly guys paled next to the monumental albums being produced 3000 miles to the east.

At Your Own Risk (1990) was better, particularly the fearsome collection of battle verses on "Ruff Rhyme (Back Again)", the cheating tale "Skanless" and the drunkard's anthem "Jay Fay Dray". Still, Tila's embrace of harmless pleasures and unintimidating music couldn't match the sheer force of neighbours NWA and Ice-T, and King Tee was relegated to the background. **Tha Triflin' Album** (1993) found the St. Ides pitch man cold-rockin' the party with gratuitous shout-outs to his favourite brand of malt liquor and introducing protegés Tha Alkaholiks on the great "Got It Bad Y'All". The album also found Tee embracing LA's ruling Funkadelicized sound, finally matching his mic skills to state-of-the-art production.

IV Life (1994) sounded hung-over after the party antics of **Tha Triflin' Album**. "Dippin'" was all bloodshot and queasy, but the great "Super Nigga" updated the old Richard Pryor routine for Compton set-trippers. **Thy Kingdom Come** (1999) came and went with little fanfare; unfortunately the lack of response was justified.

⊙ **Ruff Rhymes**   Capitol, 1998

This retrospective takes most of the best tracks from his first three albums (although the inclusion of "Diss You" is unconscionable) and should go some way towards rescuing the reputation of one the West Coast's forgotten pioneers.

KMD

Originally put on by 3rd Bass, KMD were like an Islamic De La Soul. Screwing around with narrative, following a logic all their own, toying with the art of making records, KMD delivered black pride lessons with a wit and originality rare in hip-hop or any other form of popular music.

Zev Love X made his debut on 3rd Bass's Beasties dis "Gas Face" (1990), but it was KMD's debut, **Mr. Hood** (1991), that marked him out as one of hip-hop's great maverick talents. With brother Subroc and childhood friend Onyx, Zev created a Five Percent *Sesame Street* on **Mr. Hood**. Détourning snippets from a language instruction record, **Mr. Hood** found KMD taking the uptight title character on a tour through the ghetto, interrogating black stereotypes along the way. It was far from preachy or teachy, however, as the language was anything but direct, the metaphors skewed and the beats mellow but trippy like a Monet painting of the corner of 125th and Lexington.

KMD tried to continue the "humrush" on **Black Bastards** (2000), which was originally scheduled to be released in 1994. During the making of the album, Subroc was hit by a car and killed. When the album was finally completed, Elektra refused to release it because of the album's controversial cover art (a cartoon of Little Black Sambo in the gallows). Although the album had been bootlegged numerous times, and bits and pieces emerged on Fondle 'Em, when the full album was released it proved to be another masterpiece. On "It Sounded Like a Roc", Subroc poignantly said, "If I be a ghost, expect me to haunt." The rest of the record relied on snippets of some Last Poets albums for its emotional and intellectual weight, creating a heavier, less quirky atmosphere than **Mr. Hood**.

On "Gas Drawls" (1997) Zev mutated into MF Doom, a comic book persona based on the metal-faced character from *Fantastic Four*. Doom's **Operation Doomsday** (1999) followed the KMD tradition by twisting comic book records and '80s R&B like Atlantic Starr and the SOS Band into a disorienting aural haze, creating a sci-fi hallucination set in East Harlem without all of the lame futuristic trappings. Doom's flow is about as graceful as his steel mask, but it's effective – like he's freestyling to passing car radios. **Operation Doomsday** evoked loss and, well, doom better than any hip-hop in years: as he rhymed on "Rhymes Like Dimes", "Only in America could you find a way to earn a healthy buck/And still keep your attitude on self-destruct".

○ **Mr. Hood**   Elektra, 1991

Like De La Soul without the hooks, this was one of the most challenging and rewarding albums of hip-hop's avant-garde golden age.

Kool Moe Dee/ Treacherous Three

A long with Spoonie Gee, Kool Moe Dee (aka Mohandas Dewese) was the only member of the original old school to graduate into the new school. As part of Treacherous Three with Special K and LA Sunshine, he helped move hip-hop from the confines of the New York City Parks Commission into uptown and Bronx clubs like Disco Fever and T-Connection. With their matching red silks and upturned collars, the Treacherous Three were the old school's sophisticates, a position they reinforced by teaming up with hip-hop's original loveman, Spoonie Gee, for their debut record. "The New Rap Language" (1980) was the flip of Spoonie's "Love Rap", and against a beat courtesy of Pumpkin and Pooche Costello it introduced freestyling to wax and introduced the world below 125th Street and west of the Hudson River to Kool Moe Dee's rapid-fire rhyming style.

"At the Party" (1980) rocked a synth beat that imitated the kazoo beat that Grandmaster Flash had lifted from Freedom's "Get Up and Dance", while Kool Moe Dee shouted out the zodiac signs just like Rahiem and Melle Mel. "Body Rock" (1980) had boasts like "I got more rhymes than Mother Goose", and a chorus that went "Rock the body-body/Rock the body-body/Rock the body-body/Rock" – shame about the sub-Eddie Van Halen guitar line and lumbering bassline. The group's biggest record, however, was "Feel the Heartbeat" (1981), which used New York's second favourite beat of all time, Taana Gardner's "Heartbeat". Treacherous Three's earlier records had suffered from awkward production, but here they had music that was sleek enough to accommodate their sophisticated rhymes and vocal interplay. A true classic.

After the seriously lame "Put the Boogie in Your Body" (1981), the group moved from Enjoy to Sugar Hill. Their first Sugar Hill single, "Yes We Can-Can" (1982), was a cover of Allen Toussaint's Nworlins classic and featured a vocodered intro and socially conscious rhymes that "Hit your head and made your body rock". But, as Sugar Hill was eclipsed by Def Jam and Profile, the Treacherous Three's fortunes similarly went south after "Action" (1983).

In 1986 Kool Moe Dee went solo with the skeezer-hating (disguised as an STD awareness track) "Go See the Doctor", and an eponymous debut album produced by Teddy Riley. With the title track of his next album, **How Ya Like Me Now** (1987), he achieved considerable notoriety by dissing LL Cool J, whom he accused of biting his style. On top of Riley's cutting-edge production, Moe Dee also bragged about his elder statesman status on "Way Way Back" and gave Will Smith an idea or two on "Wild Wild West". Cool J responded with "Jack the Ripper" and Moe Dee followed suit with "Let's Go", claiming that "LL" "stood for lousy lover". The best moments of **Knowledge Is King** (1989), however, had Moe Dee espousing black pride rhetoric ("Pump Your Fist") and claiming that he was anything but a lousy lover ("I Go to Work").

With Riley, Moe Dee had gone platinum, but when Riley left Moe Dee lost the commercial and creative battle to LL. "Death Blow" from his 1991 album, **Funke Funke Wisdom**, didn't live up to his title and Moe Dee had long since faded by the time of **Interlude** (1994). A reunion with the Treacherous Three, **Old School Flava** (1994), didn't help matters any.

⊙ **Knowledge Is King**   Jive, 1989

With producer Teddy Riley at the height of his powers, it almost didn't matter what Moe Dee said, but he managed to keep pace with the beats.

Leaders of the New School/Busta Rhymes

I n the age of keeping it real, how is it that one of hip-hop's biggest stars is a hyperactive court jester, a whirling dervish harlequin, the tasmanian Devil with a sore throat? Busta Rhymes (né Trevor Smith) is certainly its most personable and charismatic star, but he is more than just the clown prince of hip-hop. With his ridiculous energy levels, dancehall-inspired rhyming style, outrageous videos, Five Percent (an offshoot of the Nation of Islam) beliefs and obsession with the apocalypse, Busa-Bus is hip-hop's most conflicted personality this side of Tupac, and thus its most iconic presence.

Busta first came to attention in the early '90s as a member of the Leaders of the New School with Charlie Brown, Dinco D and Cut Monitor Milo. Their debut album, **A Future Without a Past** (1991), took the terminology of old and new schools literally and the record was divided into "Homeroom", "Lunchroom" and "Afterschool" sessions (you could get away with shit like that back then). Despite this, lifting routines from the Cold Crush Brothers and rhymes like "Causing aggravation, I'll never pause/Pushing out spit balls with plastic straws", **A Future Without a Past** managed to make such schoolboy antics very agreeable, due largely to production by the Bomb Squad's Eric Sadler and an irrepressible group energy on tracks like "Case of the PTA" and "International Zone Coaster".

"Case of the PTA" was a minor hit, but it was a show-stealing cameo on A Tribe Called Quest's "Scenario" that made Busta a star. His lion roar soon popped up on tracks by everyone, and the Leaders' second album, **T.I.M.E. The Inner Mind's Eye** (1993), suffered from both group dissension and the changing times. The group disbanded later that year minutes before a scheduled TV appearance.

After more guest appearances than anyone aside from Big Pun, Busta's solo career finally took off with his double-platinum debut album, **The Coming** (1996), and its massive single, "Woo-Hah!! Got You All in Check". Built on a loop from Galt McDermot's "Space", "Woo-Hah!!" had great production, but it was dominated by Busta's personality (and definitely not his rhymes). Elsewhere, with help from EPMD's DJ Scratch, "Do My Thing" was similarly cartoonish, while "Keep it Movin'" was a reunion of the LONS.

When Disaster Strikes (1997) was equally successful and featured another anthem in the form of the awesome "Put Your Hands Where My Eyes Can See". "Turn it Up/Fire it Up" (1998) found Busta cruising on the *Knight Rider* theme to the top of the charts. **Extinction Level Event** (1999) had the ultimate harbinger of millennial apocalyspe: Busta collaborating with both Ozzy Osbourne for a version of Black Sabbath's "Iron Man", and Janet Jackson on the lame, Timbaland-biting "What's it Gonna Be?!"

After introducing his Flipmode Squad (Rah Digga, Lord Have Mercy, Spliff Star, Rampage and Baby Sham) on "Cha Cha Cha" (1998) and then overexposing them like Cameron Diaz, he actually found time to record his fourth album, **Anarchy** (2000), which suffered from Busta being unable to change his flow one iota and the world not ending. Meanwhile, the remaining Leaders of the New School, who hadn't been heard from since the group broke up, attempted a comeback with **That's How Life B** (1999), but sadly they remained unheard by just about everyone.

⊙**Extinction Level Event**   Elektra, 1999

It's pretty one-dimensional, but it's Busta's most consistent album.

Lil' Kim

Millie Jackson called herself "The Queen of Rap" long before any-one but locals had ever heard of Kool Herc, but in nearly thirty years she's had very few heirs apparent to her throne. Although she often seemed like nothing more than a succession of costume changes and ludicrous wigs, the potty-mouthed, pint-sized Kimberly Jones is perhaps the closest anyone's come. Abandoned by her parents while still in her early teens, Jones started hanging out on Bed-Stuy street corners with a gang of drug dealers led by Christopher Wallace. When Wallace trans-formed into the Notorious B.I.G. and signed to Bad Boy, he signed his crew to the Atlantic imprint he started with Lance "Un" Rivera, Undeas.

As Junior M.A.F.I.A., the crew exploded on to the scene with their debut single, "Player's Anthem" (1995), which became exactly that. Aside from Biggie's cameo, Lil' Kim dominated the track, forcing other M.A.F.I.A. members (Klepto, Lil' Cease, Larceny, Chico, Trife, Nino Brown, D-Roc) into the background. The group's second single, "Get Money" (1995), based on a sublime Sylvia Striplin loop, was a duet between Biggie and Kim that found Kim threatening to "come down your throat" with some of the most ferocious vagina dentata imagery since the Middle Ages.

Kim was linked both romantically and artistically to Biggie and she later admitted to sharing both his bed and his pen. Whoever was responsible for the rhymes on **Hard Core** (1996), the arrogant poses, piercing sexuality and sheer bitchiness were exhilarating. The Queen Bee "kick[ed] shit like a nigga do/Pull[ed] the trigger too" and "[did] shit to you Vanessa Del Rio be ashamed to do". The album went plat-inum and helped do away with the R&B diva and usher in the age of the self-proclaimed hip-hop bitch.

GEORGE DESOTA

Aside from providing the hook for The LOX's "Money, Power, Respect" (1998), Kim laid low (at least on wax, no one in hip-hop attracts more press without new product than Puffy) in the wake of Biggie's death and label troubles. She re-emerged in 2000 with Puffy now replacing B.I.G. as her mentor on **The Notorious K.I.M.** As befitting her status as one of the inaugural players in hip-hop's Ice Age, Kim kept the same focus on mercenary materialism and sex that had some dubbing her the Anti-Lauryn Hill, but "Suck My D!#k" was a castration anthem that would have Gloria Steinem nodding in appreciation.

⊙ **Hard Core**   Undeas/Atlantic, 1996

Despite some pretty appalling production, the Queen Bee proved she
was the baddest bitch since Millie Jackson.

LL Cool J

There may have been brighter hip-hop supernovas – MC Hammer,
Tone Loc, Vanilla Ice and Coolio – but LL Cool J (Ladies Love
Cool James) is hip hop's biggest, most enduring and greatest pop star.
James Todd Smith first came to the attention of Def Jam co-founder
Rick Rubin after one of the Beastie Boys heard the fourteen-year-old's
self-produced demo tape. He then exploded on to the scene with his
first single, "I Need A Beat" (1984), a withering drum machine break-
down that hit with the force of a Harlem wrecking ball. As Def Jam's
first 12" release, it provided the minimalist blueprint that would
become the label's stylistic hallmark for the next couple of years.

The follow-up, "I Can't Live Without My Radio" (1985), remains the
ultimate b-boy anthem: the lines "Terrorizing my neighbours with the
heavy bass/I keep suckers in fear by the look on my face" and "My
name is Cool J, I devastate the show/But I couldn't survive without
my radio" say everything you need to know about the hip-hop aesthetic. Both singles were found on his immortal debut album, **Radio**
(1985), along with the dozens cut, "That's A Lie". The album's best
cut, though, was "Rock the Bells", a devastating collage of urban
noise, b-boy attitude and overmodulated bass. **Radio** was, along with
Run DMC's debut, the first hip-hop album whose music bragged as
hard as its raps.

LL Cool J was the neighbourhood kid made good, but the celebrity bit went to his head and his next album, **Bigger and Deffer** (1987), was a meddled attempt to keep up with the musical advances that he and Run DMC had made possible. Although it contained pure hip-hop like "Go Cut Creator, Go" and the OK bragging cut, "I'm Bad" (which suffered from music that had nowhere near the power of his debut), the album will be remembered for his first ballad, the utterly wretched "I Need Love".

"I Need Love" was a huge hit – the first hip-hop record to top the

R&B charts – but LL quickly became a metaphorical punching bag. Kool Moe Dee savaged him on "How Ya Like Me Now" and LL hit back with the awesome "Jack the Ripper" (1988). However, LL didn't learn his lesson and his ego got even bigger on **Walking With a Panther** (1989), whose smarmy ballads suggested that he actu-

ally believed everything he rapped. Aside from "Jack the Ripper", the album's other highlight was the slow, moody, eerie "Goin' Back to Cali", written for the *Less Than Zero* soundtrack, which sounded like a slowed-down Miami Bass track.

With the burgeoning conscious hip-hop movement, the hip-hop community no longer loved Cool James, but producer Marley Marl stepped in to provide the solution. Preceded by the seriously hyped "Jingling Baby", **Mama Said Knock You Out** (1990) saw Cool J going back to his roots and, not surprisingly, provided his biggest record. **Mama Said** is probably hip-hop's greatest pop album: it's not innovative in the slightest, but nails every generic convention on the head, even Cool J's quiet storm pillow talk ("Around The Way Girl", "Milky Cereal" and "Jingling Baby"). Most of all, though, it was LL back to doing what he did best: "Rolling over punks like a redneck trucker". The title track was the best song he ever did and remains one of hip-hop's best singles.

Inevitably, **14 Shots to the Dome** (1993) was a huge letdown. **Mama Said** was all about Cool J coming back, but having successfully come back he now had nothing to rap about. Cool J's second, and probably permanent, slide into irrelevance worsened with the execrable **Mr. Smith** (1995) and **Phenomenon** (1997). Slicker than Hammer's big-budget fiasco, these albums represented the worst excesses of Cool J's obsession with his sexual persona.

When Canibus attacked LL on 1998's "Second Round KO", it looked like it might revitalize Uncle L's career. He gave as good as he got on "The Ripper Strikes Back" (1998), but Cool J quickly settled back into his comfortable middle-age acting career and churned out dull action flick after dull action flick. With Cool J spending more time in Hollywood than Queens, **G.O.A.T.** (2000) (standing for "Greatest Of All Time"), despite beats from Timbaland and DJ Scratch, was the hip-hop equivalent of those '80s albums from Bruce Willis, Don Johnson and Eddie Murphy.

⊙**Mama Said Knock You Out**   Def Jam, 1990

It's not as sonically innovative as PE, rhythmically dexterous as De La Soul, or smart as Eric B & Rakim, but as a consolidation of hip-hop's turf it's damn near perfect.

LORD FINESSE • HIP-HOP

⊙ **All World**   Def Jam, 1997

This has too many of his ego trips to be a perfect greatest hits package, but given the chart success of his recent output, which is as crass and idiotic as anything by Puff Daddy, this is probably the best we'll get.

Lord Finesse

R arely has a mic name been so appropriate as that of Robert Hall. Upholding the traditions of The Bronx, Lord Finesse is one of the great pure MCs in hip-hop. Despite being blessed with an abundance of skills, however, Finesse hasn't been blessed with an abundance of great records and his reputation doesn't match his ability.

He has made one undeniably classic record, though. "Funky Technician" (1990) began with a brilliant scratch of Craig G's "Mmm-Mmm-Mmm ain't that somethin'" line from "The Symphony" by DJ Mike Smooth and then settled into a groove based on a choked guitar line. Finesse proceeded to drop rhymes like "Now I'm the man with intellect/Know when to disrespect/I kick a rhyme and make MCs want to hit the deck", "Keep the crowd listening, I'm so magnificent/It even says 'Finesse' on my birth certifcate" and "Using bad words/Pronouns and adverbs/Puttin' English together just like a mad nerd".

Funky Technician (1990) featured similarly styled mellow grooves like "Strictly for the Ladies", over which Finesse showed off his mastery of the mic device. While the album is notable for his freestyling skills and funky wordplay, it also marked the beginning of one of East Coast hip-hop's most enduring partnerships, the Diggin' In the Crates Crew. AG matched Finesse verse for verse on tracks like "Keep It

Flowing", produced by Diamond D, and "Back to Back Rhyming", which was produced by AG's partner Showbiz.

Return of the Funky Man (1992) was more of the same, but the grooves were less inspiring. While Finesse was as good as ever on tracks like "Show 'Em How We Do Things", "Isn't He Something" and "Return of the Funky Man", the production wasn't as bright as the debut and, as a result, Finesse just didn't sound as imposing. **The Awakening** (1996) compounded the problem with sparser beats and a hardcore vibe that didn't do Finesse any favours.

⊙**Funky Technician**   Wild Pitch, 1990

With beats by the cream of the New York scene (Diamond D, Premier, Showbiz), this is the one time Finesse has had production equal to his rhyme skills.

Lost Boyz

The Lost Boyz are one of the very few hip-hop crews to have it both ways. They made their commercial breakthrough with materialistic party jams, but the bulk of their material actually deals with the flip-side of the ghetto fabulous lifestyle.

Freaky Tah (Raymond Rogers) and Mr. Cheeks (Terrence Kelly) made names for themselves at hip-hop jams held in Jamaica, Queens' Baisley Park in the early '90s. With childhood friends Pretty Lou (Eric Ruth) and DJ Spigg Nice (Ronald Blackwell) in tow, the Lost Boyz signed to Uptown and released their debut album, **Legal Drug Money**, in 1995. **Legal Drug Money** went gold on the strength of the anthems "Lifestyles of the Rich and Shameless" and "Jeeps, Lex Coups, Bimaz & Benz". Produced by Easy Mo Bee, "Jeeps, Lex Coups, Bimaz & Benz" had an easy-flowing beat and an undeniable "throw-your-hands-in-the-air" chorus that absolutely destroyed clubs. Acknowledging that this kind of obsession with money had its dark side, "Renee" was a chilling morality tale about a lover who was lost to the kill-or-be-killed code of the streets. Paralleling this dialectic between glamour and grime was the interplay of Freaky Tah's grating, almost screaming cadences and Mr. Cheeks' smooth eloquence.

With tracks like "Music Makes Me High" and "Me & My Crazy World" being blasted from SUVs throughout New York, **Love, Peace and Nappiness** (1997) followed **Legal Drug Money** into gold territory. On March 28, 1999, however, Freaky Tah was shot in the back of the head outside of a party in Queens. The Lost Boyz continued as a trio and released **LB Fam IV Life** (1999). Although the group desperately missed Tah, "Let's Roll Dice" was an effective anthem of the trife life, while "Only Live Once" and "LB Fam IV Life" mourned the fallen rapper with characteristic poignance.

⊙ **Legal Drug Money**   Uptown/Universal, 1995

An engaging album that managed to be both hardened and compassionate, party-hearty and chilling.

Luniz

The partnership of Yukmouth and Numskull started in Oakland, California in 1992 as the Loony Tunes. After garnering a reputation in the Bay Area, the duo changed their name to the Luniz and signed to Noo Trybe. Featuring super-slick, Bay Area funk production, their 1995 single, "I Got 5 On It", was one of the year's biggest hits. Incredibly hypnotic and instantly catchy, "I Got 5 On It" was based on a loop from Club Nouveau's "Why You Treat Me So Bad" and horn stabs from Kool & the Gang. Over these perfect, radio-friendly beats, Yukmouth and Numskull drawled about splitting the cost of a bag of weed, creating a ganja-smoking anthem every bit the equal of Cypress Hill's "Stoned Is the Way of the Walk" or the Pharcyde's "Pack the Pipe".

Unfortunately, the Luniz's debut album, **Operation Stackola** (1995), couldn't maintain the same standards. "Playa Hata" (which was aimed straight at Too \$hort's head) and "Blame a Nigga" were both OK tracks, but **Operation Stackola** was generic East Bay rap without any personality to differentiate Luniz from the rest of Oakland's hustler's convention. Marred by its desperate search for another hit, **Lunitik Muzik** (1997) was lowest common denominator gangsta rap and was even worse than their debut. It was perhaps notable only for "Funkin' Over Nuthin'", in which the Luniz and Too $hort made peace after the deaths of 2Pac and Biggie.

Yukmouth went solo in 1999 with a double CD, **Thugged Out: The Albulation**, recorded for Houston's Rap-A-Lot. Harder than **Lunitik Muzik**, **Thugged Out** was a big hit with the *Murder Dog* crowd, but it

also saw him broaden his range with "Revalationz", an uncompromising track about losing his parents to AIDS. Of course, the baller wasn't completely reformed and "Stallion" featured MC Ren remaking NWA's godawful "Just Don't Bite It". While Yukmouth has claimed that the Luniz are still together, "Falling" seemed to be

a fairly definitive statement to the contrary: "My old record company is trying to sue me/Is it because I quit the Luniz/And left they ass broke as fuck in the boonies?"

⊙ **Operation Stackola**   Noo Trybe, 1995

The only Luniz track worth owning is "I Got 5 On It", but if you can't track down the single, it's here.

Mack 10

Gangsta rap's critics complain that it's the same ol' shit time after time, that the OG is the same as the new G. For empirical evidence, you don't have to look any further than Inglewood, California's Mack 10. Ever since being put on by Ice Cube in 1993, Mack 10 has gone gold by towing the West Coast party line and sounding a lot like his mentor.

Cube produced Mack Dime's debut album, **Mack 10** (1995), which was just like much of the second wave of gangsta rap in that it took the rage out of the music in favour of smooth-rolling gangsta funk and a laidback, almost blasé delivery – lo-cal SoCal. The only notable tracks were "Westside Slaughterhouse" (which introduced the Westside Connection team of Mack, Cube and WC, who would make their regional pride full length on the **Bow Down** album) and the hit "Foe Life", but Mack was largely kicking the same game Cube did six or seven years earlier.

Aside from the utterly pointless remake of "Dopeman", which only increased the accusations of copyright infringement, **Based on a True Story** (1997) managed to find some humour and fresh angles in a genre that was more tired than Rip Van Winkle, particularly on the Kool & the Gang pastiche "Inglewood Swangin'". **The Recipe** (1998), however, saw Mack trying to break out of LA with guest appearances by everyone from Foxy Brown to Master P to the late Eazy-E. The problem was that, while **The Recipe** had plenty of ingredients, it didn't have much flavour.

The following year Mack introduced his Hoo-Bangin' label with the **Hoo-Bangin' Mix Tape** (1999). Aiming to fill the gap left by Death Row's absence, Mack signed MC Eiht to Hoo-Bangin' along with artists like the Road Dawgs and CJ Mac. Like his *Thicker Than Water* movie (a straight-to-video story of life in LA in the time-honoured tradition of Master P), however, Hoo-Bangin' suffered from a lack of ideas and formulaic production. Unfortunately, Mack's **The Paper Route** (2000) extravaganza couldn't stop the rot.

⊙**Based on a True Story**   Priority, 1997

It may not be saying much, but this might be the best G-Funk album of the second half of the '90s.

Main Source

Main Source may be Canada's finest contribution to hip-hop, but most of the action came from Brooklynite Paul Mitchell (aka Large Professor) who has also worked on tracks for Eric B & Rakim, Nas, Biz Markie, Intelligent Hoodlum and Kool G Rap. Extra P's standing among hip-hop heads can be gauged from the fact that, next to Tupac, he's the most bootlegged hip-hop artist. While Large Professor may be hip-hop's most potent triple threat (on the decks, on the mic and behind the desk), brothers Sir Scratch (Shawn McKenzie) and K-Cut (Kevin McKenzie) both added a little something to the Main Source sound.

The group debuted on the incredibly rare "Think/Watch Roger Do His Thing" single (1989) on Actual Records. They also appeared on a Canuck hip-hop comp, but it was **Breaking Atoms** (1991) that established their rep. While Extra P's production is often compared to Pete Rock's, the Prof's use of jazz is much more disorienting. Check the denuded keyboard and horn samples on "Live at the

Barbeque" (1991) (the track that introduced both Nas and Akinyele) and the epic "Peace Is Not the Word to Play". "Peace ..." was a sophisticated examination of hypocrisy, a topic which would crop up again on the remarkable racist metaphor "A Friendly Game of Baseball" and the woman-trouble narrative "Looking at the Front Door".

Breaking Atoms sold only 130,000 copies despite being hailed as a classic, and the critique of hip-hop commercialization, "Fakin' the Funk" (1992), would be the original line-up's last record. Originally found on the *White Men Can't Jump* soundtrack, "Fakin' the Funk", thankfully, did not live up to its title, with its clever Kool & the Gang and doo-wop samples. Soon after, the crew split amidst recriminations and Sir Scratch and K-Cut carried on with Mikey D replacing Extra P. Their album, **Fuck What You Think** (1994), was never officially released, which probably turned out to be a good thing after some weak tracks emerged on a Japanese collection, **The Best of Main Source** (1996).

Large Professor signed to Geffen in the aftermath and released two fine (if not as good as the original Main Source material) singles, "Mad Scientist" and "I Wanna Chill" (both 1995), but his proposed **The LP** was shelved. Various tracks have appeared on any number of bootlegs, but the only legit releases to feature his name as an artist have been collaborations with Chris Lowe and the man who shared the mic with him on "Fakin' the Funk", Neek the Exotic. Most notable of these was Neek's excellent EP, **Backs 'N Necks** (1999).

⊙ **Breaking Atoms**   Wild Pitch, 1991

After years of being unavailable, this classic has been reissued so it can get the props it never got first time around.

Mantronix

" **M** an plus electronics equals Mantronix" may not be the most promising of equations for hip-hop success, but back in his day Kurtis Khaleel was one of the most important producers in hip-hop. Born in Jamaica in 1965, Khaleel moved to New York from Vancouver, Canada in 1980. After the usual tale of being inspired by Bambaataa and Grandmixer D.ST and making pause-button edits at home, Kurtis Mantronik and MC Tee cut a cheap demo, which they gave to Sleeping Bag's Will Socolov. Sleeping Bag promptly released "Fresh Is the Word" (1985) which became a size-able hit in New York thanks to Mantronik's ground-breaking use of the SP-1200 sampler.

In addition to "Fresh Is the Word", **Mantronix** (1985) contained the massive "Bassline", an awesome union of circuitry and flesh. Mantronik became one of the most sought after producers in New York. Sleeping Bag's Fresh imprint was started with Mantronik's drum machine masterpiece, Tricky Tee's "Johnny the Fox" (1985). Mantronik also produced Just Ice's staggering **Back to the Old School** (1986) album, which included the classics "Cold Gettin' Dumb" and "Latoya", and the chopped-up "Mardi Gras" break on T La Rock's "Breaking Bells" (1986), which also featured the mind-boggling edits of Chep Nunez and Omar Santana, who would both contribute to the Mantronix sound in the future. Mantronik also predated New Jack Swing's combination of hip-hop and soul with his electro-soul productions for Joyce Sims.

"Scream" from **Music Madness** (1986) remains one of the few hip-hop records that borrowed both Kraftwerk's synth lines and their icy detachment. Where Afrika Bambaataa and the Soulsonic Force decorated their Kraftwerk thievery with dance-as-transcendence lyrics, on "Scream" MC Tee sounds like he'd rather be playing Ms. Pac-Man. "Who Is It?" similarly prefigured Mantronik's move towards dance music with withering synth stabs and subdued, streamlined beats. **In Full Effect** (1988) found Mantronix struggling to keep up with a changing hip-hop scene, but managed to stay ahead of the times on one track, the immortal "King of the Beats". Again aided by Nunez's editing, "King of the Beats" was a cut-up of classic and soon-to-be classic breaks that managed to be both futuristic (it introduced the "Amen" break that would become the cornerstone of the drum 'n' bass scene) and sound as close to Kool Herc wrecking the decks as anyone had in several years.

This Should Move Ya (1990) and **The Incredible Sound Machine** (1991) found Mantronix moving inexorably towards club music, a trend which continued to his 1998 comeback record, **I Sing the Body Electro**.

⊙ The Best of Mantronix (1986–1988)   Sleeping Bag, 1990

Long out of print, but this features the best of Mantronik's work, without the filler that ruined his early records.

Master P/No Limit

I f nothing else, you've got to admire Master P. Not only for his business acumen and empire-building skills, but for the fact that the Alexander the Great of hip-hop has stayed true to no-nonsense, no pretence hip-hop. While all around him ran away from gangsta rap and ghetto sentimentality in favour of "futuristic" beats and ridiculous space-age garb, Master P and his No Limit soldiers almost single-handedly brought back the medallions and garish jewellery of the old school and the metaphorical meat and potatoes of Tupac and his ilk. It may very well be nothing but "give the people what they want" pragmatism (best exemplified by Skullduggery's "Where You From", in which Skullduggery brags about being from everywhere in the US except Alaska), but P's version of the Motown fairy tale is somehow more admirable, more likable than that of other inner-city media moguls. Shame about the music, though.

Percy Miller grew up in the Calliope Projects in New Orleans, but he moved to Richmond, California along with brothers Zyshonne and Corey after their brother Kevin was murdered in 1988. Percy opened a record store there and the three started making tapes that sold well in the Bay Area. The Millers moved back to Louisiana in 1994, setting up a home base in Baton Rouge. With Master P's West Coast connections, No Limit released the **West Coast Bad Boyz** (1994) and **Down South Hustlers** (1994) compilations. Although Master P released his first two albums, **The Ghetto's Trying to Kill Me** and **99 Ways to Die** at around the same time, No Limit wouldn't start attracting attention until TRU's (Master P and his brothers now known as Silkk the Shocker and C-Murder) "I'm Bout It, Bout It" (1995). Although the synth whine was lifted wholesale from the Dr. Dre songbook, "I'm Bout It, Bout It", produced by No Limit's Beats By the Pound team (Mo B. Dick, Carlos Stephens, KLC, O'Dell and Craig B), was slower and scarier than anything from Cali, especially with that detail about dipping cigarettes in formaldehyde to get high.

As brutal as P's storytelling was, it was the cameo from Mia X (Mia Kristen Young) that stole the show. Even though she sounded a lot like Yo-Yo, Mia X's precise enunciation and street sass contrasted perfectly with P's molasses mumbling. Mia X had a local hit in New Orleans with "The Big Payback" (1993) before Master P snapped her

up for No Limit and released the so-so **Good Girl Gone Bad** (1995). Far better was **Unlady Like** (1997), which included a savage remake of Salt 'n' Pepa's "I'll Take Your Man". **Mama Drama** (1998) had too many love interludes, but the over-the-top theatrics of the title track made up for the poorly conceived slow ones and the duet with The Gap Band's Charlie Wilson.

With the death of Tupac, Master P saw an opening. On albums like **Ice Cream Man** (1996) and **Ghetto D** (1997), Master P combined the most saccharine, Hallmark card sentimentality ("I Miss My Homies") with unrepentant gangstaisms, shout-outs to the projects with the most garish production values this side of a Siegfried & Roy spectacular ("Make 'Em Say Uhh"). Sounding like James Brown passing a kidney stone (particularly on the abominable "I Got the Hook-Up!"), Master P's "unnggh" might just be the most unappealing catchphrase in living memory.

Master P's triumph isn't an artistic one, however. In 1998 P made something like $56.5 million. With his remake of Run DMC's "Dumb Girl", "Thug Girl", **MP Da Last Don** (1998) went quadruple platinum; P poached Snoop Dogg from Death Row and released his **Da Game Is to Be Sold, Not to Be Told** (1998) and **Top Dogg** (1999); his *I'm Bout It* film went straight to video, but was one of 1997's best-selling videos, while *I Got the Hook-Up* netted $7 million from the cinemas; his sports management agency signed high-profile clients like Heisman Trophy winner Ricky Williams; he started clothing, real estate and, believe it or not, petrol station businesses; he even had two tryouts with NBA teams.

Another commercial coup was luring Mystikal away from Jive. Mystikal had previously released **Mind of Mystikal** (1995), with the impressive "Here I Go" introducing his style: with the old Southern soulman grunt merged with a rapid-fire rhyming style, Mystikal doesn't rhyme for the sake of Ritalin. His No Limit debut, **Unpredictable** (1997), turned his already hyper flow into an unremitting torrent of noise. Mystikal also appeared on what is probably Beats By the Pound's least workmanlike production, Silkk the Shocker's cyberdelic Mardi Gras chant, "It Ain't My Fault" (1999).

1999, however, saw a change in fortune for No Limit. Having lost momentum to cross-town rivals Cash Money, "It Ain't My Fault" and TRU's *Exorcist* sampling and OutKast biting "Hoody Hoo" were the label's only two hits. P's sports management enterprise negotiated bad deals for its clients and was struggling, and P's **Only God Can Judge Me** (2000) extravaganza, featuring the most blatant Tupac rips of his career and sub-Cliff Richard version of the Lord's Prayer, limped to gold. One measure of just how far the No Limit empire had fallen could be found on the **WWF Aggression** album (2000), where C-Murder had the awful task of recording the third-rate Gangrel's theme song, while Method Man got The Rock, and comparative nobodies Dame Grease and Meeno got The Undertaker. Master P tried a change of nomenclature with the 504 Boyz (basically TRU plus Mystikal and newcomer Krazy), but their **Goodfellas** (2000) was riddled with remakes and a paucity of ideas. It seems like only God can save P now.

⊙ **TRU – True**   No Limit, 1995

The album that put No Limit on the map is probably the label's most palatable, and the rallying cry "I'm Bout It, Bout It" is certainly No Limit's best track.

MC Eiht/Compton's Most Wanted

O f all the groups that followed in NWA's bullet trail, Compton's Most Wanted might have been the best. Formed by former Crip member Aaron Tyler (aka MC Eiht), ex-World Class Wreckin' Cru member The Unknown DJ and DJ Slip, CMW's first single was "Rhymes Too Funky" (1988), which appeared on the Sound Control Mob's **The Compton Compilation**. Signing to Orpheus, CMW dropped the landmark **It's a Compton Thang** (1990). While the album featured the debut of Eiht's trademark "geeyaahh" phrase and his unique, oddly punctuated flow, **It's a Compton Thang** is perhaps most notable as the instigator of hip-hop's most notorious and brutal beef with the DJ Quik dis "Duck Sick".

Now signed to Epic, the group continued to make gangsta tales of surprising emotional depth thanks to Slip's slick production on **Straight Checkn' 'Em** (1991). But, for all of Eiht's harrowing tales of ghetto alienation and Slip's graceful pimp limp on "Growin' Up in the Hood" and "Compton Lynching", **Straight Checkn' 'Em**'s best track was another DJ Quik bitch-slap, "Def Wish". The dark, edgy and cinematic **Music to Driveby** (1992) was CMW's best album and a bona fide street classic thanks to "Hood Took Me Under", "Compton 4 Life" and "Dead Men Tell No Lies".

In 1993 Eiht starred as A-Wax in the Hughes Brothers' *Menace II Society*, and provided the soundtrack's best moment on "Streiht Up Menace", which managed to overcome its saccharine production with a precisely detailed narrative. Getting used to his name up in lights, CMW became MC Eiht featuring CMW for **We Come Strapped** (1994). Despite largely uninspiring production that resulted from Slip's downplayed role, **We Come Strapped** went gold and was Eiht's biggest hit.

Death Threatz (1996) and **Last Man Standing** (1997), however, were both artistic and commercial disappointments. In the wake of the deaths of Tupac and Biggie and his own commerical death, Eiht quashed his beef with DJ Quik and dropped his gang affiliation by signing to former Blood Mack 10's Hoo Bangin' label. **Section 8** (1999) marked a decade in the industry for Eiht and it sounded like it: the production was a pale imitation of the dark jazz Slip used to provide for him and Eiht sounded positively octogenarian on tracks like "Hood Still Got Me Under". **N' My Neighborhood** (2000) similarly lacked the intensity of his earlier joints and sounded like an old, reformed G sitting on the porch, sipping lemonade and telling little G's stories of the good, old days.

⊙ **Music to Driveby**   Epic, 1992

Probably the best gang-banging album not produced by Dr. Dre.

MC Lyte

mbodying both gum-snapping sass and gun-clapping blasts, MC Lyte is, aside from her one-time rival Roxanne Shanté, hip-hop's nicest female MC. Of course, the erstwhile Lana Moorer borrowed a trick or two from Audio Two's MC Milk – close your eyes and that could easily be her on "Top Billin'" – but considering he is her half-brother, it isn't much of a crime. In fact, Lyte's wax debut was an inspired summit with Milk and his partner Giz, "I Cram to Understand U (Sam)" (1987), a scathing indictment of a crackhead ex.

"I Cram to Understand U" featured on her superlative debut album, **Lyte as a Rock** (1988). The fearsome "10% Dis" was a savage response to Antoinette's "I Got an Attitude", which included the devastating couplet, "30 days a month your moon is rude/We know the cause of your bloody attitude". "Paper Thin" was even better: "Ooohs" from a male chorus, grinding guitars, menacing minimal beats and more choice epithets for former paramour, Sam.

Eyes on This (1989) was just as good and more popular. On top of more fleshed-out beats and some of the best scratching of the era (courtesy of DJ K-Rock), Lyte continued the Sam saga on "Not Wit' a Dealer", warned against rising above your station on "Cappuccino" and got raucous on "Cha Cha Cha". However, for her next album, **Act Like You Know** (1991), Lyte didn't heed her message on "Cappuccino" and got a makeover, swapping the b-girl attitude for cosmetic airbrushing and sweetening. Aside from the Toto-sampling "Poor Georgie", the album was a commercial and critical bomb.

With hardcore ruling the roost, she returned to her tough-chick image on **Ain't No Other** (1993). While the move was a commercial success (the single "Ruffneck" was the first gold single by a female solo rapper), all the expletives and bad behaviour seemed forced. Strangely, she abandoned the mack slapping for slow jamming on **Bad as I Wanna B** (1996), which featured production by Jermaine Dupri and R Kelly. Despite the effort, the album's only hit was Puffy's remix of "Cold Rock a Party", which liberally used a sample of Diana Ross's "Upside Down" and became Lyte's biggest hit. **Seven & Seven** (1998) was even worse, particularly the remake of Audio Two's "Top Billin'", which was just paper-thin.

⊙ **Lyte as a Rock**   First Priority/Atlantic, 1988

Classics like "10% Dis", "I Cram to Understand U" and "Paper Thin" make this one of the finest albums of the era, by a male or female.

Miami Bass

That gut-churning rumble you feel coming from those neon-lit IROCs and Cherokees that crawl the malls in the Southern US is Miami Bass. The guiltiest of guilty pleasures, Miami Bass is about one thing, and one thing only – booty. With more unrepentant ribaldry than Rudy Ray Moore, Redd Foxx and Blowfly put together, the collected works of Miami Bass serve as a *Satyricon* for the late twentieth century. What's interesting about booty music, though, is not so much that it's lasted for some fifteen years (with its subject matter focusing entirely on the female posterior), but that its earthiness is expressed exclusively through the most purely electronic sound this side of Iannis Xenakis.

The preponderance of thongs in south Florida made booty inevitable, but the obsession with the bottom end didn't start until the electro-bass cruised down the I-95 autobahn from New York in Afrika Bambaataa's jerry-rigged Kraftwerk hooptie "Planet Rock" (1982). While "Planet Rock" introduced the Roland TR-808 drum machine, Juan Atkins, the kingpin of Detroit techno, and Richard Davis, aka 3070, moved with a machinic glide and truly dropped the BOOM with Cybotron's "Clear" (1983).

As if kids from The Bronx and Detroit grooving to Teutonic man-machine music wasn't bizarre enough, MC ADE (Adrian Hines) imagined what Kraftwerk's Ralf and Florian would sound like cruising south Florida's strip malls in their bass-booming rides. Basically a cover of "Trans-Europe Express" with additional 808 claves, archaic scratching, a vocoded voice listing the equipment used to make the record, a snippet of the *Green Acres* theme and an overmodulated synth bassline, "Bass Rock

➡

Express" made booty bounce all over the South in 1985 and became one of the founding records of Miami Bass even though it came from Fort Lauderdale.

From even further afield, Riverside, California's 2 Live Crew relocated to Miami and defined the sound and subject matter of Bass with "Throw the D" (1986). With DJ Mr Mixx's primitively scratched Herman Kelly break and its megaton bass, "Throw the D" was probably the Crew's best record, but it was 1989's "Me So Horny" from the **As Nasty As They Wanna Be** (1989) that brought the group, and Bass music in general, to public attention. Based around samples of Mass Production's "Firecracker" and *Full Metal Jacket*, "Me So Horny" got exposure on MTV and embroiled the group in a whirlwind of controversy. As a solo artist, 2 Live Crew's Luke (originally Luke Skyywalker) released the all-time classic "I Wanna Rock" in 1992, which set Luke's scurrility to a beat with so much relentless forward momentum that you'd forgive him for spending the rest of the record talking about his favourite position from the *Kama Sutra* (which, in fact, he does).

Afro-Rican's "Give it All You Got" (1988) and "Just Let It Go" (1989) and DJ Magic Mike's **Drop the Bass** (1989) followed "Me So Horny" as commercial successes for Bass, but it would require a journey up north to Atlanta and Jacksonville for Bass's biggest hits. With less of an emphasis on the 808 sound, tracks like Tag Team's "Whoomp! There It Is" (1993) and Quad City DJs' Barry White-sampling "C'mon 'N Ride It (The Train)" (1996) had more fluid basslines and cleaner catch-phrases than their Miami rivals and became two of the best-selling records of the '90s.

While Bass might have had its commercial apotheosis elsewhere, Miami is still the undisputed centre of a sub-genre called Boom 'n' Bass. The overlord of this bizarre subculture is The Dominator, who is responsible for arming a militia of Camaros, Jeeps, vans and drop-top Cadillacs with bowel-damaging infrasound riffs. Played almost exclusively at competitions that serve to test the lower limits of automotive bass bins, Boom 'n' Bass is the ultimate example of music as a toy for boys.

While Miami producers like Beatmaster Clay D (responsible for MC Cool Rock & Chaszy Chess's "Boot the Booty" (1988)), Tony Mercedes (B-Rock & the Bizz's "My Baby Daddy" (1996), 69 Boyz's "Tootsie Roll" (1994) and Duice's "Dazzey Dukes" (1993)), DJ Smurf and Peter "Shy-D" Jones perked up their spartan 808scapes with light-speed scratching and party-hardy samples, Bass music's position as the quintessential postmodern genre was realized 1000 miles to the north. Picking up from where Dynamix II's mind-boggling, genre-bending throwdown "Just Give the DJ a Break" (1987) left off, Detroit's DJ Assault christened his brand of Bass "ghetto tech" and unleashed a flurry of supersonic samples and scratches on

→

229

his awesome **Straight Up Detroit Shit** mix compilations.

Bass may be known for its limp, too fast MCs like Shy-D and Prince Rahiem, but in Poison Clan (JT Money, Uzi, Debonaire, Trigga and Drugzie) Miami had a group as hardcore as anything coming from Compton. On their debut album for Effect/Luke Records, **2 Lowlife Muthas** (1990), they busted caps at anyone for any reason, bitch-slapped ho's up and down South Beach and rapped lines like "It's too late to straighten up because you blew it/If smoking crack makes you feel good, do it!", making them perhaps the kings of the ignorant rhyme. Nevertheless, **Poisonous Mentality** (1992) gave the group two hits with "Dance All Night" and "Shake Whatcha Mama Gave Ya". In 1999, JT Money would have a solo hit with "Who Dat?", perhaps signalling a Miami renaissance, following the success of Trick Daddy's "Nann Nigga" (1998).

⊙ **Various Artists – Booty Super Party**   Lil' Joe, 1999

A fine compilation of down South booty hits, from "Throw the D" to "Dance All Night".

Mobb Deep

With their drug dealing, beatdown delivering, thug tales from the Queensbridge housing project, Mobb Deep's Havoc and Prodigy are the poet laureates of the trife life. But, while no one would ever be foolish enough to question the veracity of their rhymes, Kejuan Muchita and Albert Johnson actually got together as students in rather different environs, the Manhattan School of Art and Design. The duo was signed to 4th & Broadway while they were both still students and both just fifteen years old. Despite production from DJ Premier and other A-list beat-makers and a bona fide underground classic in "Hit it From the Back", **Juvenile Hell** (1993) was marred by the duo's youth and dropped like the proverbial tree in the forest.

Undeterred, the Queensbridge dunns took the means of production into their own hands and unleashed "Shook Ones (Pt. II)" (1995). Against a Wu-Tangy zither loop, Havoc and Prodigy turned some fairly average battle rhymes into a gruesome parable about needing to be numb to survive the streets. "Shook Ones" was the Mobb Deep appeal in miniature: unoriginal but savage rhymes delivered with ice water in the veins that didn't have to resort to any gimmicks to make you believe them. **The Infamous** (1995) was that same formula writ large: minor chord piano loops, Grim Reaper strings and brutal lyrics that reflect the bleakness of their surroundings. In addition to "Shook Ones", the album included such classics as the collaboration with Raekwon, "Eye for an Eye (Your Beef Is Mine)".

Hell on Earth (1996) was no great (or any) stylistic leap and was similarly teeth-grindingly intense. "Animal Instinct", "Drop a Gem on 'Em" and the title track were all brutally effective and followed the style established by **The Infamous** letter for letter. **Murda Muzik** (1999) was a comparative disappointment. Instead of the unflinching tales of old, much of the album was marred by a kind of sentimentality on tracks like "Streets Raised Me" and "Spread Love". Of course, the fact that the rest of **Murda Muzik** was the same album they'd been making for the previous four years didn't help matters any. "Quiet Storm", however, managed to be everything you'd expect while pushing their sound to new dimensions with an eerie, gurgling synth-bassline and a big, dark space in the track where their hearts should have been. Perhaps sensing the stagnation,

Prodigy went solo for **HNIC (Head Nigga In Charge)** (2000), which expanded on the standard Mobb Deep sound with tracks from Alchemist, Rockwilder and Bink, as well as beats from Havoc.

⊙ **The Infamous** Loud, 1995

The no-nonsense deliveries and arrangements make this a bone-chilling classic of Rotten Apple hardcore.

M.O.P.

P erhaps the most revealing statistic about Brownsville, Brooklyn's Mash Out Posse and their status among real hip-hop heads is that their **First Family 4 Life** album was the most stolen album from New York City's HMV stores in 1998. With so many boosted units, M.O.P. have yet to translate their rep into sales, but with their tales of cathartic violence they probably have more respect on the streets of the Rotten Apple than any other hip-hop artist. Lil' Fame may be like an "orthopedic shoe/[He's] got mad soul", but it's Billy Danze and his Son of Sam-inspired alias, William Berkowitz, that epitomizes M.O.P.'s approach.

While they first appeared on an underground comp called **The Hill That's Real** (1992), they really burst on the scene with the awesome "(How About Some) Hardcore" (1993). The track, produced by Laz-E-Laz, may have featured a galvanizing horn riff, but it was the dirty bassline and no-nonsense drums that created a stark background over which Lil' Fame and Billy Danze spitted (literally) ferocious battle lines like "I used to pack slingshots, but now I'm packing heavy metal". "(How About Some) Hardcore" was included on their debut album, **To the**

Death (1994), which also included the similarly brutal "Rugged Neva Smoove" and the mean and moody bell-ringer, "Downtown Swinga".

Although it didn't have a single as devastating as "(How About Some) Hardcore", **Firing Squad** (1996) was a better album. Their verbal gunplay was adorned with more fully realized tracks and the album featured production by the one and only DJ Premier. "Dead & Gone" and "World Famous" took their weapon-fetishism-as-battling-technique to the absolute limit of metaphorical plausibility and proved that no one, not even Mobb Deep, was as hard as they were.

First Family 4 Life (1998) was even better, but it was equally slept on. The single, "4 Alarm Blaze", sampled Survivor's "Eye of the Tiger" (!) and an unrelenting siren sound to create a savage portrait of urban claustrophobia that, amazingly, wasn't ruined by Jay-Z's cameo. "Breakin' the Rules" had what may be the scariest line in all of hip-hop – "Before you test me/Know that I feel that the impact from a gat when it kicks back is sexy" – while "Real Nigga Hillfiguz" was a more introspective Preemo track that had Billy Danze admitting "I've always been afraid to die". **Warrior** (2000) featured more inner-city war chants and proved that M.O.P are true hardcore; everyone else is just Zalman King.

⊙ **First Family 4 Life**   Relativity, 1998

Violent, uncompromising, frightening rhymes that epitomize underground, street-level hip-hop.

Nas

Main Source's "Live at the Barbeque" (1991) may have marked the debut of Akinyele, but no one remembers it for that.

Instead, everyone knows "Live at the Barbeque" for the lines, "When I was 12 I went to hell for snuffing Jesus/Nasty Nas is a rebel to America/Police murderer, I'm causin' hysteria". One of the most powerful MCs ever to bless a mic, Nasir Jones, the son of jazz trumpeter Olu Dara, is hip-hop's chosen one. After several false messiahs, the Queensbridge standard bearer was anointed Rakim's successor when he dropped one of the greatest albums ever, **Illmatic** (1994).

Nas had also released "Half Time" (1992) on the *Zebrahead* soundtrack and appeared on MC Serch's "Back to the Grill Again" (1993), but it was **Illmatic** that heralded the coming of New York hip-hop's saviour. Not since **Straight Outta Compton** had there been such a potent evocation of life on the street; not since **Fear of a Black Planet** had there been such a devastating match between lyrics and production; and not since **Paid in Full** had there been a new MC who so fully commanded the microphone. Over an unbearably tense beat from Premier, "New York State of Mind" was an intense, visceral tale of a hustler who "never sleep[s] because sleep is the cousin of death". Elsewhere, Pete Rock ("The World Is Yours"), Q-Tip ("One Love"), LES ("Life's a Bitch") and Large Professor ("It Ain't Hard to Tell") all contribute some of the best beats of their careers and Nas moves from chilling nihilism to moving neighbourhood newscasting with ease.

Illmatic was the work of a precocious man-child (he was only nineteen when it was made), but, unfortunately, Nas seems to have regressed ever since. Although his remake of Kurtis Blow's "If I Ruled the World" made more of the implied politics of the "Imagine that" hook than the original, most of **It Was Written** (1996) was a garish celebration of the thug life, rather than an examination of it. His intensity on the mic made **Illmatic** so vital, but here he sounded complacent, moving into a comfortable middle age at twenty-one, resting on his laurels, clinking champagne flutes with Prada-clad honies in the club's VIP room. His album with his Firm posse (Foxy Brown, Cormega and AZ), **The Firm** (1997), was even worse, bringing label-whoring to new heights of excess.

He toned down the flossin' to more realistic Johnson & Johnson levels on **I Am ...** (1999), which had a couple of OK tracks in the form of Primo's "Nas Is Like" and the ridiculously over-the-top "Hate Me Know", but it felt like a schizophrenic battle between the Nasty Nas of old and the new Nas Escobar. **Nastradamus** (1999), too, suffered from an obsession with shiny things and a lack of interesting subjects for his beat journalism now that he's moved out of the projects.

⊙ **Illmatic**   Columbia, 1994

On 1999's "Hate Me Now", Nas bragged that he was the "most critically acclaimed/Pulitzer Prize winner/Best storyteller/Thug narrator". This album is why.

Naughty By Nature

On first glance East Orange, New Jersey's Naughty By Nature seem little more than no-frills professionals in a genre filled with ego-trippers, divas and big willies. Dig deeper, though, and NBN quickly reveal themselves as perhaps the finest pop-rap group of the '90s. They certainly have all the ingredients: a sex symbol lead MC in Treach (Anthony Criss) whose rapid-fire mic style is capable of delivering both simple hooks and epiphanies; a decent hype man in Vinnie Brown; and Kay-Gee's (Keir Gist) Puffy-inspiring production comprised of easy-to-digest, easy-to-recognize samples.

Vinnie and Kay-Gee were originally in a group called New Style until they joined forces with Treach and rechristened the crew Naughty By Nature. Coming under the wing of Queen Latifah, NBN signed with

Tommy Boy and released one of the most auspicious debut singles ever. "OPP" (1991) was an enormous pop hit, largely thanks to a sizeable chunk of the Jackson 5's "ABC" and an aggressive sticker-ing campaign in the New York metropoli-tan area. Of course, the sly, cleverly con-structed cheating tale didn't hurt either. Similarly chunky piano samples and easy-rolling drums featured on "Guard Your Grill" and "Uptown Anthem" from **Naughty By Nature** (1991), which proved that Treach was capable of twisting metaphors as well as tongue-twisting hooks.

19NaughtyIII (1993) featured the mind-numbingly facile hit "Hip Hop Hooray", but, with the inclusion of tracks like "The Hood Comes First", it was hard to hate them. By this time, NBN had become one of the first hip-hop groups to start their own line of clothing, Naughty Gear, and Treach's acting career started to take off with roles in *Juice* and *Jason's Lyric*. On **Poverty's Paradise** (1995), however, the group seemed to lose their focus and, despite a moderate hit in "Feel Me Flow", it was their least successful album. Nevertheless, they won the largely irrelevant rap Grammy for **Poverty's Paradise**.

After a four-year absence, NBN returned with more hip-hop cheerleading on **Nineteen Naughty Nine: Nature's Fury** (1999). The Buppie production hadn't changed any, but what once sounded fresh and invigorating was now as tired and lazy as a vat of relaxer.

⊙ **Naughty By Nature**   Tommy Boy, 1991

Designed the blueprint for cross-over hip-hop in the '90s.

Nice & Smooth

Singing back-up for New Edition and Bobby Brown might not be the most promising of starts for a career in hip-hop, but Darryl Barnes (aka Smooth Bee) rose above his R&B origins to become a mainstay on the early '90s scene with his partner in rhyme Gregg Mays (aka Gregg Nice). Like labelmates EPMD, Nice & Smooth specialized in light-hearted party rhymes that balanced out the hardcore politics and self-righteous consciousness dominating New York hip-hop at the time.

The duo's eponymous debut album (1989) was the last record to be released on Sleeping Bag's Fresh subsidiary. Despite virtually non-existent promotion and distribution, the album had two semi-hit singles in the Mary Jane Girls-sampling "More and More Hits" and the great "Funky For You", which has probably featured in more DJ routines than any other record this side of the *Kung Fu* soundtrack. With their exaggerated, cartoonish deliveries (they sounded not unlike butlers on American sitcoms) and Partridge Family and Tommy Roe samples, Nice & Smooth managed to stay just on the right side of the novelty artist line.

Moving to Russell Simmons' empire, Nice & Smooth released **Ain't a Damn Thing Changed** (1991). While "Hip Hop Junkies" and its great "I dress warm so that I won't catch pneumonia/My rhymes are stronger than amonia/I'm a diamond, you're a cubic zirconia" line showed that their style hadn't changed much, the Tracy Chapman-sampling, anti-drug track, "Sometimes I Rhyme Slow", betrayed a creeping maturity. Although "Sometimes I Rhyme Slow" was a big hit, the group's finest moment came as guest stars on Gang Starr's "DWYCK", the stoopidest posse cut of them all.

While **Jewel of the Nile** (1994) had Smooth Bee going back to his R&B roots on the truly awful "Cheri", the deep-funk production and a cameo from Slick Rick saved the album from congealing into a smarmy ooze. Not even a truncated version of "DWYCK", however, could prevent **Blazing Hot Vol. IV** (1997) from being as wack as its ageing (ungracefully) lovemen cover. Tellingly, it was released on Scotti Bros., former home of groups like Survivor.

⊙ **Nice & Smooth**   Fresh, 1989

Like nearly everything from this period, it now sounds hopelessly dated, but age hasn't dulled its effervescence.

Notorious B.I.G.

ike Tupac, the yin to his yang, Christopher Wallace was a bundle of contradictions. The former Bed-Stuy drug dealer was the
gregarious court jester who used his quick wit to stave off his heart of
darkness. Notorious B.I.G. made his money with MTV-friendly, overweight lover party raps, but made his rep with his pure mic skills: cinematic details, a hardcore sensibility tempered by a remorseful pathos
and a voice that enveloped the beat.

Biggie's vinyl debut was on the remix of Mary J. Blige's "Real
Love" (1992). His solo debut was the uproarious "Party and Bullshit"
(1993) from the *Who's the Man* soundtrack. After seemingly endless
remix appearances, Biggie dropped **Ready to Die** (1994) on Puffy
Combs' newly formed Bad Boy label. Showcasing his skills on the
smoking, Premier-produced "Unbelievable", rocking Mtume's "Juicy
Fruit" on the hopeful "Juicy", blowing his brains out on "Suicidal
Thoughts", Big Poppa embodied hip-hop's new playa lifestyle tempered with the fear of death, the knowledge that it could all come
crashing down any second. Going platinum, **Ready to Die** was the
album that put New York back on the map commercially and the subsequent beef with Death Row would haunt the rest of Biggie's life.

Biggie reinforced his commercial instincts with his Junior M.A.F.I.A.
crew and his production and guidance of Lil' Kim's career. Released
just days after he was murdered outside of a music industry party,
Life After Death (1997) was a sprawling double album that tried to be
all things to all people. While Big Poppa proved that he had "been
smooth since days of Underoos", an MC no matter how great was
often only as good as his producer's beats. **Life After Death** was, like
Biggie himself, too padded. Tracks like "Kick in the Door" and those

239

produced by Premier were gritty East Coast underground hip-hop that could hold its own against any of New York's all-time greats. Elsewhere, though, he rode Hammer-sized chunks of Diana Ross on "Mo Money Mo Problems", tried to out-mack Too $hort and attempted Bone Thugs-N-Harmony's tongue-twisting cadence on "Notorious Thugs". While this wasn't much different from the formula of his first album, it just sounded like a bunch of tracks; there was no tension, no pathos and not enough humour.

Like other pop music martyrs, Notorious B.I.G. had his musical

carrion picked bare by scavengers out to make a quick buck on **Born Again** (1999). Unlike Bob Marley, Jimi Hendrix and Tupac, who all left behind mountains of unreleased material, however, Biggie's master-tape estate was blessedly small. In fact, in order to turn the scant amount of material featured on **Born Again** into a full-length album, Bad Boy had to call in favours from Juvenile, Mobb Deep, Sadat X, Redman, Nas, Missy Elliott and, amazingly, since he was banished from the fold, Craig Mack. There were so many cameo appearances here that Biggie sounded like a guest star himself. There was little of the humour or sense of a person wrestling with their demons that made Biggie such a star and, with a couple of exceptions, **Born Again** was as crass as you'd think it would be.

⊙**Ready to Die**   Bad Boy, 1994

The reason that this album revitalized New York hip-hop was that he managed the trick that Dre had perfected on *The Chronic*: he tempered an unremittingly bleak vision with high jinks and *joie de vivre*.

NWA

Hip-hop in 1988 was a lot like rock circa 1970. While many rock critics were championing artier, "progressive" groups like Genesis and King Crimson, the real action (which would prove far more influential) was happening with the reviled Black Sabbath. In 1988, critics were lauding the political rage of Public Enemy while denigrating NWA's apolitical nihilism. While Public Enemy made some undoubtedly great records, history, as usual, has proven the critics wrong. While both PE's radical soundscapes and engaged rhymes have been ignored by virtually everyone, the hardcore rap which NWA more or less pioneered has become the lingua franca of hip-hop.

In 1986 Eric Wright decided he wanted to start a record company as a way to get paid. Hooking up with the World Class Wreckin' Cru's Dr. Dre (Andre Young) and DJ Yella (Antoine Carraby) and former CIA rapper Ice Cube, Eazy-E recorded "Boyz 'N the Hood" as a demo. Written by Ice Cube, produced by Dre and rapped by Eazy-E

(the first time he ever
blessed a mic), "Boyz 'N
the Hood" took LA by
storm and soon Eazy-E's
Ruthless Records got a
distribution deal with
Priority. With MC Ren
(Lorenzo Patterson) and
Arabian Prince (Kim
Nazell), Niggaz With
Attitude recorded a com-
pilation album, **NWA and
the Posse** (1987), whose
highlight was Ice Cube's
"Dopeman". Most of
NWA and the Posse,
however, was, like Eazy-
E's solo debut, **Eazy Duz
It** (1988), made up of
unnoteworthy party raps.

Straight Outta
Compton (1988), on the
other hand, was the most
uncompromising vision of
life that popular music

had yet produced. Unlike heavy metal's cartoon depictions of the dark
side, NWA sounded like they had first-hand knowledge of everything
they talked about. They never flinched, never embellished; they even
called it "reality rap". The first three tracks of **Straight Outta
Compton** – "Straight Outta Compton", "Gangsta Gangsta" and "Fuck

Tha Police" – were the most powerful records hip-hop had produced, not only lyrically, but sonically: Dre's drum machines knocked you in the solar plexus like a gun butt.

After a contract dispute, Ice Cube (who had written most of **Straight Outta Compton** and **Eazy Duz It**) left the group in 1989. In 1990 NWA returned with the **100 Miles and Runnin'** EP, which found Dre and Yella imitating the Bomb Squad, who had just produced Ice Cube's **AmeriKKKa's Most Wanted** (1990). "Real Niggaz", a savage dis of Cube, however, was a breakthrough: Dre's drums were funkier and the track was dominated by an eerie wah-wah riff that presaged Dre's future direction.

While Ice Cube responded with the equally no-holds barred "No Vaseline" (1991), NWA, and particularly Dre, would get the last laugh. **Efil4zaggin** (1991) defined the sound of popular music for the next decade. With its whining synth lick and rolling rhythm, "Alwayz Into Somethin'" was the blueprint for G-Funk, while "Just Don't Bite It" laid the foundation for the wave of blue raps and skits that would mar hip-hop in the future.

After another dispute over publishing rights, Dre left NWA, leaving Eazy-E to pursue an uninspiring solo career. He joined up with his protegés Above the Law for a series of brutal Dre disses contained on the

It's on **(Dr. Dre)** **187um Killa** EP (1993). While his albums became increasingly irrelevant, Eazy-E kept releasing solo albums by Ren (**Kick My Black Azz** (1992), **Shock of the Hour** (1993), **The Villain in Black** (1995) and **Ruthless For Life** (1998)) and introduced Bone Thugs-N-Harmony. Ruthless Records stayed relatively healthy until his death from AIDS in 1995.

⊙ **Greatest Hits**   Ruthless/Priority, 1996

While **Straight Outta Compton** is unquestionably their best album, all of its great tracks are here along with some choice moments from **100 Miles and Runnin'** and **Efil4zaggin**.

Onyx

Don't let their origins as a dance troupe fool you – Jamaica, Queens' Onyx weren't about genie pants, funny haircuts and piccaninny grins. Instead, with their black hoodies, shaven heads and roughneck scowls, Onyx brought hip-hop into the mosh pit. While groups like UTFO and Public Enemy collaborated with Anthrax, NWA remade hip-hop as punk rock and Esham camouflaged his rhymes in corpse paint, Onyx brought with them a slam-dancing, shock-tactic, locker-room bragging male camaraderie reminiscent of AC/DC into hip-hop.

Stciky Fingaz, Fredro Star, Big DS and Suave Sonny Seeza were discovered and signed by Run DMC's Jam Master Jay, who also produced their first album, **Bacdafucup** (1993). Filled with shouty, sing-along choruses, lame sexual innuendo and a drunken primitivism, **Bacdafucup** could have been an Oi! album if it was made by ale-swilling British dollies in the early '80s. But Peter & the Test Tube Babies were never funky enough to sample The Mohawks' "Champ" as Onyx did on their mega-hit, "Slam". The thrashing male energy continued on tracks like "Throw Ya Gunz" (a very funny take on hip-hop's worst cliché, "throw your hands in the air and wave 'em like you just don't care"), "Bichasniguz" and the really dumb "Blac Vagina Finda".

Losing both Big DS and Jam Master Jay, Onyx applied their "grimee" rhyming style to their own beats on **All We Got Iz Us** (1995). Without Jay's simple but effective production or the soccer terrace esprit de corps, though, the album failed miserably at attempting "shocking" stories from the naked city and was totally outclassed by their neighbours from Queensbridge. **Shut 'Em Down** (1998) went back to the raucousness of the first album and wasn't a bad attempt at recovering lost ground, but by this point people like Limp Bizkit and Kid Rock had reclaimed their territory for skate punks and bored suburbanites. The group soon disbanded and Sticky Fingaz went solo with **Black Trash: The Autobiography of Kirk Jones** (2000), but he wasn't making anyone bacdafucup any more.

⊙ **Bacdafucup**   RAL/Columbia, 1993

Given the success of Run DMC's collaboration with Aerosmith, it's a wonder no one thought of this sooner, but fitting that Jam Master Jay was behind it all.

Organized Konfusion

O riginally protegés of legendary producer Paul C, calling themselves Simply 2 Positive, Pharoahe Monch and Prince Poetry thankfully changed their name and became one of hip-hop's greatest and most radical groups. Due to both a climate that demanded "realness" and an uncompromising complexity, Organized Konfusion languished in obscurity until the duo split and Monch "blew the fuck up" with "Simon Says" in 1999.

As their name suggests, Organized Konfusion's self-titled debut album (1991) was a schizophrenic mishmash of styles that didn't do them any favours in finding an audience. "Fudge Pudge" found Prince Poetry imitating both an answering machine and the *Hong Kong Phooey* theme over a mellow, jazzy beat, while Monch bragged about his dick and fucking Heather Hunter. "Who Stole My Last Piece of Chicken?" found Monch making like Marcel Proust and reminiscing on things past. The album's highlight, though, was the mind-boggling "Releasing Hypnotical Gases". Based around a crazy Weather Report sample, "Releasing Hypnotical Gases" was a collection of sci-fi battle rhymes that would have left Einstein dumbfounded ("It's ironic when a demonic government utilizes bionics in a six million dollar man/To capture me, clever, however, you can never, ever begin to apprehend a hologram") that predated a decade of self-conscious avant-garde black futurism.

Stress: The Extinction Agenda (1994) found Monch recovering from the death of his father and the duo wrestling with their label. On tracks like the intro, "Stress" and "Maintain", they vented their anger by "crush[ing], kill[ing] and destroy[ing]" racist cab drivers and anyone else who walked into their path. As Monch says, "[he] like[s] the taste of radioactive waste", and the music is thick, fetid, noxious, more like electric Miles Davis than the cool bop favoured by most hip-hop producers. "Black Sunday" used a loop from A Tribe Called Quest, but they elongated it, stretching it to breaking point, replacing Quest's languid insouciance with an enervated survival instinct. "3-2-1" was a joyous celebration of skills, but the album's defining track was "Stray Bullet": a gruesome narrative written from the point of view of a bullet that lodges itself into a six-year-old girl's head.

Equinox (1997) was perhaps their most challenging album. Although it veered perilously close to Yes and ELP territory, **Equinox** was a concept album that just about succeeded despite itself. The story about two characters named Life and Malice was pretty lame, but the songs themselves were often extraordinary, particularly the stunning "Hate", in which Monch and Prince Po adopt the personas of two white supremacists.

Tired of respect but no cream, Monch changed tack on his solo debut **Internal Affairs** (1999). Instead of trying to move butts, the production of "Simon Says" tried to bludgeon you into submission, a plan which came to fruition when the track blew up in New York. The rest of the album was equally brutal and unforgiving. While it's hard to begrudge this most underrated of MCs' success, **Internal Affairs** was disappointingly one-dimensional.

⊙ **Stress: The Extinction Agenda**   Hollywood Basic, 1994

It may be challenging, but even people who want their music to be as easy as a Jackie Collins novel can appreciate the pure skills of "Bring it On" and "Let's Organize" and the ghastly storytelling of "Stray Bullet".

Paris

B orn in San Francisco and raised in Oakland, Oscar Jackson has tried to uphold the Bay Area's tradition of radicalism in rhyme. While an Economics student and radio DJ at the Universtiy of

California-Davis, he became influenced by both the Black Panthers and the Nation of Islam, renamed himself Paris and started his own Scarface label. Scarface released his first single, "Scarface Groove" (1988), which got him signed to Tommy Boy.

His first single for Tommy Boy was "Break the Grip of Shame" (1989). Housed in a sleeve of a white cop grabbing a screaming black boy in a choke hold, "Break the Grip of Shame" had all the lyrical poses of black militancy, but didn't actually say much. Instead, the message was in the music: fearsome, plastic funk synth stabs, scathing guitar riffs and devastating scratching from DJ Mad Mike (not to be confused with Underground Resistance's techno rabble-rouser). His debut album, **The Devil Made Me Do It** (1990), was a bit uneven skillswise, but it was uniformly intense, making it one of the classics of the short-lived black nationalist trend in hip-hop.

Sleeping With the Enemy (1992) kept the message confined to the lyrics. While the production was fairly standard and dull West Coast funk, his rhymes on "Guerrillas in the Mist", "Conspiracy of Silence" and "Make Way For a Panther" were scathing. The album, however, attracted notoriety only for "Bush Killa", an interlude in which Paris dreams of assassinating President Bush, and the cop-killing fantasy, "Coffee, Donuts & Death", which forced the Time-Warner-owned Tommy Boy to drop the album in the wake of Ice-T and Body Count's "Cop Killer" fiasco.

Guerrilla Funk (1994) saw Paris trying to make G-Funk explicitly political with mixed results, especially on the title track, which was little more than watered-down rapping on top of a Puff Daddy-sized chunk of Funkadelic's "(Not Just) Knee Deep". Paris continued to provide funk for the trunk with his production of the Conscious Daughters **Ear to the Street** (1993), which featured the bumping, if not very conscious, "Something to Ride to (Fonky Expedition)". Paris's much-delayed **Unleashed** (1998) followed the same formula to even more disappointing, increasingly irrelevant results.

⊙ **The Devil Made Me Do It**   Tommy Boy, 1990

Not perfect, but a ferocious blast of righteous rage nonetheless.

Pharcyde

Representing the LA underground, the Pharcyde managed to see the funny side of hip-hop, while all around them was the aftermath of Darryl Gates' policies, St. Ides and crack. The nucleus of the group – Imani Wilcox, Tre "Slimkid" Hardson and Romye "Booty Brown" Robinson – met while they were working as dancers and choreographers, and they even briefly featured on *In Living Color*. Hooking up with Derrick "Fat Lip" Stewart, the Pharcyde signed a deal with Delicious Vinyl in 1991.

The group's debut album, **Bizarre Ride II the Pharcyde** (1992), was a carnival of silliness, group camaraderie, goofy gags, dusty samples and inventive flows. "Ya Mama" was an update of street-corner pastimes snapping and the dozens. On top of a neat organ riff, the Pharcyde dropped a series of classic snaps ("Your Mama's got a peg leg with a kickstand", "Your Mama got a glass eye with a fish in it") and original insults destined to become standards ("Your Mama's got an afro with a chin strap", "You was beatboxin' for Lou Rawls"). However, when the carnival left town, these hip-hop nerds got introspective and self-deprecating, talking honestly about sexual frustration on the awesome "Passing Me By" and "Oh Shit".

Typically, though, the Pharcyde suffered from hip-hop's blight and

they become more sombre and more "real" on their follow-up, **Labcabincalifornia** (1995). "Somethin' That Means Somethin'" and "Devil
Music" recounted their difficulties with their label and moaned about the
dark side of fame over subdued jazz samples. "Runnin'" continued the
bad trip and was accompanied by a Spike Jonze video that shot the
band moving backwards with the tape running in the reverse direction,
giving it an off-kilter, slightly queasy feel that fit the music perfectly.

The Pharcyde were troubled by internal strife as well as record label
differences and Fat Lip left the group shortly after **Labcabincalifornia**
was released. Slim Kid, Imani and Booty Brown re-emerged in 1999
with the **Testing the Waters** EP on the tiny Chapter One Records. The

title was unfortunately accurate, as it found the group tentatively rapping in a similar style to **Labcabincalifornia**. Fat Lip, meanwhile, got self-conscious and rapped about the plight of the MC who fell off on "What's Up Fat Lip?" ("Yeah I'm a brother but sometimes I don't feel black/My girl is white/My game ain't tight/Niggas who ain't seen me in a while be like, 'Dude, you aiight?'") from **Revenge of the Nerd** (2000).

⊙ **Bizarre Ride II the Pharcyde**   Delicious Vinyl, 1992

Taking hip-hop on a ride through the fun house, the Pharcyde made one of the best, most original albums of the '90s.

Poor Righteous Teachers

Spiritual descendants of Clarence 13X, Trenton, New Jersey's Poor Righteous Teachers were, along with Brand Nubian, among the best of the wave of Five Percent rappers that emerged at the beginning of the '90s. Wise Intelligent, Culture Freedom and Father Shaheed attempted to tackle ignorance by dropping lessons into their raps, unsurprisingly attracting much controversy with their belief in the godhood of black men.

Despite their commitment to the Koran and to Clarence 13X's teachings, it was the very profane art of production that initially attracted attention their way. "Rock Dis Funky Joint" from their debut album, **Holy Intellect** (1990), was a supremely groovalicious cut-up of War's "Slippin' Into Darkness", whose body-rockin' rhythms made this potentially tedious lesson far more interesting and effective than memorizing the times tables with Miss Crabtree. Most of **Holy Intellect** followed suit with Wise Intelligent's ragga styled chit-chit-chatter and producer Tony D's ricocheting funk championing inclusive pop values over strict dogma.

Pure Poverty (1991) was nearly as good, with a more pronounced dancehall flavour and another semi-hit in the R&B-tinged, but still pretty decent, "Shakiyla (JRH)". **Black Business** (1993) had more nods to Kingston DJs in the form of "Nobody Move", but the didacticism which always threatened to rear its ugly head did and made the album less fun than Ramadan. **The New World Order** (1996) was a slight return to form (particularly the storming "Gods, Earths and 85ers", which turned a recital of the Five Percent creed into a street anthem), but it was bogged down by too many awkward cameos (KRS-One, Miss Jones, Junior Reid and The Fugees, who borrowed the sing-jay style of "Shakiyla") and too many crap skits. PRT have been quiet ever since, although a poorly selected best-of, **Righteous Grooves**, appeared in 1999.

⊙ **Holy Intellect**   Profile, 1990

Too many Five Percenters didn't seem to understand that nation-building requires a populist vision, but, on this album at least, PRT balanced their pedantry with galvanizing grooves.

Profile Records

Started by Steve Plotnicki and Corey Robbins in 1981, Profile Records is probably the most important independent label of the last quarter century. Not only was Profile the label that graduated hip-hop into the new school, but, while all of its contemporaries have sold out to the corporate dollar, Profile has remained firmly independent.

Plotnicki and Robbins were both established players on the Big Apple club scene, so their label began with so-so disco records. Their first hip-hop signing was Lonnie Love (Alonzo Brown), who released "Young Ladies" (1981) to little fanfare. With the label rapidly running out of money, Lonnie Love mutated into Mr. Hyde and teamed up with Dr. Jeckyl (Andre Harrell) for "Genius Rap" (1981). One of the first hip-hop records to jack the beat from Tom Tom Club's "Genius of Love", "Genius Rap" featured Brown and Harrell bragging about being in *Jet* magazine and having "jazz, pizzazz, razzamatazz" and became the label's first hit.

Profile continued to have moderate success with tracks like Disco Four's "We're at the Party" (1982), Fresh 3 MCs' "Fresh" (1983), Pumpkin's awesome "King of the Beat" (1983) and Rammellzee Vs. K-Rob's all-time great, "Beat Bop" (1983). However, with the release of Run DMC's "It's Like That/Sucker MCs" (1983), the label changed the face of hip-hop and subsequently all of popular music. Housed in a brittle, mechanical, absolutely booming drum machine armour, "Sucker MCs" was no yes, yes, y'allin', hotel-motel-Holiday Inn track; it was pure b-boy braggadocio, calling names with savage aggression and

→

even bragging about eating "chicken and collard greens" – this was no fantasy, this was "reality".

While Run DMC continued to redefine hip-hop, Profile hit with novelty records like Dana Dane's Slick Rick-biting "Nightmares" (1985) and "Cinderfella Dana Dane" (1987) and Spyder D's "Buckwheat Beat" (1985). However, with Word of Mouth featuring DJ Cheese's mind-boggling early scratch record, "King Kut" (1985), the label proved that it was no one-hit wonder. K-Rob returned in 1986 with the in-your-face "I'm a Homeboy", which featured DJ Cheese on the cuts, the Latin Rascals on the edits and Duke Bootee behind the boards. It may have been based on James Brown, but Sweet Tee & Jazzy Joyce's "It's My Beat" (1986) was as loud, as geometrical as any drum machine anthem by Run DMC.

Rob Base & DJ E-Z Rock, Special Ed and Poor Righteous Teachers kept the label's profile high as hip-hop became more sampladelic. They mined the New York underground with records from King Sun and Twin Hype, reached out to the West with DJ Quik, and even bogled in the dancehall with records from Daddy Freddy and Asher D.

Partially because of legal wrangles between Robbins and Plotnicki, the label lost its footing in the early and mid-'90s, and records from Nine, Smoothe Da Hustler and Camp Lo couldn't fully stop the rot.

⊙ **Various Artists – Diggin' in the Crates**　　　Profile, 1994

An impeccable collection from the label's glory days featuring Run DMC, Rammellzee, Pumpkin and DJ Cheese.

Public Enemy

Hip-hop fundamentalists may think otherwise, but Public Enemy were unquestionably hip-hop's greatest group. No other hip-hop crew has had such an impact on popular music and popular culture in general. Before PE, hip-hop only flared up in the mainstream consciousness when the Beastie Boys got busted for their frat boy antics or when Run DMC shared the stage with Aerosmith. PE made hip-hop the most vital cultural form of the last 25 years and made everybody from college professors to newspaper columnists to lunkhead guitarists come to terms with hip-hop. PE attracted the most controversy for their embrace of the teachings of the Nation of Islam, but with Chuck D's forceful delivery and the Bomb Squad's radical sonics, they would have attracted notoriety if they were supporters of Billy Graham.

Public Enemy came together in the early '80s around Bill Stephney's radio show on Adelphi University's WBAU. Stephney was joined by the Spectrum City DJ crew – Hank and Keith Boxley (later Shocklee) – and Graphic Design student Carlton Ridenhour. The crew would mix tracks on air with Ridenhour (aka Chuck D) rapping over the top in a stentorian boom. One of these on-air jams made its way to Def Jam's Rick Rubin and the abrasive "Public Enemy No. 1" made an immediate impact on his rabble-rousing sensibilities.

With DJ Norman Rogers (Terminator X), Minister of Information Professor Griff (Richard Griffin) and hype man Flavor Flav (William Drayton), an expanded Public Enemy signed to Def Jam in 1987. Produced by the Bomb Squad (the Shocklees and Eric Sadler), their first single, "Public Enemy No. 1" (1987), proved Rubin's instincts correct. With the buzzing Moog intro from the JB's "Blow Your Head" looped into a fierce dissonance, "Public Enemy No. 1" sounded like nothing else – with their very first record they had achieved their ambition: to hit like a Led Zeppelin power chord. **Yo! Bum Rush the Show** (1987) was the sound of a group just finding its feet, nonetheless tracks like "Public Enemy No. 1", "Miuzi Weighs a Ton" and "Rightstarter (Message to a Black Man)" hinted at a group with prodigious talent. It would be realized on their next album.

Like many of hip-hop's biggest celebrities, PE were wracked by paranoia, but instead of wallowing in it like Biggie or Tupac they pro-

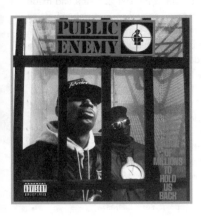

jected it outward on hip-hop's greatest album and one of popular music's true masterpieces, **It Takes a Nation of Millions to Hold Us Back** (1988). Hip-hop as urban noise, as black rage, as punk rock, as revenge fantasy, as community activism, as intellectual rigour – the album was organized chaos. Chuck D embraced Farrakhan, criticized urban radio for backing away from the group's

pro-black politics, slammed drug dealers, declared he was "an un-Tom" and sprayed militant graffiti over the FBI building. Swarming with feedback drones, James Brown horn riffs turned into air-raid sirens, shards of thrash metal guitar, no group had so perfectly matched words and music since the Velvet Underground. But, for all the agit-prop, it was still as funky as hell: "Louder Than A Bomb" sampled and borrowed the dynamics of Kool & the Gang's "Who's Gonna Take the Weight", while Flav threw around surrealist asides like Richard Pryor in a Dali landscape.

The homophobic and anti-Semitic bullshit of Professor Griff got the group in trouble with the media and the spotlight only intensified with the release of the incredible Elvis-dissing "Fight the Power" (1989), which many commentators read as an incitement to violence. Their response to the controversy was "Welcome to the Terrordome" (1990). Perhaps the most radical single to achieve significant sales, "Welcome to the Terrordome" was the Bomb Squad at their most amelodic, intense and seething. **Fear of a Black Planet** (1990) was just as incendiary, and in its way just as awesome, as **It Takes a Nation ...**, even if it lacked its head-spinning sonic invention.

Apocalypse 91 ... The Enemy Strikes Black (1991) was a definite retreat. The dissonance had been replaced by a streamlined funk that, while it still walloped, didn't have anywhere near the force of their previous albums. The group, reeling from media scrutiny, personnel strife and Flavor Flav's personal problems, released the poorly conceived **Greatest Misses** (1992) and the messy, trying-too-hard **Muse Sick-N-Hour Mess Age** (1994). Hip-hop is ruthless: if you miss a step and fail to keep up for even a second it swallows you whole, and the music's standard-bearers fell victim to the very thing that made it so vital. The group fell apart and Chuck released a poorly received solo album, **The Autobiography of Mistachuck** (1996).

After they reunited to work on the soundtrack to Spike Lee's *He Got Game*, they released **There's a Poison Goin' On ...** (1999). They may not have had the millennial fervour of old, but, like Christopher Hitchens, Chuck D was naming names and it wasn't pretty. Everyone from Puffy to Funkmaster Flex to Def Jam came under the gaze of Chuck's rhetorical cross hairs and no one survived intact. No wonder it was almost released exclusively on the Internet. Being pissed off at the industry will never produce music as great as being pissed off with the world, but then again there is no more awesome sound in the world than a pissed off Chuck D, no matter what the reason. As Chuck said, quoting fifteen-times world heavyweight champion, Ric Flair, "If you want to be the man, you got to beat the man." No one has yet.

⊙ **It Takes a Nation of Millions to Hold Us Back**   Def Jam, 1988

Quite simply, the best hip-hop album ever.

Quannum Collective

Running counter to the prevailing reality politiks of rap, the San Francisco Bay Area's Quannum Collective – DJ Shadow, Latyrx and Blackalicious – had their lives saved by hip-hop and want to save yours too. Recognizing the limitations of throwing their guns in the air, the Quannum crew try to get their transcendental groove on with mics and the wheels of steel as their only weapons.

The main players – Shadow, Lyrics Born, Lateef, Chief Xcel and Gift of Gab – first got together in the early '90s while most of the members were attending the University of California at Davis. Turning the college radio station, KDVS, into their own personal clubhouse, the crew raided the record library for rare grooves and spent endless hours in the booths freestyling to the latest instrumentals. While Shadow had material released on Dave Funkenklein's Hollywood Basic label (his remix of Lifers' Group's "Real Deal" and "Lesson 4" in 1991, and the "Legitimate Mix" of Zimbabwe Legit in 1992) as well as work for Tommy Boy, Wild

Pitch and Big Beat, the future for the crew began in 1993 when they formed their own label, Solesides. Their first record was Lyrics Born's (then known as Asia Born) "Send Them" with Shadow's "Entropy", a seventeen minute discourse on why hip-hop culture was dying, on the flip.

Blackalicious (Gift of Gab and Chief Xcel) followed in 1995 with the **Melodica** EP, which featured the classic "Swan Lake", an almighty

MIKE LEWIS

rumination on The Stylistics' "People Make the World Go Round". After some detours on Mo' Wax (Shadow's "Hardcore Hip-Hop" b/w Blackalicious's "Fully Charged on Planet X" and Shadow's landmark **Endtroducing** album (both 1996)), Latyrx (Lateef and Lyrics Born) followed with their self-titled album, featuring wonderful lines like "Suckas steer clear of me like feminists do car shows", and the **Muzapper's Mixes** EP in 1997.

At the end of 1997, however, Solesides was shut down and the crew reorganized as the Quannum Collective with a new label, Quannum Projects. Since making the Quannum leap, they have released two albums, the label showcase **Spectrum** (1999), and Blackalicious's magnificent double album, **Nia** (1999). A sprawl of styles encompassing the sci-fi gamma-tek blasts of "Divine Intervention" (complete with a stentorian rap from the black mystic Vincent Price, Divine Styler), the dystopian claustrophobia of "Looking Over a City" with Company Flow's El-P, straight-up old-school funk on "I Changed My Mind" and "People Like Me", the cheeky ode to the '80s that is "Hott People" and good old-fashioned hip-hop on "Concentration" (with Jurassic 5) and "The Extravaganza" (with Souls of Mischief), **Spectrum** was the sound of the collective showing off their multifaceted skills. **Nia**, meanwhile, and its accompanying **A2G** EP, were showcases for Gift of Gab, who is a walking encyclopedia of MCing styles.

⊙ **DJ Shadow – Endtroducing ...**   Mo' Wax, 1996

An album that proved that trip-hop or instrumental hip-hop or blunted beats, or whatever else you want to call it, wasn't just an excuse for bohemians to drop out.

Queen Latifah

Dana Owens' strength is also, unfortunately, her weakness. With a big, engaging personality, she's a born entertainer, a fact which shines through the mic. But she's an entertainer (and a businesswoman) first and MC second – something that also shines through the mic.

Owens got her start in the rap game as a beatboxer for a high-school rhyme troupe calling themselves Ladies Fresh. After meeting The 45 King, she transformed into Queen Latifah ("Latifah" means "fine, sensitive and delicate" in Arabic) and quickly became the leading light of the Flavor Unit posse. She signed to Tommy Boy and released the landmark **All Hail the Queen** (1989). With her regal mien, Afrocentric dress, charisma and womanist rhymes, Latifah projected an original persona on tracks like "Ladies First" (with Monie Love), "Wrath of My Madness", "Evil That Men Do" (with KRS-One) and "Mama Gave Birth to the Soul Children" (with De La Soul). It was a critically acclaimed album, but went nowhere commercially. However, Latifah clearly made her mark on popular culture and one measure of this is how often she appeared in comedian Sandra Bernhard's routines.

Nature of a Sista (1991), however, was a retreat into the usual roles accorded to women in showbiz and its move into R&B was paradoxically a commercial disaster. Latifah would realize her ambitions, though, by landing a star-ring role on the Fox network's long-running *Living Single* sitcom, not to mention silver-screen appearances in *Jungle Fever*, *Juice*, *House Party 2* and *Set it Off*. **Black Reign** (1993) took Latifah out of the R&B penthouse and back on to the street. That street may have been Fifth Avenue, but at least the excellent "U.N.I.T.Y. (Who

You Calling a Bitch?)" had some royal badness in it and won her a Grammy. **Order in the Court** (1998), however, once again clad Latifah in velvet instead of head wraps as she attempted to go into Lauryn Hill territory on the "Heard it Through the Grapevine"-sampling "Paper".

⊙ **All Hail the Queen**   Tommy Boy, 1989

Both righteous and bumptious, this seemed to the beginning of one of the most promising careers in hip-hop.

Rammellzee

Rapper, wildstyle visual artist, screenwriter and Garbage God cosmologist Rammellzee is one of hip-hop's true originals. Nobody has taken the figurative implications of hip-hop culture as literally or as far out as Rammellzee. He is the prophet of Ikonoklast Panzerism and Gothic Futurism, two homemade philosophies that attempt to make hip-hop's basic tropes – obsession with sci-fi and horror imagery, ritual name-calling, "double-dutch remanipulation" of language and ethos of recreating ready-mades in its own image – the bedrocks of a culture war against a society that has refused to acknowledge the existence, let alone genius, of African and Asian ways of life. He came up with these ideas in 1979 and has doggedly pursued them in a peripatetic career that has included one of the greatest hip-hop jams on wax, symbolically bombing the New York City transit system, gallery exhibitions in New York and Europe, a stint collaborating with Bill Laswell and a screenplay for what he calls an "intellectual horror film".

Aside from his "E.G." (Evolution Griller) tag that plagued Gotham straphangers on the IRT subway line in the '70s, Rammellzee first came to public attention in 1983 with his duel with fellow rapper K-Rob, "Beat Bop". Dressed in a prototypically schematic black and white Jean-Michel Basquiat sleeve that proclaimed its place of origin as "New Yoke, NY", "Beat Bop" picked up where Grandmaster Flash and the Furious Five's "The Message" left off and turned it into a "death, death, death jam y'all". Simultaneously funny, frightening and indecipherable, "Beat Bop" was all about rap as the invention of a new way of speaking: "Like a .38 shootin' real straight/ Because I'm down like a double-dutch remanipulation on the beat Grandmaster make a move when I'm shootin' to the boom-boom". And "Beat Bop" created a new musical language as well. Where most hip-hop tracks of the time had beats that were as subtle as cement shoes, "Beat Bop" was a spongy, dubby, stringy masterpiece that felt like it was flitting in and out of consciousness: off-kilter violins crept into the mix like they were stalking Ramm and K-Rob; everything was surrounded by water-drop percussion and bubbles of sound; the bongos belied, rather than shaped, the groove; one moment Rammellzee sounded like he was rapping from the catacombs, only to surface with pinpoint clarity for the next word. It did indeed sound like "the beat from the depths of Hell".

Ramm then worked with Bill Laswell on his own Gettovets project and provided the hip-hop element in the diasporic funkathon of Sly & Robbie's **Rhythm Killers** (1987) album. **Missionaries Moving**, the 1988 Gettovets album, was pure beatbox treachery. Featuring Ramm, Laswell, Bootsy Collins, Grandmixer D.ST, Nicky Skopelitis and Shock Dell, the album took Rick Rubin's Def Jam experiments with the similarities between the booming systems of metal and hip-hop even further by appending explicit politics to the ensuing collision. "The Lecture" featured Ramm donning his "Master Killer" mask and dropping some demented science over some patented Laswellian industrial funk grooves.

He has spent his time since working on a screenplay/performance art extravaganza called *Letter Racers and Monster Models*. Using graffiti's guerrilla assault on "standard" English and rap's B-movie sensibility as starting points, he has created a mythology of hip-hop in which the taggers' rhetorical bombing raids on subway cars become tangible in an imagined world where the letters of the alphabet are spaceships made of plastic, skateboard wheels, hood ornaments, disused telephones, scrap metal and discarded clothing; a world where rappers are superhero librarians and the wordplay of comic-book characters hits with the ideological force of an Elijah Muhammad hip to Derrida.

⊙ "Beat Bop"   Profile, 1983

Housed in a Jean-Michel Basquiat sleeve, this may be one of the most expensive records in the world, but it's also one of the best. It's available on the *Beat Classic* (DC Recordings, 1997) compilation.

Rawkus Records

Like politics, hip-hop makes strange bedfellows. Indie standard-bearer Rawkus Records allegedly got off the ground with start-up capital from Rupert Murdoch and began its life by releasing records by mobile phone terrorist Scanner. However, after records from the Brick City Kids (aka the Artifacts), B-One and Black Attack, Brian Brater and Jarret Myer's label hit its stride with three of underground hip-hop's biggest anthems.

Featuring Ravi Shankar tuning up on top of funkless drums and brutal scratching, Indelible MCs' (Company Flow with Juggaknots) "Fire in Which You Burn" (1997) had a beat that didn't let record buyers forget about the label's experimental origins and pushed hip-hop about as far as it could possibly go. Reflection Eternal's (Talib Kweli and DJ Hi-Tek, and featuring Mos Def and Mr. Man) "Fortified Live" (1997), on the other hand, was more conventional, but it was still far out enough for Mos Def to utter lines like "Sipping wishing well water imported from Pluto" on top of icicle pianos and ultra-processed guitar. The record that really put Rawkus on the map, though, was Mos Def's "Universal Magnetic" (1997). After reminiscing about *Ten Speed and Brown Shoe* and "Planet Rock", Mos Def mumbled like a depressed Craig Mack with a cold and "kept it raw boned like Skeletor" on top of a sublime Fender Rhodes loop courtesy of Shawn J Period.

MIKE LEWIS

12s from Shabaam Sahdeeq, Sir Menelik, L-Fudge and RA the Rugged Man followed along with Company Flow's boundary-breaking **Funcrusher Plus** album (1997). Black Star's **Mos Def & Talib Kweli Are Black Star** (1998) found Mos Def still sipping the "wishing well water imported from Pluto" and, judging from the vivid rhymes on this record, he was spiking Talib Kweli's Hennessey with it too. While staying true to the eternal verities of hip-hop, Black Star skewered the myth of "keeping it real" ("He was out chasing cream and the American Dream/Trying to pretend that the end justifies the means") and savage "Hater Players" ("You should retire, get that complimentary watch, be out"). More importantly, as their name implied, Black Star imparted hip-hop with some of roots reggae's liberation morality and some of dancehall reggae's guitar licks. The bass sounds – dyspeptic rumbles, snapping elastic thwacks, busted woofer flatulence – would have satisfied Jamaica's low-end theorists, while Shawn J. Period's toy Casio keyboards sent the UK's '70s kitschmeisters back to the schoolyard where they belonged.

Lyricist Lounge (1998), a composite portrait of the art of MCing (freestyling, hip-hop poets, ciphers of MCs hustling for record deals, beatboxing), was a fine survey of underground hip-hop's unique homiletics. The most accessible track was the mightily smooth old-school throwdown "Body Rock", featuring Mos Def, Q-Tip and Tash from The Alkaholiks. Far less polished was the gruff "Famous Last Words" by Word A' Mouth, which used a Tom Waits sample to compensate for some numbskull tough-guy rapping. The album's second disc was hosted by inspired lunatics Kool Keith and Sir Menelik "live at Shea

→

Stadium". The silliness was punctuated by Lord Have Mercy & D.V. alias Khrist's brilliantly bizarre combination of work-song chanting and messianic delusion on "Holy Water". Typically, though, Indelible MCs stole the show with the sequel to their furiously atonal "Fire in Which You Burn": a beat made out of an incredibly harsh drum

machine and the smart bomb sound from an ancient Defender video game.

Rawkus blew up in 1999 with Mos Def's brilliant **Black on Both Sides** album and Pharoahe Monch's "Simon Says" from his **Internal Affairs** album. With a new distribution deal with Priority,

Rawkus moved away from the more radical aspects of underground hip-hop (prompting stalwarts Company Flow to leave the label), although they kept a commitment to the streets with albums from old faves like Kool G Rap and Big L and *Ego Trip* magazine's excellent compilation of obscure hip-hop, **The Big Playback** (2000).

⊙**Soundbombing II**   Rawkus, 1999

All three instalments of the **Soundbombing** series are essentials, but the combination of the outrageous (Pharoahe Monch's "The Mayor" and Company Flow's "Patriotism"), the funky (Dilated Peoples and Tash's "Soundbombing") and slamming (Eminem's "Any Man" and Sir Menelik's "7XL") make this the best of the bunch.

Pete Rock & CL Smooth

" **T**he Chocolate Boy Wonder", Pete "Rock" Phillips is one of the most revered producers in hip-hop. As one of the first hardcore beat diggers to make a name as a producer, Rock has been able to perform a high-wire act by precariously balancing raw beats with melodic loops. Along with A Tribe Called Quest, Rock helped institute hip-hop's love affair with smooth basslines and jazzy horns.

Growing up in money-earnin' Mount Vernon, New York, Rock began his career in the '80s under the aegis of Marley Marl and his cousin Heavy D. After some run-of-the-mill remixes for the likes of Johnny Gill and his incredible remix of Public Enemy's "Shut 'Em Down", Rock teamed up with MC CL Smooth (Corey Penn) for the **All Souled Out** EP (1991). On tracks like "The Creator" and "Go With the Flow", the easy horn stabs blended perfectly with Smooth's technically unblemished, if unincisive, delivery. On "Good Life", they even managed to make their style signify by commenting on the perils of being a middle-class African American in the US.

Dedicated to Heavy D dancer Trouble T-Roy, who died when he fell from a rafter before a concert, "They Reminisce Over You (T.R.O.Y.)" anchored **Mecca and the Soul Brother** (1992) and was the duo's best track. Rock's jazz stylings, which could often be just too damn suave, here imbued Smooth's semi-autobiographical musings and mourning with an emotional depth that very few hip-hop tracks before or since have managed. While not as good, "Ghettos of the Mind", "Straighten it Out", "Lots of Lovin'" and "For Pete's Sake" showed that "T.R.O.Y." was no fluke.

The Main Ingredient (1994) was fine on the skills quotient (nasty breaks and loops, on-point rhymes), but it never went beyond sheer professionalism and the sound was even slicker than before. Soon afterwards the duo split, with Smooth fading into history and Rock working with everyone from Nas and Slick Rick to Common and Janet Jackson. Rock re-emerged from behind the boards on **Soul Survivor** (1998), which found him toning down his horn samples in favour of sparser, less adorned drum beats, but remaining as funky as ever.

⊙ **Mecca and the Soul Brother**   Elektra, 1992

The style may have been eclipsed by hardcore posturing, but this was state-of-the-art hip-hop in the early '90s.

The Roots

The Roots are one of those groups that people respect to the hilt, but don't necessarily like. There's no doubt that they're one of the most original, consistently creative crews around, but their coffee-shop self-righteousness and talkin'-all-that-jazz arrogance alienates much of the hip-hop community, making them pretty much the exclusive property of the bohemian fringe.

The group first took root when MC Black Thought (Tariq Trotter) met beat-maker Ahmir "?uestlove" Thompson (he was originally dubbed B.R.O.theR ?uestion) at Philadelphia's High School for the Creative and Performing Arts in 1987. The duo originally called themselves the Square Roots and acquired a local rep by busking around the City of Brotherly Love. Lacking money for turntables, ?uestlove would imitate classic breakbeats on his drum kit, instilling in the group

MIKE LEWIS

a commitment to performance and live instrumentation. With MC Malik B (Malik Abdul Basit) and bassist Hub (Leonard Hubbard) on board, The Roots recorded their rough debut album, **Organix** (1993), and released it themselves on the Remedy label.

With the mind-boggling human beatboxer Rahzel the Godfather of Noyze and keybs man Kamal, The Roots released **Do You Want More?** in 1995. Drenched in watery Fender Rhodes riffs, **Do You Want More?** perfectly caught the vibe of the jazzy, black bohemian intelligentsia. Although there were no samples, tracks like "Mellow My Man" and "? Vs. Rahzel" proved that their embrace of live instruments wasn't a retrograde step. Nevertheless, they were lumped in with the likes of Digable Planets, a fate which they partially brought on themselves with their "we're giving you what you need, not what you want" rhetoric. The banging "Clones" from **Illadelph Halflife** (1996), however,

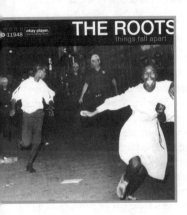

was the best riposte the group could have made. Unfortunately, the rest of the album didn't really go anywhere and they failed to convince that they were anything other than the best live act in hip-hop.

Named after Chinua Achebe's book about the effects of colonialism, **Things Fall Apart** (1999) was the group's most fully realized album and, in spite of its "death of hip-hop" theme, it managed not to sound too convinced of its own magnificence. Although they were unable to escape their own arty ghetto, **Things Fall Apart** engaged more with the real world and the production had emotional depth, not just a patina of cool. Meanwhile, Rahzel released a fine solo album, **Make the Music 2000** (1999), while **The Roots Come Alive** (2000) was a good document of their fearsome prowess on stage, but was let down slightly by some under-par performances.

⊙ **Things Fall Apart**   MCA, 1999

Melancholic but hopeful, this is The Roots' best album by some distance.

Run DMC

T hey may have stopped rocking long before they retired, but Run
DMC will always be hip-hop's Kings of Rock. With drum machine
minimalism like Bruce Lee's one-inch punch, the Hollis, Queens trio of
Run (Joseph Simmons), DMC (Darryl McDaniels) and Jam Master
Jay (Jason Mizell) made music that was as hard as New York liked to
think it was.

Rendering all precursors old hat with one fell swoop, Run DMC's
first single "It's Like That/Sucker MCs" (1983) completely changed hip-
hop. Previously, hip-hop records were pretty much party jams done to
live funk tracks laid down by studio bands. With a spartan, loud, really
loud, rhythm from Orange Krush (Larry Smith) and nothing else,
"Sucker MCs" redefined the b-boy as all attitude: a hard rock with his
arms crossed, a scowl hidden behind his Cazal glasses, untied sneak-
ers, rockin' a fedora like a Hasidic diamond merchant. Their third single, "Rock Box" (1984), featured guitarist Eddie Martinez tearing
through some metallic shards, making their drum machine matrix even
more potent. **Run DMC** (1984) was a collection of their singles, but it
was still hip-hop's first great album.

King of Rock (1985) was a slight disappointment, but the title track
made the implicit message of "Rock Box" crystal clear: Phil Collins and
Bruce Springsteen need to move over and call us "sire" because this is
our time now. In case anyone missed it, they found Aerosmith in the
rehab clinic, dusted them off and released a cover of "Walk This Way"
(1986), which would bring hip-hop to the mainstream for the first time
since the novelty effect of "Rapper's Delight" wore off. While **Raising
Hell** (1986) had obvious cross-over numbers like "Walk This Way" and
"You Be Illin'", it was the pure hip-hop of "Peter Piper", "Perfection",

"It's Tricky" and "My Adidas" that made the record the best early hip-hop album. Co-produced by Def Jam's Rick Rubin and Russell Simmons, **Raising Hell** was the first rap album to go platinum, eventually selling three million copies.

Run DMC opened the doors for hip-hop (even contributing to the album that kicked the door down, the Beastie Boys' *License to Ill*), but

they were locked out almost instantaneously. The Juice Crew, Boogie Down Productions and Public Enemy took hip-hop beyond anyone's expectations and Run DMC couldn't keep up. There was some pretty good music on **Tougher Than Leather** (1988) – "Run's House", "Beats to the Rhyme", "I'm Not Going Out Like That", even the Monkees-sampling "Mary, Mary" – but it was like Perry Como compared to **It**

Takes a Nation of Millions to Hold Us Back or **Straight Outta Compton**.

Back From Hell (1990) found them lagging behind the times, ironically they were trying to sound hard when only seven years earlier they had been meaner than anyone else. Run became Reverend Run for **Down With the King** (1993), and the Christian theme made them hip-hop exiles even though the Pete Rock-produced title track hit the charts. Their **Crown Royal** album was much delayed and seemed doomed to make little impact as architects were about as respected as the Mayor in the hip-hop community.

⊙ **Together Forever: Greatest Hits 1983–1991**   Profile, 1991

The records that made hip-hop hip-hop.

Salt'n'Pepa

The careers of hip-hop's most enduring female rappers can be traced to the Sears Roebuck store on Fordham Avenue in The Bronx. Former Queensborough College students Cheryl James and Sandy Denton were working there when they met co-worker Hurby "Luv Bug" Azor, who persuaded them to record an answer record to Doug E Fresh's "The Show". Credited to Super Nature, "The Show Stoppa (Is Stupid Fresh)" was released on Pop Art three months after "The Show" came out in 1985. Less vitriolic than Roxanne Shanté's "Roxanne's Revenge" (the record's clear inspiration), "The Show Stoppa" was pretty lame, except when they dissed MC Ricky D and his "plastic Ballys and fake gold tooth".

"The salt and pepper MCs" renamed themselves Salt'n'Pepa (adding Spinderella Mark I, Pamela Greene) for their debut album, **Hot, Cool & Vicious** (1986). Including such classics of b-girl attitude as "Tramp" and "Push It", the album went double platinum, making them the first female rappers to achieve such commercial success. For the disappointing **A Salt With a Deadly Pepa** (1988), Dee Dee Roper wore Spinderella's glass slipper, but the change of personnel couldn't help such dire material as a cover of "Twist and Shout" and the ill-advised rock-rap of "I Gotcha".

Abandoning the leather jackets, rope chains and basketball sweats of b-girldom in favour of the push-up bras, high heels and slinky black dresses of R&B, Salt'n'Pepa evolved into the best urban pop group of the first half of the '90s. **Blacks Magic** (1990) was far from a perfect album, but in "Expression" and "Let's Talk About Sex" it featured two singles that out-sassed and out-sexed Madonna on her own turf. **Very Necessary** (1993) followed the same formula, but was even better and eventually sold five million copies thanks largely to the singles "Shoop" and the inspired remake of Lynda Lyndell's "What a Man" featuring En Vogue.

Very Necessary, however, was the group's commercial and artistic peak. **Brand New** (1997) was anything but, and suffered from the group severing ties with Azor, who had produced all of their previous records. Salt now seems more interested in working with Kirk Franklin, while Pepa has concentrated on motherhood after having a child with Naughty By Nature's Treach. Spinderella, meanwhile, is still waiting to release a long-delayed solo project.

⊙**Very Necessary** Next Plateau/London, 1993

Probably the only acceptable union of hip-hop and R&B until Missy Elliott burst on the scene.

Schoolly D

Philadelphia may be known as the City of Brotherly Love and its most famous musical export may be the lush proto-disco of the Philadelphia International label and its theme song, "Love Is the Message", but in hip-hop circles it will go down as the birthplace of gangsta rap. Accessorizing like a b-boy Alexis Carrington and rhyming about street gangs, Schoolly D almost single-handedly invented hardcore hip-hop and "reality rap". It wasn't just Schoolly's lyrics and his matter-of-fact style of reportage that created a new genre, but his music's unrelenting drum machine tattoo and vicious scratching from DJ Code Money that sounded like yanking a jagged knife out of a freshly killed carcass.

Although he had released two singles in 1984, "Gangster Boogie/Maniac" and "CIA/Cold Blooded Blitz", the former Jesse Weaver really exploded on the scene in 1985 with his self-produced, self-released, self-titled EP. Giving shout-outs to Gucci and Fila as well as Philly's notorious Park Side Killers in his trademark "dusted" style, Schoolly was the kind of pitchman corporations have nightmares about. "P.S.K.

'What Does That Mean?'" is the ground zero of gangsta rap: its tale of casual violence and brutal sex was contained by a unbelievably loud boomscape of kick drums, rat-a-tat-tat cymbals and acidic scratching

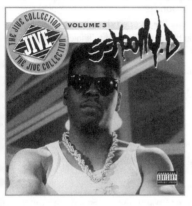

– a sheer powerhouse of sound that wouldn't be equalled until NWA's **Straight Outta Compton**.

Hooking up with engineer Joe "The Butcher" Nicolo, Schoolly released the classic **Saturday Night – The Album** (1987). Introduced by a catchy cowbell pattern and a biting wah-wah guitar, "Saturday Night" was "better" produced than his debut,

but just as raw. Nothing else on the album was as memorable, but "Parkside 5-2" was an obvious model for the Left Coasters, "B-Boy Rhyme and Riddle" was a radical reconstruction of a Sly Stone keyboard riff, and "Housing the Joint" was a response to Spoonie Gee's "The Godfather".

Schoolly signed to Jive and released the disappointing and over-produced **Smoke Some Kill** (1988). Like Philly's favourite son, Rocky Balboa, Schoolly was trying hard now to keep up with the times and **Am I Black Enough For You** (1989) managed to incorporate Schoolly's gangsta persona in the vogue for black nationalism. Tracks like "Livin' in the Jungle", "Gangsta Boogie" and "Black Jesus" were hardly groundbreaking message tracks, but they didn't sacrifice Schoolly's b-boy brio for the sake of political correctness.

How a Black Man Feels (1991), however, did, and the album sucked. **Welcome to America** (1994) returned to criminality, and although the production was good it was obvious that Schoolly was well past his prime. **Reservoir Dog** (1995) found Schoolly going back to producing his own damn self. The stripped-down feel of the tracks certainly framed his gruff style better than any new-fangled production methods, but the Park Side Killer was no longer a thriller.

⊙ **The Jive Collection Series Volume 3**   Jive, 1995

Featuring the pick of both Schoolly D and Saturday Night, this is the best available Schoolly comp.

Slick Rick

Born in the London suburb of Wimbledon in 1965, Ricky Walters moved to The Bronx in 1979, where he became immersed in hip-hop culture. Five years later he met beatboxer extraordinaire Doug E Fresh and the following year Fresh and MC Ricky D changed hip-hop with "The Show/La Di Da Di" (1985), the greatest two-sided single since "Hound Dog/Love Me Tender". "The Show" largely belonged to Fresh's raspberry percussion, but it was clear even in his short rhymes that the real mic talent was Ricky D. Even though it too featured Fresh spittin' like Gene Krupa, "La Di Da Di" was the greatest rap since "The Message". While Rick introduced such immortal lines as "La di da di, we like to party/We don't cause trouble, we don't bother nobody", "La Di Da Di" was so important because of its narrative structure and Rick's understanding of how crucial little sonic details like his female voice and his yawning rap were to hip-hop style.

After splitting with Fresh, Ricky D reinvented himself as Slick Rick and reinforced his reputation as one of hip-hop's greatest MCs with **The Great Adventures of Slick Rick** (1988). Speaking the Queen's English with a gangster lean, Rick told stories like a Homer decked out in an eyepatch, a Kangol and Mr. T chains. Most of his mini-epics were dodgier than Bernard Manning ("Treat Her Like a Prostitute", "Indian Girl (An Adult Story)", "Mona Lisa"), but when he broke into impromptu impressions of King Pleasure and Dionne Warwick he was funnier than Rudy Ray Moore or Redd Foxx. The album's most enduring track was "Children's Story", a cautionary tale that was hip-hop's version of Johnny Cash's "Don't Bring Your Guns to Town".

Unfortunately, Rick didn't heed his own words and on July 3, 1990 he was arrested for attempting to shoot his cousin, who he thought had shot at him two months earlier at a club in The Bronx. He was sentenced to three to ten, but Russell Simmons posted his bail and in marathon recording sessions recorded **The Ruler's Back** (1991). Understandably, given its circumstances, the album wasn't a patch on his debut. **Behind Bars** (1994) was largely recorded while Rick was on work release, but Rick was better at relating the comic-book strips that ran in his head than at telling reality tales.

While Rick was on lockdown (he was released in 1996), hip-hop moved away from

Rick's urban Brothers Grimm style to something more akin to Alain Robbe-Grillet, so when **The Art of Storytelling** arrived in 1999 it sounded as archaic as dixieland jazz. With a glittering cast of thousands, including OutKast, Nas, Snoop and Raekwon, **The Art of Storytelling** was built around simple, Morse Code drum loops that played Rick's straight lines against the new blood's non-planar geometry.

⊙**The Great Adventures of Slick Rick**   Def Jam, 1988

Perhaps the ultimate example of hip-hop's golden rule: it's not what you say, but how you say it.

Snoop Dogg

Announcing his arrival on the scene by bragging about killing an undercover cop, the former Calvin Broadus burst on to the hip-hop scene fully formed. While he had been in the group 213 with Warren G and Nate Dogg, Snoop Doggy Dogg wasn't a local mix-tape legend paying his dues for years before he blew up, unlike so many of his MC peers. Instead, Dre heard one of the group's demos and put Snoop on one of hip-hop's true landmarks. "Deep Cover" (1992), from the Jeff Goldblum movie of the same name, was a menacing track built from an off-kilter piano stab, stunted JB horns, a grimly insistent drum beat, a monotonous bassline and Snoop's shockingly original flow – as if Slick Rick had been born in South Carolina instead of South London.

Snoop was also the star of Dr. Dre's monumental **The Chronic** (1992). Where "Deep Cover" was the heart-stopping, water-rushing-to-the-mouth moment of violence, **The Chronic** was the day leading up to it, making clear the brutality and anger that hid behind the smooth camouflage of much African-American music. Snoop's **Doggystyle** (1993) was the night afterwards. Snoop cruised around sipping on gin and juice, smoking chronic and hitting skins to blunt his pain and blot out his surroundings. On the G-Funk remake of P-Funk's "Atomic Dog", "Who Am I (What's My Name?)", and "Doggy Dogg World" Snoop put the gangsta persona down to talk shit. Elsewhere, he showed where his style came from by covering Slick Rick's "La Di Da Di" (as "Lodi Dodi") and descended into juvenilia on "The Shiznit" and the truly atrocious "Ain't No Fun". Despite its abundant failings, **Doggystyle** was the best-selling hip-hop debut album ever, even outselling **The Chronic**.

Doggystyle's best track, the Tupac-style death fantasy "Murder Was the Case", was remixed and turned into a pointless short movie and soundtrack by Dre. Notable only for Dre's reunion with Ice Cube, **Murder Was the Case** (1994) sold two million, proving just how much Snoop and Dre ruled the roost. However, when his label Death Row started to fall apart and Dre left the label, Snoop foundered. **Tha Doggfather** (1996) was an absolute mess. Produced by a gang of producers like DJ Pooh and Dat Nigga Daz, the album lacked the consistency and quality of Dre's boardwork. Despite the end of the G-Funk era and an abominable cover of Biz Markie's "The Vapors", **Tha Doggfather** still went platinum.

In 1998 Snoop escaped Death Row for a ride in Master P's No Limit tank. With his molasses drawl, Snoop, now calling himself Snoop Dogg, seemed a perfect match for the Beats By the Pound production team's bayou gumbo, but **Da Game Is to Be Sold & Not Be Told** (1998) had too much filler, and "Still a G Thang" showed just how much Snoop needed Dre's effervescence. **No Limit Top Dogg** (1999) was equally tired, the only highlights being the scandalous "B Please"

MICHEL LINSSEN

with Xzibit and the remake of Dana Dane's "Cinderfella Dana Dane", "Snoopafella".

He reunited with Dre on **Dr Dre 2001** (1999), killing it on the album's only good track, "Still D.R.E.". His Doggystyle Records label introduced the platinum-selling Tha Eastsidaz, while his **The Last Meal** (2000) featured potentially a track made in heaven, an NWA reunion with Timbaland producing.

⊙ **Doggystyle**   Death Row, 1993

Snoop's funkiest and best album by some distance.

Special Ed

Edward Archer may have taken his mic name from American slang for the classes for kids with learning difficulties, but his rhyme skills are anything but remedial. Ever since he burst on the scene as a precocious sixteen-year-old in 1989, Special Ed has been regarded as one of hip-hop's most gifted MCs. Ed not only had a flair for rhyming boasts, but, along with Kid from Kid'N Play, he had the definitive hi-top fade (complete with racing stripes).

His debut album, **Youngest In Charge** (1989), was produced by Hitman Howie Tee and featured at least four stone-cold classics. "I Got it Made" was a minimal masterpiece of braggadocio, as was the Dave and Ansel Collins-sampling "I'm the Magnificent". "Taxing" liberally sampled The Beatles' "Sgt. Pepper's Lonely Hearts Club Band" and featured a pretty ridiculous rhyme scheme, while the title track cemented Ed's reputation for arrogance. The only weak cut on **Youngest In Charge** was the truly abysmal "Club Scene".

Legal (1990) saw Ed celebrating the fact that he had reached voting age. While the title track and the spy fantasy "The Mission" showed that he was as fresh as ever, the production and lyrics of numbers like "Come On Let's Move" were stagnant at a time when hip-hop was moving in leaps and bounds. After a couple of years of bit-part acting roles on *The Cosby Show* and *Juice*, Ed re-emerged as part of the Crooklyn Dodgers (with Masta Ace, Buckshot and, later, Chubb Rock) for the classic "Crooklyn" (1994) (from the soundtrack to Spike Lee's *Crooklyn*) and the less classic "Return of the Crooklyn Dodgers" (1995).

With the success of the Crooklyn Dodgers project, Ed released the solo album, **Revelations** (1995). Although it was met with resounding indifference, **Revelations** was a decent attempt at offering an alternative to thug life. The only problem was that Ed's flow, once among the dopest in hip-hop, was now as archaic as a Louis Armstrong scat. Undeterred, Ed forged ahead with his own label, Sure Shot, and got some underground props for "Think Twice" (1997), but he has done little of note since.

⊙ **Youngest In Charge**   Profile, 1989

Special Ed's flow is hopelessly dated now, but at the time this represented the pinnacle of mic skills.

Spice 1

C alling his brand of hip-hop "suicide rap", Spice 1 is one of the best gangsta rappers around. Although he has only contributed one real innovation (his rapid-fire delivery), Spice 1 deserves gangsta canonization for consistency and staying power. He may have been born in Texas, but by chronicling the horrors of the streets in Hayward and Oakland, California, Spice 1 ranks just below Too $hort as an East Bay original.

In fact Too $hort gave Spice (when he was still calling himself MC Spice) his start by signing him to his Dangerous Music label in 1987. Although Spice appeared on a Dangerous compilation, it wasn't until 1991's **Let it Be Known** EP that he made a name for himself. Over the top of trademark slippery East Bay funk from producer Ant Banks, Spice 1 unleashed a ragga-tinged, light-speed, tongue-twisting flow that would become a key weapon in gangsta rap's arsenal, influencing such artists as Bone Thugs-N-Harmony and Three 6 Mafia. The EP's hit, "187 Proof", reappeared on his debut album, **Spice 1** (1992), along with the equally influential "East Bay Gangster", "Peace to My Nine" and "Money Gone".

187 He Wrote (1993) didn't push his style into any new directions, but it did feature one of the all-time gangsta classics, "Trigga Gots No Heart". Over a whining synth and a dramatic blaxploitation strings/bass beat, Spice relates his tale of carefree murder with a chilling flow that was the diametric opposite of the cartoonish excesses of most West Coast street bards. The track was so brutally effective that it would later appear on the soundtrack to *Menace II Society*. Elsewhere, "The Murda Show" saw Spice and  Compton's MC Eiht prove that G-Funk was the universal language throughout California.

Amerikkka's Nightmare (1994) followed pretty much the exact same formula. Nonetheless, it had one classic moment in the collaboration with long-time friend 2Pac, "Jealous Got Me Strapped". **1990-Sick** (1996) continued along the same lines as he collaborated again with MC Eiht on the gruesome title track and removed the metaphors from Run DMC's "Sucker MCs" and remade it as the no-holds-barred "Sucka Ass Niggas". **The Black Bossalini (aka Dr. Bomb From Da Bay)** (1997) didn't go anywhere new either, but "Playa Man" found Spice getting pimp-silly over a Curtis Mayfield-esque beat from Paris.

Although the production from Rick Rock was somewhat dated, his sixth album, **Immortalized** (1999), attempted to keep up with the East Coast sound, with a cameo from Noreaga and Spice now calling his rhymes "thug poetry".

⊙ **Spice 1 Hits**   Jive, 1998

Featuring all his hits from "187 Proof" to "Sucka Ass Niggas", there's no reason to buy another Spice 1 album.

Spoonie Gee

As Cheryl the Pearl from The Sequence said, "MC Spoonie Gee/Ain't a man quite like he". Credited with inventing the term "hip-hop" along with "yes, yes y'all" and "One for the trouble, two for the time/Come on y'all, let's rock that ...", Spoonie Gee was perhaps the first great MC. Even though his speciality was crowd-rocking non-sense rhymes, he saw himself as a loveman in the tradition of Marvin Gaye and Nat "King" Cole, and his extensions of the tradition of street-corner boasting brought sex talk into hip-hop.

Gabe Jackson was twelve when his mother died and he was raised by his uncle, Bobby Robinson, head of the Enjoy label. Although Spoonie (his *nom de mique* was his childhood nickname, derived from his habit of eating only with a spoon) inspired Robinson to start releasing rap records, Spoonie's own debut was on the Sound of New York USA label. "Spoonin' Rap" (1980) was a dense layering of percussion over which Spoonie introduced many of early hip-hop's catch phrases. Spoonie's next record was released on Enjoy and is one of the true landmarks of the genre. "Love Rap" (1980) found Spoonie telling tall tales about his prowess, on top of Pumpkin's drums, and congas by Spoonie's brother, Pooche Costello. Unlike just about every other hip-hop record of the period, "Love Rap" was just beats and rhymes and helped inaugurate the minimalism that would characterize the music over the next several years. The flip, "New Rap Language", featured Spoonie trading rhymes with LA Sunshine, Kool Moe Dee and Special K, aka the Treacherous Three, and it too, with its rapid-fire freestyle feel, changed the face of hip-hop.

A year later Spoonie moved to cross-Harlem rivals Sugar Hill, where he re-recorded "Spoonin' Rap" and teamed up with The Sequence for "Monster Jam" (1981), one of the great old-school throwdowns. "Spoonie's Back" (1981) followed, before Spoonie moved once again to Aaron Fuch's Tuff City label and released the DMX masterpiece, "The Big Beat" (1983). After a few more tracks produced by Davy DMX and Pumpkin, Spoonie laid low before re-emerging with **The Godfather** (1987). The title track was produced by Marley Marl, and the rhymes that attacked Schoolly D for biting his style demonstrated that Spoonie had made the transition from old to new school with ease. While nothing else on the album could match "The Godfather"'s rumbling bassline and JB guitar lick production, "Take it Off" had sprightly production backing Spoonie's slightly stale chat-up lines, while "Hit Man" featured boardwork from a young Teddy Riley. Unfortunately, Spoonie's been in and out of jail ever since.

⊙**The Godfather of Hip-Hop**   Tuff City, 1997

This compiles almost all of Spoonie's early and best hits. An essential document.

Stetsasonic/ Prince Paul

From the time Prince Paul Houston started DJing for fellow Long Islander Biz Markie as a thirteen-year-old, it's been clear that he was one of hip-hop's true originals. Comprised of rearranged ready-mades, hip-hop is the ultimate postmodern form, but it took the boy-genius from Amityville, Long Island to bring a playful self-consciousness and a stylistic promiscuity to the music. Taking his inspiration from the deranged cinematic sweep of George Clinton's Parliafunkadelicment Thang, Prince Paul has viewed hip-hop as his own playground and is one of the few producers to make hip-hop hit as hard conceptually as it does sonically.

Prince Paul first caught the attention of Stetsasonic (Daddy-O, Delite, Fruitkwan, DBC and Wise) during a DJ battle in Brooklyn in 1984 and they asked him to be the group's DJ. Stetsasonic had just won the Mr. Magic talent contest and with Paul on turntables they recorded "Just Say Stet" (1985) – a showcase for beatboxer Wise – for Tommy Boy. **On Fire** (1986) advertised the group as "the world's only hip-hop band" and, with an infectious group camaraderie fleshing out the sparse 808 beats on tracks like "Go Stetsa 1", "My Rhyme" and "A.F.R.I.C.A.", they helped usher in hip-hop's most creative period.

In Full Gear (1988) was the group's masterpiece. Using the bassline from Lonnie Liston Smith's "Expansions", "Talkin' All That Jazz" was not only the best defence of sampling this side of Public Enemy, but it anticipated the jazzmatazz of Guru, Us 3 and the Dream Warriors. "Sally" was just as musically rich and became a big radio hit, while Paul's "Music For the Stetfully Insane" was stunningly abstract and prefigured his mind-bending productions for De La Soul. "Freedom or Death" followed "A.F.R.I.C.A." as a revolutionary message that would inspire a mini-generation of "conscious rappers". While most New York-based hip-hop acts had a similar outlook to the famous *New Yorker* cartoon showing the Manhattanite's world view more or less ending at the Hudson River, Stetsasonic ventured into the Jamaican dancehall on "The Odad" and gave props to "Miami Bass".

Although it was pleasant enough, **Blood, Sweat and No Tears** (1991) suffered from Paul's involvement with De La Soul and was achingly complacent at a time when the best hip-hop was all about breaking paradigms. At the time Paul had become the most in-demand producer in hip-hop, working with MC Lyte, 3rd Bass, Big Daddy Kane and Boogie Down Productions as well as his famous partnership with De La Soul. Stetsasonic soon dissolved, with Daddy-O going on to work with Mary J. Blige and the Red Hot Chili Peppers among others.

In 1994 Prince Paul joined up again with Fruitkwan, along with the RZA and Poetic, to form the Gravediggaz. Ingesting bad vibes, splatter flicks and Grim Reaper tales, Paul spat out the Gravediggaz' debut album, **6 Feet Deep** (1994), as an act of catharsis. Finding himself suddenly a hip-hop outcast after the commercial failure of De La Soul's **Buhloone Mindstate** and enduring a custody battle over his son, Paul rewrote the black American experience as a shoddy horror flick with really bad special effects and **6 Feet Deep** was shunned by critics as a "horrorcore" gimmick. **The Pick, The Sickle and The Shovel** (1998) followed in a similar style, but this time it really was a gimmick.

With the hip-hop skit which he invented on De La Soul's first album and the cartoon gothic imagery of the Gravediggaz, Paul's individual signature as a producer was the sight gags and scenarios that he conjures from purely sonic information. This was writ large on **Psychoanalysis (What Is It?)** (1996). With its evocations of raunchy Rudy Ray Moore party albums and distillation of every crap skit from every hip-hop album of the previous six years into a handful of comic gems, **Psychoanalysis** was one of the more successful explorations of scatalogy since NWA's **Straight Outta Compton**.

Paul's widescreen vision achieved its fullest expression on his **A Prince Among Thieves** (1999) album. Although hailed in many quarters as a work of genius, the narrative of this hip-hop musical (conceived as a film soundtrack) was a bit forced and a bit trite. The music, however, was anything but, and there are some good moments (particularly De La Soul's "More Than U Know") here. His next project, Handsome Boy Modeling School, saw him team up with Dan "The Automator" Nakamura. The fashion-lounge-lizard concept of **So ... How's Your Girl?** (1999) may have been a bit pointless, but the music was as suave, stylish, sophisticated and lovely as the Handsome Boys thought they were. With gorgeous torch songs, wild turntable cut-ups, mondo bizarro sci-fi and a glittering line-up of cameos, **So ... How's Your Girl?** showed that the catwalk was just as vital to hip-hop as the streets and that Prince Paul's imagination knows no bounds.

⊙ **Stetsasonic – In Full Gear**   Tommy Boy, 1988

Aside from the awful remake of The Floaters' "Float On" with Full Force, this is one of the most influential, and most slept on, albums in hip-hop's history.

⊙ **Handsome Boy Modeling School –**
So ... How's Your Girl?   Tommy Boy, 1999

Not one for the hip-hop purists, but as an expansion of boundaries it was Paul's best since De La Soul.

Stone's Throw

Indie standard-bearer Stone's Throw Records was formed by Chris Manak (aka Peanut Butter Wolf, a name he got from an old girlfriend's kid brother's name for the bogeyman) in 1993 after the murder of his partner in rhyme, Charizma. The label's first couple of releases were taken from tapes Charizma and PBW had made in 1992, but the Wolfman didn't really make a name for himself until his contribution to the **Return of the DJ** (1995) compilation. A response to Common's "I Used to Love H.E.R.", "The Chronicles (I Will Always Love H.E.R.)" was an optimistic collage that moved from Mr. Magic to Jeru the Damaja. Given his upbringing in the suburban wasteland of San Mateo, California – the stronghold of Van Halen and Slayer – it is perhaps surprising that "The Chronicles" remains the definitive hip-hop history lesson on wax.

Particularly among Europe's trip-hop fraternity, PBW garnered more attention for his production work, most notably his **Peanut Butter Breaks** LP and the **Lunar Props** EP (both 1996). These collections of fleshed-out beats were the remnants of his pre-maturely halted collaboration with Charizma. Stone's Throw, however, really established itself with Rasco's big indie hit, "The Unassisted" (1996). With minimal production based around a stunted guitar stab, "The Unassisted" led the way for under-ground hip-hop's challenge to the jiggy good life fantasies of the mainstream. Rasco's fine album **Time Waits For No Man** (1998) showed him to be a gravel-throated battle-rhymer capable of smoking just about any kind of beat. Even better was his **The Birth** EP (1999) (released on Britain's Copasetik label) on which Rasco traded Peanut Butter Wolf's beats for the more direct, more neck-snapping rhythms of Moleman His-Panik. The more streamlined, less adorned beats on **The Birth** highlighted Rasco's awesome skills. Not much of a wordsmith, Rasco got over solely on the strength of one of the purest flows in the business. Teaming up with Planet Asia as Cali Agents, Rasco bit the hand that fed him (if not his daughter) on **How the West Was Won** (2000): "I'm telling your ass that I'm out to make cash/I'm a revoke your little hip-hop pass ... I'm not in the game for tryin' to break my neck/My little baby girl can't eat your respect".

While the label was developing some fine MCs, they also gave plenty of space for turntablists with Babu's **Super Duck Breaks** and Rob Swift's **Soulful Fruit** (1997) and the technics summit, "Tale of Five Cities", on PBW's **My Vinyl Weighs a Ton** album

→

(1999). On **Sound Pieces – Da Antidote** (1999) the Likwit Crew's Lootpack defined the underground's mind-set: they weren't afraid to admit that they still went to open-mic nights to keep their flows tight; they turned the "Crate Digga" into a superhero; they "break MCs on contact" by using the "laws of physics"; and they realized that not being down with them didn't mean that you weren't real. Although it tied MCs Wildchild and Madlib in knots, the production on "Friends Vs. Ends" was a killer cut-up of a rare groove track. Best line: "I'm going to carbonate your flow because it sounds flat". Madlib's alter ego, Quasimoto, released the excellent **The Unseen** (2000), which featured a flow that sounded like Q-Tip played at about 39 rpm.

In 1999 Stone's Throw instituted a 7" series with Breakestra's revivalist "Getchyo Soul Togetha", A-Trak's "Enter Ralph Wiggum", and the E-40/electro piss-take, El Captain Funkaho's "My 2600".

⊙ **Rasco – The Birth**   Copasetik, 1999

The pleasures of this EP are strictly formal: you won't remember one word he says, but his flow is pretty devastating.

⊙ **Lootpack – Sound Pieces –**
    Da Antidote   Stone's Throw, 1999

They may not be making any great stylistic leaps, but zingers like "Your mom rhymes better than you/She's deaf and mute" make this worth a spin or two.

Sugar Hill

Growing out of a soul/disco label called All Platinum, Joe and Sylvia Robinson's Sugar Hill (from the Sugar Hill area of Harlem) was hip-hop's most important early label. The irony of Sugar Hill's position, though, was that many of its artists were not part of the early hip-hop scene and its use of an admittedly awesome house band pushed hip-hop away from its roots as a genre based on breakbeats.

Sugar Hill was not the first label to release a rap record (that was Spring, who released The Fatback Band's "King Tim III (Personality Jock)" a few months earlier), but their October 1979 release of Sugar Hill Gang's "Rapper's Delight" was truly when hip-hop moved out of the South Bronx and Harlem. Based on the groove of Chic's "Good Times", it remains one of the most infectious records ever made, but its success had very little to do with "Big Bank Hank" Jackson, Guy

"Master Gee" O'Brien and Wonder Mike Wright: it was largely the product of Nile Rodgers' guitar riffs, Bernard Edwards' bassline and lyrics lifted from the Cold Crush Brothers' Grandmaster Caz's rhyme book.

Sugar Hill's next release was The Sequence's "Funk You Up" (1979). Although they had their own rhymes (well, sort of – a lot of their lyrics were based on nursery rhymes and classic street-corner toasts) and were, along with Paulette and Tanya Winley, the first women to record hip-hop, Cheryl "The Pearl" Cook, Gwen "Blondie" Chisholm and Angie B. Brown were interlopers from outside of the core hip-hop scene. The group was discovered in South Carolina by the Sugar Hill house band (bassist Doug Wimbish, guitarist Skip McDonald, drummer Keith LeBlanc, percussionist Duke Bootee, keyboardist Nate Edmunds and the Chops horns) and brought to New York to record such classics as "Funk You Up", "And You Know That" (1981) and "Monster Jam" with Spoonie Gee (1981).

With the release of Grandmaster Flash & the Furious Five's "Freedom" (1980), Sugar Hill had finally released a record by one of hip-hop's true innovators. Flash & the Five released some of hip-hop's greatest records on Sugar Hill: "Adventures of Grandmaster Flash on the Wheels of Steel" (1981), "The Message" (1982), "Flash to the Beat" (1982), "Scorpio" (1982), "It's Nasty (Genius of Love)" (1982), "New York, New York" (1983) and "White Lines (Don't Do It)" (1983). Flash and crew's defection from the Enjoy label meant that others soon followed: Spoonie Gee, Treacherous Three and Funky Four + 1. The Funky Four + 1 (Lil' Rodney Cee, KK Rockwell, Keith Keith, Jazzy Jeff, Sha Rock and DJ Breakout) had previously recorded the remarkable "Rappin' and Rockin' the House" on Enjoy. Their first record for Sugar Hill was "That's the Joint" (1981), a reworked version of "Rappin' and Rockin' the House" that features a sublime interaction between a complex arrangement and party-rockin' rhymes.

As a result of using a live band to back MCs, Sugar Hill's records actually had more in common with Washington DC's go-go scene than it did with hip-hop. One of go-go's leading bands, Trouble Funk, recorded such classics as "Pump Me Up", "Drop the Bomb" and "Hey

Fellas" (all 1982) for Sugar Hill. Members of Trouble Funk had previously been part of Chuck Brown's Soul Searchers, whose "Ashley's Roach Clip" is one of the all-time hip-hop beats.

The Incredible Bongo Band's "Apache" is *the* hip-hop beat and it appeared on West Street Mob's b-boy scratchfest, "Break Dancin' – Electric Boogie" (1983). By this time, though, Run DMC had emerged and Sugar Hill's style was rapidly becoming passé. They managed to delay the inevitable with records like Crash Crew's Bob James cut-up, "Breaking Bells (Take Me to the Mardi Gras)" (1982), and "We Are Known As Emcees (We Turn the Party Out)" (1983), Busy Bee's Kid Rock-inspiring "Making Cash Money" (1982), Reggie Griffin's fearsome "Mirda Rock" (1982) and Kevie Kev's Jones Girls pastiche, "All Night Long (Waterbed)" (1983).

With the possible exception of Treacherous Three's "Turning You On" (1984), however, Sugar Hill was quickly replaced at the top by Profile and Def Jam in the mid-'80s and the label faded into obscurity. Still, with their innocence and charm, Sugar Hill's records remain some of the greatest pop music ever made.

⊙ **The Sugar Hill Story –**
   Old School Rap to the Beat Y'All   Sequel, 1992

Compiled by old-school chronicler David Toop, this three-CD set is pretty much definitive.

Three 6 Mafia

A long with New Orleans, Memphis is the cradle of American music, but ever since Al Green went gospel M-Town hasn't had a lot to shout about. Although their success is strictly regional, Three 6 Mafia and their Hypnotize Minds Crew (Gangsta Boo, Indo G, Project Pat, Pastor Troy and Killa Klan) are just about the only names Memphis has had to brag about recently (unless you count lo-fi indie rockers The Grifters). And while their guardians-of-morality-baiting tales of pimping, ho-slapping and murder don't exactly take the high-road, their subject matter isn't really all that different from the group that originally put Memphis on the map, The Memphis Jug Band.

Three 6 Mafia started courting the devil when Juicy J met DJ Paul in the early '90s. With Paul's brother Lord Infamous in tow, they formed the Triple Six Mafia and quickly became mix-tape legends in Memphis. Early tracks like Kingpin Skinny Pimp's "One Life 2 Live" (1995) were largely imitative of the Cali sound, but with even more brutal fatalism. In 1995 they changed their name to Three 6 Mafia and released their first album, **Mystic Styles**, which featured more uninspiring remakes of the West Coast gangsta/mack formula like "Throw Your Set". After two more underground albums, **Live By Yo Rep** (1996) (the title track was a savage dis of Bone Thugs-N-Harmony) and **The End** (1997), the Mafia blew up with **Chapter 2: World Domination** (1997). A remix of "Tear Da Club Up" (which had first appeared in 1995 and would reappear again and again) epitomized the new sound emerging from the Dirty South: Juicy, Paul, Infamous and Gangsta Boo rapped in rapid-fire cadences that mirrored the skittering drum machines firing off in the background, while the slow and low bassline was aimed at Memphis dancers doing the gangsta walk. With its mournful piano line and huge, victorious synth washes, "Tear Da Club Up" was as garish as Siegfried & Roy, but it was crunker than anything Master P could come up with. Even bigger in the clubs was "Hit a Muthafucka" which has surely the most outrageous murder/killing a crowd metaphor ever: if you weren't listening close it sounded like they were bragging about murdering the audience, literally – even Johnny Rotten never went that far.

Capitalizing on their success the Mafia renamed themselves Tear Da Club Up Thugs for the **Crazyndalazdayz** album (1999), but the real action was on Indo G's **Angel Dust** (1998) and Gangsta Boo's **Enquiring Minds** (1998). Recalling Organized Noize's productions for Outkast and Goodie Mob, Indo G's "Remember Me Ballin'" was a gangsta's prayer to rank with Ice Cube's "It Was a Good Day" and "Dead Homiez", while Gangsta Boo's "Where Dem Dollars At" was a slow-rolling Southern bounce track that was a big hit in strip clubs. Project Pat's **Ghetty Green** (1999) featured "Ballers", which was produced by Cash Money producer Mannie Fresh, and an ill-advised interpolation of The O'Jays' "Back Stabbers". Throwing taste out the door altogether, **Three 6 Mafia Presents Hypnotize Minds Camp Posse** (2000) was a collection of blue humour and really dirty jokes ("Azz & Tittiez", "D_ck Suckin' Hoes") that were so nasty that they would have been bowdlerized by Blowfly. **When the Smoke Clears – Sixty 6, Sixty 1** (2000) took their Southern gothic style to even more outrageous levels: after some Bible verses and a Portishead sample, "Sippin' On Syrup" was an ode to the most bizarre hip-hop tipple since formaldehyde syrup (a concoction of cough syrup, vodka and, wait for it, milk of magnesia).

⊙ **Chapter 2: World Domination**   Hypnotize Minds/Relativity, 1997

As they say, "We ain't talkin' about bustin' pimples", but this violent, misogynist and bouncing album epitomized Southern hip-hop.

Timbaland

I f hip-hop was all about the lyrics, Timbaland (aka Tim Mosley) would be somewhere in line between Candyman and Father MC to get into this book. But, while Timbaland has made most of his noise in the R&B world, he's still the most important and influential producer of the last half of the '90s. Hip-hop's obsession with space hopper funk, digital tics, what journalist Sasha Frere-Jones has called "typewriter Funk", it's all down to Timbaland.

The Virginian Björk fan got his start in Da Bassment, a posse of producers, songwriters and MCs who worked in the background behind hot-tub lovemen Jodeci. He stepped out on his own in 1996 on two R&B albums that kicked tired slow-jammers out of the penthouse: Ginuwine's **The Bachelor** and Aaliyah's **One in a Million**. Then, Tim dropped the album that would change R&B forever, Missy "Misdemeanor" Elliott's **Supa Dupa Fly** (1997). The wild futurism – hyper-syncopated beats, almost surreal digital sheen and cyberdelic Kingston dancehall feel – on tracks like "Hit 'Em Wit Da Hee" and "The Rain (Supa Dupa Fly)" has since been appropriated by every producer in the business.

On his debut album as an artist, Timbaland & Magoo's **Welcome to Our World** (1997), he made you ignore how bad his lyrics were by layering skittering high-hats, Gothic synth-string stabs and liquid-mercury keyboards on "Up Jumps Da Boogie", and remaking James Brown as the protagonist of *Tron* on "Luv 2 Luv U". **Tim's Bio: Life From Da Bassment** (1998) found him mining funk from the themes to *Spider-Man* and *I Dream of Jeanie* and disguising his mic incompetence with appearances from Nas, Jay-Z and Mad Skillz.

It was his outside productions, however, that made Timbaland's name in 1998. Aaliyah's "Are You That Somebody?" was a stunning record constructed out of bionic human beatboxing, gurgling babies and a Swiss cheese rhythm track, while "Paper Chase" and "Jigga What, Jigga Who" from Jay-Z's **Volume 2 ... Hard Knock Life** album

took him out of the ghetto and into orbit. Tim reappeared on Jay-Z's **Vol. 3 ... Life and Times of S. Carter** (1999) to make the dark hole of "It's Hot" and the Gulf of Mexico synth zephyrs on "Big Pimpin'". Missy Elliott's **Da Real World** (1999) was disappointing, aside from its incredible trio of singles, "She's a Bitch", "All in My Grill" and "Hot Boyz", but Tim-

baland's so hot it's entirely likely he'll reinvent R&B and hip-hop again before he's through.

⊙ **Tim's Bio: From Life From Da Bassment**   Blackground, 1998

Eventually Tim will get a retrospective, but until that time this half-mind-boggling album will have to do.

Tommy Boy

Like a surprisingly large number of New Yorkers at the time, in 1979 Tom Silverman was the publisher/editor/writer of a dance music 'zine, *Disco News*. Stumbling across the nascent hip-hop culture in a Times Square record store, Silverman journeyed up to White Plains Road in The Bronx to hear Afrika Bambaataa spin at the T-Connection club. After his conversion experience, Silverman soon set up his own label, Tommy Boy, which he ran from his apartment on the Upper East Side.

His first signing was Bambaataa and his Cosmic Force MCs, who released their first record for the label under the name of Bon Rock and Cotton Candy ("Junior Wants to Play" (1981)). The group had previously recorded for the Winley label, but the record that established Bambaataa (outside of The Bronx at least) and Tommy Boy was "Jazzy Sensation" (1981), credited to Afrika Bambaataa & the Jazzy 5. The record was produced by Arthur Baker and mixed by Shep Pettibone and, although it was based on Gwen McRae's "Funky Sensation", its Casio clavé and synth-dominated instrumental B-side marked the move away from the live instrumentation of the Sugar Hill sound. Even more of an upheaval, however, was Bambaataa & Soulsonic Force's "Planet Rock" (1982), whose electro-funk single-handedly started the Electro and Miami Bass genres and became one of the most important records of the '80s.

With records by Planet Patrol ("Play at Your Own Risk" (1982)), Jonzun Crew ("Pack Jam" (1982) and "Space Cowboy" (1983)), the Force MDs ("Let Me Love You" (1983)) and Keith LeBlanc/Malcolm X ("No Sell Out" (1983)), Tommy Boy quickly

→

replaced Sugar Hill as the leading hip-hop label. Despite its pre-eminence, the label's greatest record was never released, being the victim of corporate copyright robber-barons. The winner of a contest held by Tommy Boy for mastermixes of G.L.O.B.E. & Whiz Kid's 1983 single "Play That Beat Mr. DJ", Double Dee & Steinski's "The Payoff Mix" (1984) became an enormous cult hit in New York by virtue of its prescient reading of sampling as the

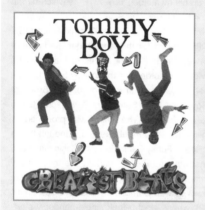

modern equivalent to the call-and-response that characterized African-American music. The work of studio engineer Doug DiFranco and advertising jingle producer Steve Stein, "The Payoff Mix" was the result of endless hours in the studio literally cut-ting and pasting together tapes of Spoonie Gee, "Soul Power" chants courtesy of Bobby Byrd, Funky Four +1 "It's the Joint", the World Famous Supreme Team radio show, Incredible Bongo Band's "Apache", Culture Club, Little Richard, exercise routines, Humphrey Bogart, Herbie Hancock's "Rockit", The Supremes' "Stop in the Name of Love", Grandmaster Flash, Chic

→

and about a hundred other things, not to mention "Play That Beat Mr. DJ". "The Payoff Mix" was scheduled to be released on an EP with the equally mind-boggling "Lesson Two: The James Brown Mix" and "Lesson Three: The History of HipHop", but they have only ever appeared on bootlegs.

As hip-hop matured, Tommy Boy kept pace with landmark releases by Stetsasonic, De La Soul, Queen Latifah, Digital Underground, House of Pain, Naughty By Nature, Paris, Coolio, Screwball and any number of Prince Paul projects. Closing in on their twentieth year of operation, and now run by Monica Lynch, Tommy Boy started the Tommy Boy Black imprint to showcase underground talent like The Jigmastas, Self Scientific, Natural Elements and DV Alias Khrist.

⊙ Tommy Boy – Greatest Beats	Tommy Boy, 1998

Housed in a mini-milk-crate, this four-CD, 56-track compilation is easily the best label overview available.

Too $hort

He may have only one subject, but no one in hip-hop has had a longer career than Oakland's Too $hort. Despite the East Coast bias of most hip-hop histories, for better or worse Too $hort will eventually go down as one of the three or four most important hip-hop artists. The entire West Coast style can be traced back to Too $hort's obsession with P-Funk, synth hooks and, of course, "beeeyitches".

Todd Shaw was born in 1966 in Los Angeles, but at fourteen he moved to Oakland to escape LA's gang culture. The Bay Area may not have had the gang problems, but it was awash with prostitution. Inspired by his surroundings, Shaw invented a character called Too $hort (aka $horty the Pimp, $hort Dog, etc), a game-talking, bitch-slapping, dank-smoking mack. With schoolmate Freddy B, $hort made like an African praise singer and made customized tapes for specific customers, which glorified their customers' deeds in music. Soon enough, $hort and Freddy could be found on buses selling their tapes for $5 a pop and the two quickly became Bay Area celebs.

In 1983, $hort released **Don't Stop Rappin'** and **Players** on the tiny 75 Girls label. Nothing coming out of New York sounded anything like this: although there were booming drum machines and Bambaataa-styled vocoders, with whining synths straight out of the Bernie Worrell songbook, tracks like "Don't Stop Rappin'" sounded closer to Prince than Grandmaster Flash, while $hort's blue lyrics couldn't have

been further from the social commentary and "Yes, yes y'all"-ing coming from the Rotten Apple.

Raw, Uncut and X-Rated (1985), however, really set Too $hort apart. Over a bass-heavy groove, "Flat Booty Bitches" laid out $hort's nightmare: he crosses over the border into Berkeley and "sees nothing but bitches with no ass". "She's a Bitch", "The Bitch Sucks Dick" and "Blow Job Betty" continued the theme. Not only had no one heard such language on vinyl since Blowfly and Lightnin' Rod, but the Clintonian synth-funk had gotten even more pronounced and laid the foundation for NWA, E-40, Dr. Dre, Ant Banks, Spice 1, Eightball & MJG, etc. The best drug song since Melle Mel's "White Lines", "Girl" (1985) was $hort's first 12" and proved that he was more than just Rudy Ray Moore without a sense of humour.

Born to Mack (1986) was originally released on his own Dangerous Music label. When $hort signed to Jive Records, the album was re-released and it introduced the rest of the world to $horty the Player. Entirely self-produced, the album nailed the $hort formula and tracks like "Freaky Tales" and "Dope Fiend Beat" became landmarks of Californian hip-hop. **Life Is ... Too $hort** (1988) saw $hort work with Oakland producer Al Eaton, who fleshed out $hort's signature sound, and tracks like "City of Dope" and "Don't Fight the Feeling" benefited from the higher production values.

$hort Dog's in the House (1990) followed with a more LA-influenced sound (courtesy of co-producer Sir Jinx) and featured his biggest hit to date, a chilling, Last Poets-sampling update of Donny Hathaway's "The Ghetto". **$horty the Pimp** (1992), **Get in Where You Fit in** (1993) and the appropriately named **Cocktales** (1995) all followed in a similar style, helping $hort notch his sixth platinum album along the way.

$hort claimed that he was retiring after **Gettin' It (Album Number Ten)** (1996), but it was merely a clever ploy to renegotiate his contract with Jive. The album was pretty much business as usual, but it was notable for the title track, which saw $hort working with George Clinton. **Can't Stay Away** (1999) was $hort's "return" and, sure enough, things hadn't changed a bit. He even resorted to remaking "Invasion of the Flat Booty Bitches" (admittedly, it was pretty good) and "Freaky Tales". His eleventh album, **You Nasty** (2000), was the same old concoction of pimp shit and funk beats. Then again, after eighteen years of singing pretty much the same song, you can forgive a guy for resting on his laurels and repeating himself.

⊙ **Greatest Hits Volume 1:**
   The Player Years 1983–1988   In-A-Minute, 1993

A double-CD package that collects his 75 Girls material that no one outside the Bay Area would have heard otherwise.

A Tribe Called Quest

S tarting off by playing second fiddle to the Jungle Brothers and De La Soul as the junior members of the Native Tongues, A Tribe Called Quest quickly outstripped both in terms of commercial and artistic success. Quest simplified De La's oblique logic and hardened the JBs' breezy jazziness to produce hip-hop that was both abstract and pop savvy. With Q-Tip (Kamaal Fareed, né Jonathan Davis) providing his legendary record collection and Ali Shaheed Muhammad bringing an equally legendary production shine, A Tribe Called Quest redefined the art of crate diggin', establishing late '60s and early '70s jazz as *the* sound of East Coast hip-hop in the '90s.

Q-Tip first established himself with introductory cameos on the Jungle Brothers and De La Soul albums, but the Tribe's debut album, **People's Instinctive Travels and the Paths of Rhythm** (1990), displayed a talent, effervescence and vibe that Tip's guest appearances didn't even begin to hint at. Filled with morality plays, allegorical journeys, slice-of-life vignettes and comedic asides, **People's Instinctive**

Travels was a coming-of-age tale with Tip, Ali Shaheed, Phife (Malik Taylor) and Jarobi trying to find their way in the hip-hop game, thumb-

wrestling with role models, avoiding cholesterol, chiding friends who step out of line and calling out fools. With rich, sprightly production based on Lou Reed and Roy Ayers samples and a levity and sense of humour, the album was never bogged down by its own intentions.

Losing Jarobi, **The Low End Theory** (1991) found the new trio brimming with confi-dence. Tip's nasal, heavily

New York accent had developed into one of the best flows in the busi-ness. The exuberant jazziness of the first album had become more measured and self-assured, using snippets of jazz not just as a flava enhancer – the "low end theory" here became more than just a use of the bottom end to move butts (although it definitely was that), but a claim to history and heritage. Giving a rap the same aesthetic weight as a Coltrane solo, **The Low End Theory** went platinum on the strength of "important" hip-hop that realized it was only truly important if it was "boomin' in ya, boomin' in ya, boomin' in ya jeep".

After the classic, elastic "Hot Sex" (1992) from the *Boomerang* soundtrack, the Tribe attempted to perfect their aesthetic on **Midnight Marauders** (1993). Following the same blueprint as **The Low End Theory** but with greater density, **Midnight Marauders** was more of a production showcase, letting the message be transmitted through the beats rather than lyrics. Beat junkies were justifiably astounded by the album, but the whole thing didn't quite cohere as much as the previous two.

Before **Beats, Rhymes and Life** (1996), Phife moved to Atlanta from New York – a bad omen, considering only Cameo ever survived that journey with their brains intact. Perhaps as a result of this move to America's home of slight urban contemporary pop, **Beats, Rhymes and Life** was glossy, hi-contrast hip-hop that aspired to the quality of R&B. Typically, the music was lazy and sleepy, but the blear was gone. The hazy film of old had been replaced by a mix that featured impossibly crisp beats and razor-sharp snares. Q-Tip's flow was still impeccable, however, and Phife's talent for juxtaposition remained refreshingly unfettered: "Watch me stab up the track as if my name was OJ Simpson/I packs it in like Van Halen/I work for mine; you, you're freeloadin' like Kato Kaelin".

The Love Movement (1998) was more of a disappointment, drowning in the lifeless bohemia they'd laid out the parameters for on **The Low End Theory** and **Midnight Marauders**. There were highlights like "Find a Way", but this was the sound of a group that had run out of ideas. **The Love Movement** was the Tribe's last album. On **Amplified** (1999) Q-Tip was his own man and he had a new vitality as a result. The loping, jazzy beats of old were gone, but the in-vogue, hi-definition, sharp contrast, stop-start production style gave Q-Tip a fresh breath of life. With tracks as hot as "Breathe and Stop", "Vivrant Thing", "Let's Ride" and "Moving With U", **Amplified** was the acceptable face of jigginess. On "Bend Ova" (1999), Phife Dawg thought he was Blowfly and tried to fuck his way across Atlanta over seriously hot production (sparse drums and chicken-scratch guitar) from The Ummah's Jay Dee (who produced the Tribe's last two albums). Meanwhile, Ali Shaheed formed the boho soul group Lucy Pearl with exiles from Tony! Toni! Tone! and En Vogue.

⊙**The Low End Theory**   Jive, 1991

Less joyous than their debut, this deep, serious album redefined the
sound of East Coast hip-hop.

Tupac Shakur

Never much more than an adequate rapper, Tupac Amaru Shakur,
like so many pop stars, was a man whose contradictions made
him larger than life. With his movie-star eyelashes, "Thug Life" tattoo,
saccharine odes to women in the ghetto, X-rated tales of cocksmanship,
self-destructive impulse, sexual assault conviction, near-death experience and eventual martyrdom, Tupac was all things to all people.

Tupac first appeared on Digital Underground's "Same Song" from
This Is an EP Release (1990), uttering the inauspicious line, "Now I
clown around when I hang around with the Underground". He was also
found alongside fellow Digital Undergrounders DJ Fuze and Money B
on Raw Fusion's **Live From the Styleetron** (1991) album before his
own debut single, "Brenda's Got a Baby" (1991). This simplistic and
overly dramatic morality tale was just about the only halfway decent
track on his first album, **2Pacalypse Now** (1991).

But after his role as Bishop in *Juice*, 2Pac was becoming a star.
Strictly 4 My N.I.G.G.A.Z. (1993) was more fully realized. 2Pac was
improving on the mic and the album helped create his histrionic, self-
destructive, crazy persona. "Holler If Ya Hear Me" gave Master P most
of his ideas, although he never picked up on the fairly well-articulated
black rage. "Keep Ya Head Up" was a Hallmark card to the very
women he would viciously disrespect on "I Get Around".

After more film roles in *Poetic Justice* and *Above the Rim* and run-ins with the law, **Me Against the World** (1995) was released while he was in prison on a sexual assault charge. The sequel to "Keep Ya Head Up", "Dear Mama", was more inner-city Norman Rockwell and seemed calculated to counteract his incarceration in the minds of critics. The bitch-slapping elsewhere, though, didn't do his cause any good. The title track summed up both his paranoia and his attractiveness as an outlaw figure.

Rescued from New York's Clinton Correctional Facility by Death Row CEO Suge Knight, who paid his $1.4 million bond, Tupac signed to the label and released hip-hop's first single-artist double-disc album, **All Eyez on Me** (1996). On the most notorious label in the world, 2Pac proceeded to spontaneously combust into a scandalous, scabrous gangsta no longer dwelling in his sense of doom, but partying until the 2Pacalypse comes. The seven-times-platinum album was over-long by at least a disc and contained more than its fair share of irredeemable misogyny, but it did contain his best track, "California Love".

All Eyez on Me would be the last album he released while he was alive. With savage tracks like "Hit 'Em Up" aimed at the Bad Boy stable who Tupac claimed were responsible for his shooting in 1995, he was blamed for fanning the flames of the East–West dispute. On September 13, 1996, Tupac was murdered in Las Vegas and the recriminations have been flying around ever since. Since his death, there has been a flood of Tupac material, taking advantage of fans who can't separate art from life and are convinced that he left clues to his whereabouts after he faked his own death: **Don Killuminati: The 7 Day Theory** as Makavelli (1996), **R U Still Down?** (1997), **Greatest Hits** (1998), **Still I Rise** (1999) and some fifteen Makavelli bootlegs.

⊙ **All Eyez on Me**   Death Row, 1996

Way too long and way too unpleasant, but this is still the most convincing argument for Tupac's status.

UGK

Kickin' "trill ass lyrics", dem boys from Port Arthur, Texas UGK (aka the Underground Kingz) represent the filthiest aspects of the Dirty South. Pimp C (Chad Butler) and Bun B (Bernard Freeman) are big-ballin', shot-callin' playas who like "big birds and tight herb" and, when they're packing heat, you don't want to squab with them.

Originally in a group called Mission Impossible that put out a song called "Underground Kingz", Pimp C eventually hooked up with Bun B after several personnel changes. Taking the song's title as their new name, UGK put out a couple of local tapes before signing to Houston's

Big Tyme Records for the release of **Too Hard to Swallow** (1992). The title pretty much said all you needed to know, with the album featuring lyrics like "I don't trust the dugout 'cause I'm scared of the disease/'Cause she's passin' out the skins like government cheese", on top of Rufus and Chaka Khan interpolations.

Super Tight (1994) was more of the same, but with Pimp C's combination of live instrumentation and obvious samples and Bun B's Down South flow notably improving. "Feds in Town" and "Protect and Serve" also expanded their lyrical concerns beyond aimless gunplay and the punani. Before their best album, **Ridin' Dirty** (1996), was released, the duo collaborated with Houston's DJ Screw on the **Volume I** and **II** (1995) compilations, which found the Kingz laying down their Lone Star pimp lyrics alongside the similarly minded Point Blank and PSK-13. **Ridin' Dirty** featured more tales about rollin' down Interstate 10, but with the political slant of the title track, the details of "Pinky Ring", the fairly funny "Diamonds and Wood", and the Screw collabo, "3 'N the Mornin'", Pimp C and Bun B managed to flesh out their somewhat cheap

gangstaisms. It was "Murder", though, that broke the duo outside of south Texas with its bouncy, skittering drums and ominous gangsta lean in the synth riffs backing Bun B viciously rhyming "Pelle Pelle", "smelly red jelly" and "belly" in hip-hop's equivalent of John Woo's choreographed violence.

Ridin' Dirty got UGK noticed by Jay-Z, who invited them to contribute to "Big Pimpin'", the Timbaland-produced hit from his **Volume 3 ... The Life and Times of S. Carter** album (1999). With their newfound notoriety, **Dirty Money** (2000) was much delayed and much bootlegged, but hitting with "Pimpin' Ain't No Illusion" when it was finally released.

⊙ **Ridin' Dirty**   Big Tyme/Jive, 1996

Jayhova's favourite guest artists show why they're runnin' tings in Texas.

Ultramagnetic MCs

The intro to Ultramagnetic MCs' first demo, "Space Groove" (1984), said pretty much all you need to know about the group that practically invented underground hip-hop: "Space, the final frontier. These are the voyages of the Ultramagnetic MCs: to boldly go where no other rapper has gone before; to examine the universe and reconstruct the style of today's hip-hop culture." Before Kool Keith Thornton, Ced Gee (Cedric Miller), Moe Luv (Maurice Smith) and TR Luv (Trevor Randolph) became hip-hop's first afronauts, they were breakdancers with the New York City Breakers and People's Choice. However, for an individualist like sometime Creedmore and Bellevue resident Kool Keith, breaking didn't allow him to "travel at the speed of thought" and the Bronx residents came together to form one of the greatest crews in hip-hop history.

After a thoroughly uncharacteristic first single, "To Give You Love" (1986), Ultramagnetic would begin to make their mark with the mind-boggling "Ego Trippin'" (1986). Featuring epochal production by Ced Gee (a loop of Melvin Bliss drums and some vicious synth stabs, it was the best kind of minimalism – one that managed to fill the entire sound field), "Ego Trippin'" had Keith freestyling rhymes like "As the record just turns/You learn plus burn/By the flame of the lyrics which cooks the human brain, providing over-heated knowledge/By means causing pain/Make the migraine headaches ...". It sounded like nothing else at the time, except for Eric B & Rakim's "Eric B Is President" – hardly surprising, since Ced Gee helped out on the beats for *Paid In Full* and Boogie Down Productions' *Criminal Minded*.

"Funky" (1987), the flip-side of the Keith showcase "Mentally Mad", was another radical Ced Gee production (based on a Joe Cocker piano sample) that was so ahead of its time it would only enter the public consciousness nearly a decade later, when the beat was swiped wholesale by Dr. Dre on Tupac's "California Love". People would only have to wait a few months for the full implications of Ultramagnetic's debut album, **Critical Beatdown** (1988), to get mass awareness: the Bomb Squad has often said that **Critical Beatdown** was a major influence on Public Enemy's *It Takes a Nation of Millions to Hold Us Back* (check out "Ease Back" for proof). It may have been a stunning exposition of early sampling technology, but **Critical Beatdown** remains a devastating album in an age of 32-bit samplers and RAM-intensive sound-editing software. The music jumped and snapped with an energy reminiscent of the Cold Crush Brothers, while Kool Keith dropped abstract rhymes with cadences so bizarre they haven't been duplicated in a decade's worth of experimentalism.

The flip of the amazing "Travellin' at the Speed of Thought" (1988), "Chorus Line Pt. 1", was a sinister, bass-heavy battle cut that introduced Tim Dog, whose savage **Penicillin on Wax** (1991) would dis everyone in sight, particularly NWA and DJ Quik on tracks like "Fuck Compton" and "Step to Me".

The Ultramagnetics' delayed follow-up, **Funk Your Head Up** (1992), was largely disappointing. While Keith should have been perfectly at home with hip-hop's advanced sonics, the sex fantasies and rhymes were regressive at best. The only real highlight was the wild "Poppa Large", which had a bassline and horror strings to match Keith's dementia. **The Four Horsemen** (1993) was a return to the energies that fuelled the debut and had a range that took in the rousing ("Raise it Up"), the battling ("One Two One Two") and the poignant ("Saga of Dandy, the Devil and Day").

Unclassifiable and unruly, the group broke up in 1994, but Keith, at least, hasn't faded away. In 1995 he released the underground landmark, **Cenubites** EP, with Godfather Don. In 1996 Keith reincarnated himself as Dr. Octagon, a gynaecologist from outer space. Teaming up with Dan "Automator" Nakamura and DJ Q-Bert, Dr. Octagon released the absurd, scabrous, but completely original **Dr. Octagon** album (1996). With influences ranging from the *Love Story* soundtrack to Mantronix, **Dr. Octagon** had a beatscape that was as crazy as Keith's new persona: "Can't finetooth a dead ex, but the skin don't match", "A paramedic fetus of the East".

Without the deranged concept, Kool Keith's **Sex Style** (1997) was more awkward and just proved that he was a connoisseur of freaky porn. Cannibalism, vermin for pets, body parts in his car, "kicking your intestines like Ric Flair", listening to Slayer and the Staple Singers, borrowing toilet paper from his neighbours, "taking your dick for ransom", eating tampons with whipped cream, hanging with Jim Jones, eating raw steak, "putting used diapers on your windshield wipers", smoking embalming fluid – **First Come, First Served** (1999) was just another day at the office for Kool Keith in his new guise as Dr. Dooom. **Black Elvis/Lost in Space** (1999) continued his skewering of roach MCs with more sci-fi beats, but working on his own he wasn't as challenged as he was by the Automator or the Diesel Truckers (who produced the Dr. Dooom album).

⊙ **Critical Beatdown**   Next Plateau, 1988

"Taking your brain to another dimension", this is quite simply one of the five or six greatest hip-hop albums ever.

UMC's

A couple of years before it housed a rebuilt Shaolin Temple, Staten Island was ruled by Kool Kim and Haas G. Originally calling themselves the Universal MC's, the UMC's made their wax debut at the height of the D.A.I.S.Y. Age on a compilation released by the tiny Rough Justice label. "Invaders of My Fruit Basket" (1989) was a sprightly, jazzy record very much in the De La Soul style.

The bright, effervescent sound would reach its apex on the crew's debut album, **Fruits of Nature** (1991). "Blue Cheese" epitomized the approach, with its shuffling rhythm, cartoonish horn and flute break, and abstract raps with complex metaphors. The anthemic "One to Grow On" sounded like it was based on every Blue Note record ever released, while "Swing it to the Area" had that Memphis/Hi Records funk. Whereas the lyrics of Haas G and Kool Kim were clever, almost freestyle in nature and conception, **Fruits of Nature** belonged to producer RNS who, along with A Tribe Called Quest, defined jazzy hip-hop at the beginning of the '90s.

At the turn of the '90s, however, hip-hop was becoming ever more hardcore and the UMC's ditched their Native Tongues-styled image for their next album, **Unleashed** (1994). Track titles like "Evil Ways", "Ill Demonic Clique" and "Staten Island Comes First" told the story. While most of the tracks were clearly in thrall to the Wu-Tang Clan, "Time to Set it Straight" had fierce, organ-driven production (from Haas G and Kool Kim) that retained connections to their old sound even as it pushed in a new direction. While they tried to front at being hard, lines like "You're an anal wart" wouldn't have scared a 99-pound weakling and their uncomfortable role-playing made the UMC's seem like nothing but bandwagon jumpers.

⊙ **Fruits of Nature**   Wild Pitch, 1991

It might have been everything hip-hop was running away from – bubbly, eclectic, abstract – but this is nevertheless a great, imaginative album.

UTFO

The Kangol Kid and The Educated Rapper were originally a Brooklyn-based breakdance crew called the Keystone Dancers who popped, locked and body-rocked for Whodini. Meanwhile, Doctor Ice had released "Calling Doctor Ice" (1981) for Enjoy before joining up with Kangol Kid and the Educated Rapper. While their debut single, "Beats and Rhymes" (1984), introduced the nonsense language that would hit the big time with Fankie Smith's "Double Dutch Bus", UTFO's second single is perhaps the greatest novelty record of all time, if only for the fact that it spawned more answer records than any other single in history. Produced by Full Force, "Roxanne Roxanne"

(1984) was the tale of a beautiful woman who moves into the neighbourhood and resists the advances of the three East Flatbush lotharios.

While "Roxanne Roxanne" was an enjoyable piece of pop fluff, it and UTFO probably remain in the memory only because of what came after. Upset at its unflattering portrayal of women, a fourteen-year-old rapper calling herself Roxanne Shanté recorded "Roxanne's Revenge" (1985) with Marley Marl. Using the same Billy Squier "Big Beat" rhythm, Shanté proceeded to demolish UTFO and established herself as one of the most fearsome battle rappers in the business. In response, UTFO teamed up with a waitress called Joan Martinez and released their own answer record, "The Real Roxanne" (1985). Then producer Spyder D and his protegée, Sparky D, released "Sparky's Turn (Roxanne You're Through)" (1985), which attacked both Shanté and the Real Roxanne. A hundred records later, after Roxanne's mother and shrink had been heard from, the craze was finally over.

UTFO's response to all this was "Leader of the Pack" (1985). The implication of the title was that UTFO were the originators, but the record was really about their new DJ, Mix Master Ice. While the scratching was pretty def, UTFO proved themselves to be as bad at rapping as they were at spelling (UTFO was an anagram for Untouchable Force) and their self-titled debut album was generic at best. Over the next several years, they would try to perk up their act with gimmicks like rock licks (**Lethal** (1987)), New Jack Swing (**Doin' It** (1989)) and, finally, blue humour (**Bag It and Bone It** (1991)). Believe it or not, they're still in the biz: Mixmaster Ice is a radio DJ in Ohio, while Doctor Ice released "Phenomenon" in 1997.

⊙**The Best of UTFO**   Select, 1996

You can find "Roxanne Roxanne" on innumerable old-school comps, so only masochists and anoraks need to seek this out.

WC and the
MAAD Circle

With more than a decade in the business behind him, William
Calhoun is one of the most underrated players in the rap
game. Born in Texas, Calhoun moved in the early '80s to LA, where he
started rapping in high school. Hooking up with the mighty DJ
Aladdin, WC formed Low Profile and the duo dominated Ice-T's
Rhyme Syndicate Comin' Through (1988) compilation with "Think
You Can Hang". Signing to Priority, they released the collector's item,
We're in This Together (1989). Perhaps understandably overshadowed by NWA, **We're in This Together** is nevertheless a smoking
album of classic late '80s hip-hop: "Dub" talking about the old days
over a rumbling LA beat on "Pay Ya Dues" and getting nice over fast
tempos on "The Dub BU Just Begun", while Aladdin showed untouchable turntable skills on "Funky Song" and "Aladdin's on a Rampage",
not to mention a jaw-dropping scratch solo on "The Dub BU Just
Begun".

After **We're in This Together** failed to make any noise, the duo split
and WC formed the MAAD Circle (Minority Alliance Against Discrimi-
nation) with Big Gee, his younger brother Crazy Toones and some
guy called Coolio. With all around them in the throes of gangbanging,
on **Ain't a Damn Thing Changed** (1991) the MAAD Circle rapped
about absentee fathers and label whores, and on "Back to the Underground" WC bragged, "I'd rather go down in the book as a brother
who ripped clubs/And who told it how it was". Unsurprisingly, it too
was a commercial flop.

After industry difficulties and Coolio leaving the group, the MAAD

Circle finally returned with **Curb Servin'** in 1995. The highlight was the George Duke-sampling "West Up!", which, with Ice Cube and Mack 10, was really a Westside Connection track. Westside Connection's

Bow Down (1996) was straight up, East Coast-baiting, gangsta shit that went double platinum and finally gave WC the success he deserved. Shame he had to pander to the lowest common denominator in order to do it. Without the market imprimatur of Ice Cube, WC's **The Shadiest One** (1998) again was slept on, despite semi-classics of West Coast street funk like "Just Clownin'" and "Fuckin' Wit Uh House Party".

◉ **Low Profile – We're in This Together**   Priority, 1989
You'll have to look high and low to find it, but this is timeless, classic hip-hop.

Whodini

With the help of pioneering hip-hop radio DJ Mr.Magic, Whodini – Brooklynites Jalil Hutchins, Ecstacy (John Fletcher) and Grandmaster Dee (Drew Carter) – was the first act signed to Jive Records. Returning the favour, Whodini's first single was a homage entitled "Magic's Wand" (1982). Following in the wake of "Planet Rock", "Magic's Wand" was co-produced by Thomas Dolby and featured synth riffs, a chugging "Trans-Europe Express"-like intro and drum machine beats. Rather than the supernatural weirdness of "Planet Rock", though, "Magic's Wand", with its slap-bass groove and luxurious keyboards, easily slotted alongside disco records like D-Train's "You're the One for Me"and The Peech Boys' "Don't Make Me Wait".

Working with Run DMC and Kurtis Blow producer Larry Smith, Whodini then recorded their self-titled debut album in 1983. Where Run DMC's production could level a skyscraper at twenty paces, Smith designed Whodini as the upwardly mobile, suit-wearing suave cats who could stride right into that same skyscraper without a second glance. Aside from "Magic's Wand", the biggest hit from the record was "Haunted House of Funk", a pretty lame reworking of Bobby (Boris) Pickett's "Monster Mash".

Smith's vision really came together on **Escape** (1984). Preceded by the awesome double-sided single, "Friends/Five Minutes of Funk", it is often said that **Escape** was the first rap album to go platinum, but it has never been certified. Whatever, **Escape** was one of the best early hip-hop albums with biting electro-funk production, inoffensive R&B vocals, tasteful vocoders and clever songwriting. Aside from "Five Minutes", the album's best track was "Freaks Come Out at Night", a tale of Brooklyn meeting Greenwich Village at The Danceteria told to a video game beat.

Unlike AC/DC's victorious album of the same name, **Back in Black** (1986) showed Whodini to be in terminal decline, unable to escape from the constrictions of the old school. Tracks like "Funky Beat" and "One Love" were OK, but in 1986 the action was definitely elsewhere. **Open Sesame** (1987) was clearly not the magic word and not even Mr. Magic's wand could prevent Whodini from sounding like they were in a different century from Eric B & Rakim, Boogie Down Productions, etc. **Bag-a-Trix** (1991) was even less notable and an attempted comeback on Jermaine Dupri's So-So Def label, **Six** (1996), was little short of an embarrassment.

⊙ **Jive Collection Series, Vol. 1**   Jive, 1995

More Whodini than anyone will ever need.

Wu-Tang Clan

B randishing a remarkable mythology fashioned out of fortune-cookie versions of ancient Chinese secrets, Five Percent mathematics and chess master Gary Kasparov's Sicilian defence, the Wu-Tang Clan talk loudly and carry a big shtick. For all of hip-hop's keep-it-real rhetoric, the Wu's chimerical demi-monde demands more suspension of disbelief than James Cameron. The principal weapon in the Clansmen's bag of tricks is camouflage: from the intimidation tactics of quoting Sun Tzu's *The Art of War* to the labyrinthine obfuscation of the Wu-Tang's 36 chambers, ringleader RZA, just like his mentor Dr. Funkenstein, is often "gamin' on ya".

RZA and his charges (Method Man, Ol' Dirty Bastard, Raekwon the Chef, Ghostface Killah, Genius/GZA, U-God, Masta Killa and

Inspectah Deck) know that hip-hop is no different from a Steven Seagal flick: it's not necessarily the skills, but the facade of invincibility that counts. Fully inhabiting this fantasy world, the Wu make more out of low culture sources – Hong Kong chop-sockies, comic books, Hanna-Barbera, professional wrestling (not even WWF, but old-school NWA) – than anyone since the glory days of P-Funk. More than just comic relief, though, this bottom feeding is a survival tactic for those caught in hip-hop's metaphorical crossfire. Like his other Clansmen, Method Man (aka Johnny Blaze, The Ticalion Stallion, John-John McLain, Iron Lung, the Panty Raider, Johnny Dangerous) adopts more aliases than a Mossad agent. You could say that this name game is emblematic of W.E.B. DuBois's famous notion of the double-consciousness of African-Americans, who are forced to juggle identities by virtue of being black in a white country. But it's also a very useful ploy in hip-hop's rhetorical war games: as Meth himself says on "Dangerous Grounds" (from **Tical 2000**), "I had to kill a schizophrenic nigga twice".

MIKE LEWIS

The Wu-Tang Clan and their multiple personas dwell in a paranoiac, claustrophobic, hallucinatory, sensurround world where the city streets are crawling with visible contagion, unseen creatures scuttle and scurry in the sewers, and the pimps, hustlers and moneymakers whisper about you behind your back in backwards Satanic verses. Producers RZA, True Master, 4th Disciple and Inspectah Deck surround the MCs with swarms of hornet zithers, stinging atonal guitar licks and the Wu's trademark urban underbelly piano nocturnes.

The Wu's unique conceptual and sonic worlds were first unveiled on a self-pressed single called "Protect Ya Neck" (1992). Its enormous

impact on the underground caused a label bidding war, resulting in the Clan signing a deal with Loud that allowed each individual member to sign their own solo deals with other labels. The Clan's debut album, **Enter the Wu-Tang (36 Chambers)** (1993), is one of hip-hop's true landmarks. As hip-hop was seemingly becoming as relaxed as a Compton jheri curl, **Enter the Wu-Tang** brought a whole new kind of stylization. After a snippet from a Shaw Brothers kung-fu flick, the album began with Ghostface Killah spitting deranged verses over a distorted kick drum, detuned zithers, backwards horns and one of the most dangerous voices ever encountered on vinyl shouting, "Bring the motherfuckin' ruckus".

Elsewhere, RZA remade Southern soul horns as a rallying cry for the Rotten Apple, turned James Brown samples into aural psychosis, made the piano loop '90s hip-hop's signature sound and metamorphosed Gladys Knight and The Charmels into ghetto elegies. If you weren't convinced by the production, there were always the incredible battle rhymes like "What's that in your pants? Ahh, human faeces/Throw you shitty drawers in the hamper/Next time come strapped with a Pamper".

For a couple of years RZA's production was like Colt 45: it worked every time. Method Man's **Tical** (1994) was musically cleaner than **Enter**, but with Meth's iron-lung gust of a flow its tales of the dark side were just about as engaging as the Wu debut. Ol' Dirty's **Return to the 36 Chambers: The Dirty Version** (1995) was a collection of scatology that would make Chaucer blush (although it was nothing compared to his gloriously outrageous **N***a Please**), while Ghostface Killah's **Iron-man** (1996) featured the awesome interpretation of Bob James' "Nautilus" break, "Daytona 500", and the frighteningly intense "Winter Warz". The best Wu solo joints, however, were GZA's **Liquid Swords** (1995) – perhaps the only Wu album to get over purely on skills rather than the whole concept – and Raekwon's **Only Built 4 Cuban Linx ...** (1995), which ditched the pseudo-Asian mysticism for straight-up street tales that were as grim, nasty and heartbreaking as anything Mobb Deep ever came up with.

Just like their inspirations the P-Funk empire, though, the work rate eventually caught up with the Clan. The sprawling **Wu-Tang Forever** (1997) was a double CD with maybe one or two good ideas, while most of the ensuing solo albums have been nothing but the same old shit. Method Man's **Tical 2000** (1998) and Ol' Dirty's **N***a Please** (1999) were the best of these, but where the Wu's brutal social Darwinism used to be couched either as a survival metaphor or as Armageddon prophecy, by the late '90s it had become nothing but an end in and of itself.

⊙ **Enter the Wu-Tang (36 Chambers)**   Loud, 1993

Startlingly original, conceptually and sonically daring, and absolutely ferocious, this album almost single-handedly rescued New York hip-hop and stands as one of the genre's greatest albums.

X-Clan

Once upon a time, Egyptology in pop music meant the harmless spirituality of Earth, Wind & Fire. In the hip-hop era, Egyptology equalled the authoritative bassos and "vainglorious" grooves of X-Clan. Sure, they were riddled with contradictions and their "Nubian" garb of nose rings, ankh jewellery, wooden canes and black leather fezzes was about as African as Afros, but their embrace of the red, black and green was more thought out than the attitudes of many of their Afrocentric contemporaries and, even though they came perilously close to Leonard Stern territory, they were skilful enough never to put their feet in their mouths.

Part of the Blackwatch group, which also included YZ (of "Thinking of a Master Plan" fame) and X-Clan satellites Isis and Queen Mother Rage, X-Clan made a lot of noise with their debut single, "A Day of Outrage, Operation Snatchback" (1989), and album, **To the East, Blackwards** (1990). On top of the funkin' lessons and production of Rhythm Provider Sugar Shaft and Grand Architect Paradise, rappers/lecturers Professor X (Lumumba Carson, son of activist Sonny Carson) and Brother J dropped some dubious pseudo-science about racial politics, but they did it with panache and style, and X's trademark phrase, "The red, the black and the green, with the key, Sissy!", still resonates throughout hip-hop (check Redman and Method Man's 1999 *Blackout* album).

Laudably, the group practised what they preached and organized voter registration drives and protests against the murder of Yusef Hawkins (an African-American killed by a racist mob). **Xodus: The**

New Testament (1992) was funkier than the debut and found Professor X and Brother J dissing the "humanism" of KRS-One and taunting 3rd Bass with an amusing baseball metaphor on "Fire & Earth (100% Natural)". The album was lost, however, as the Afrocentric tide went out and the group soon dissolved. Professor X released the patchy **Puss 'N Boots ... The Struggle Continues** (1993) to little fanfare, and Brother J re-emerged quietly in 1996 with a new group, the Dark Sun Riders, on **Seeds of Evolution**.

⊙ **Xodus: The New Testament**   Polydor, 1992

Funkier and less pedantic than many of their ilk, X-Clan made their pro-black medicine go down as easy as palm wine.

Yo Yo

Discovered by Ice Cube in a shopping mall when she was still a high-school cheerleader, Yolanda Whitaker went on to become one of the most respected women in hip-hop. Treading the fine line between pop starlet, gangsta bitch, feminist role model and good-time girl, Yo Yo transcended her terrible *nom de disque* and managed to convey a woman's perspective in hip-hop without becoming a stereotype or pandering to male fantasies.

Unfortunately, Yo Yo's talent has never really matched her image and she's never been able to outdo her first appearance on wax. Acting as the feminist foil to Ice Cube's rampant misogyny on "It's a Man's World" (1990) from his **Amerikkka's Most Wanted** album, Yo Yo spit enough schoolyard insults to make Cube's dick shrivel up like a tortoise retreating into its shell. Yo Yo's debut album, **Make Way for the**

Motherlode (1991), featured the excellent single "You Can't Play With My Yo Yo" and managed to make the gangsta production of Ice Cube and Sir Jinx bounce with womanist brio.

Black Pearl (1992), on the other hand, may have been a more mature statement, but it lacked the vitality of **Motherlode**. **You Better Ask Somebody** (1993) remedied this with gangsta gender fucks like "The Mackstress", an inspired remake of Serge Gainsbourg's "Bonnie and Clyde" with Ice Cube, and the liberating "Girl With a Gun". **Total Control** (1996), however, repeated the mistakes of **Black Pearl** and went in for heavy-handed messages at a time when most hip-hop was concerning itself with delivering vicarious thrills.

⊙ **Make Way For the Motherlode**   EastWest, 1991

This is Yo Yo's most successful album because the feminist stance is couched in traditional hip-hop values like boasting, dissing and pure street attitude.

Young MC

Young MC's 1997 comeback album may have been titled **Return of the One-Hit Wonder**, but Marvin Young had at least three certifiable mega-hits to his credit – the only problem was that two of them were recorded by Tone-Loc.

Young was an economics student at the University of Southern California when he met fellow students Michael Ross and Matt Dike, who had just started up a label called Delicious Vinyl. His single, "I Let 'Em Know" (1988), was the first release on the label. In 1989, Young wrote hip-hop's biggest pop hit and one of the best-selling singles of all time, Tone-Loc's "Wild Thing". Almost as huge was the follow-up, "Funky Cold Medina", which Young also wrote. With "Bust a Move" (1989), Young MC had a platinum single in his own right. While "Wild Thing" and "Funky Cold Medina" were hits because of Loc's absurd voice and the great production by the Dust Brothers, "Bust a Move" climbed the pop charts on the back of Young MC's gentle wit and inclusiveness. Of course, the Aretha Franklin sample and Flea's monstrous bassline didn't hurt either.

"Bust a Move" was easily the best track on Young MC's double-platinum **Stone Cold Rhymin'** (1989) album, perhaps the best album by one of hip-hop's commercial flash-in-the-pans. "Principal's Office" was a Chuck Berry-ish minor hit about school mischief, while "Got More Rhymes" said that Young had more rhymes "than husbands of Elizabeth Taylor". Although "I Come Off" saw Young MC trying to be hard, he compared himself to ice-skater Dorothy Hammill – a blunder from which he would never recover. "I Come Off" also highlighted his propensity to roll his "r"s, which he repeated on the club hit "Know How", which was built on large chunks of Isaac Hayes' "Theme From Shaft" and the Incredible Bongo Band's "Apache".

Brainstorm (1991) saw Young MC wearing black medallions and trying to be socially relevant. His previous records had captured the pop *Zeitgeist*, but **Brainstorm** was about a year and a half too late, and on tracks like "Keep it in Your Trousers" he sounded pretty ridiculous. Despite production from A Tribe Called Quest's Ali Shaheed Muhammad, **What's the Flavor** (1993) fared little better with its jazzy vibes. With a title like **Return of the One-Hit Wonder**, his last album didn't promise much. It didn't deliver much either.

⊙**Stone Cold Rhymin'**   Delicious Vinyl, 1989

It might sound like a children's record nowadays, but pop-rap doesn't get much better.

NOTES

Drum 'n' bass • Hip-hop • House • Techno • Drum 'n' bass • Hip-hop • House • Techno • Drum 'n' bass •

House • Techno • Drum 'n' bass • Hip-hop • House • Techno • Drum 'n' bass • Hip-hop • House • Techno • Drum 'n' bass • Hip-hop • House

Hip-hop • House • Techno • Drum 'n' bass • 'n' bass • Hip-hop • House • Techno • Drum 'n' bass • Hip-hop • House

Sorted

ROUGH GUIDES

Techno • Drum 'n' bass • House • Hip-hop • Drum 'n' bass • Techno • House • Hip-hop • Drum 'n' bass • Techno •

100 Essential CDs

Eight titles, one name

ROUGH GUIDES

ROUGH GUIDES:
Reference and Music CDs

REFERENCE
Classical Music
Classical:
    100 Essential CDs
Drum'n'bass
House Music

World Music:
    100 Essential CDs
English Football
European Football
Internet
Millennium

**ROUGH GUIDE
    MUSIC CDs**
Music of the Andes
Australian
    Aboriginal
Brazilian Music
Cajun & Zydeco
Classic Jazz
Music of Colombia
Cuban Music
Eastern Europe
Music of Egypt
English Roots
    Music
Flamenco
India & Pakistan
Irish Music
Music of Japan
Kenya & Tanzania
Native American
North African
Music of Portugal

Jazz
Music USA
Opera
Opera:
    100 Essential CDs
Reggae
Rock
Rock:
    100 Essential CDs
Techno
World Music

Reggae
Salsa
Scottish Music
South African
    Music
Music of Spain
Tango
Tex-Mex
West African Music
World Music
World Music Vol 2
Music of Zimbabwe

AVAILABLE AT ALL GOOD BOOKSHOPS

Stay in touch with us!

**ROUGHNEWS is Rough Guides'
free newsletter.
In three issues a year we give you
news, travel issues, music reviews,
readers' letters and the latest
dispatches from authors on the road.**

I would like to receive ROUGHNEWS: please put me on your free mailing list.

NAME . . . .

ADDRESS . . . .

Please clip or photocopy and send to: Rough Guides, 62-70 Shorts Gardens,
London WC2H 9AH, England

or Rough Guides, 375 Hudson Street, New York, NY 10014, USA.

ROUGH GUIDES: Travel

ROUGH GUIDES: Mini Guides, Travel Specials and Phrasebooks

MINI GUIDES

Antigua
Bangkok
Barbados
Big Island of Hawaii
Boston
Brussels
Budapest
Dublin
Edinburgh
Florence
Honolulu
Lisbon
London Restaurants
Madrid
Maui
Melbourne
New Orleans
St Lucia

Seattle
Sydney
Tokyo
Toronto

TRAVEL SPECIALS

First-Time Asia
First-Time Europe
More Women Travel

PHRASEBOOKS

Czech
Dutch
Egyptian Arabic
European
French

German
Greek
Hindi & Urdu
Hungarian
Indonesian
Italian
Japanese
Mandarin
  Chinese
Mexican
  Spanish
Polish
Portuguese
Russian
Spanish
Swahili
Thai
Turkish
Vietnamese

Will you have enough stories to tell your grandchildren?

©2000 Yahoo! Inc.

Yahoo! Travel

Do You YAHOO!?